GREECE AND ITS MYTHS

GREECE AND ITS MYTHS

by

MICHAEL SENIOR

LONDON
VICTOR GOLLANCZ LTD
1978

© Michael Senior 1978

ISBN 0 575 02399 6

ACKNOWLEDGEMENTS

The author wishes to thank Faber and Faber Ltd. for permission to quote an extract from *Four Quartets* by T. S. Eliot, and the Hogarth Press Ltd. and Rae Dalven for permission to quote from her translation of *The Complete Poems of C. P. Cavafy*. The short extract by Willard Quine on p. 32 is from *From a Logical Point of View* published by Harvard University Press. Erich Auerbach's *Mimesis*, referred to on p. 17, is published by Princeton University Press in a translation by Willard R. Trask.

Printed in Great Britain by
The Camelot Press Ltd, Southampton

To my mother,
with thanks
for all her help

CONTENTS

ILLUSTRATIONS

(following pages 64 and 224)

Athens: the Acropolis
Plaka
Athens: a street in Monastiraki
Elevsis
Getting in the corn harvest
Corinth
Corinth: the Peirene fountain
Mycenae: Lion Gate from inside
Mycenae: Lion Gate from outside
Mycenae today
Oak trees near the Diktean Cave
Mouth of the Diktean Cave
The Diktean Cave from inside
The cave on Mount Ida
Tiryns
Nemea
Sounion: Temple of Poseidon
Fishing boats
Buying fish
Gournia
Agia Triada
Phaestos

All photographs by the author

MAPS

CHRONOLOGICAL TABLES

AUTHOR'S NOTE

This is a book about the myths of Greece viewed in the context of the places to which they are related. As such it is more than just a guidebook to the classical and pre-classical sites of Greece—though it is partly that, particularly in the cases where the myth and the site directly coincide. It also views the two matters in their own contexts: the places in their background of history and social life, and the myths within the background of mythology and of European thought. In spite of this rather ambitious-sounding programme, this is not specifically a book for scholars. No doubt in fact I have stumbled from time to time into areas where they would fear to tread.

The problem of transliteration

Many Greek names come to us through Latin sources, and hence in latinized form. The Romans were as bad as the English about making funny-sounding foreign words conform to their linguistic expectations. One of the results of this is that the Greek *k* has often become a Latin *c*. This would make little difference were it not for the habit English-speakers have of pronouncing a *c* wherever possible as if it were an *s*. By this process some names, such as Mycenae and Cyllene, have got rather a long way from their Greek originals, in these cases Mikini and Killini. It is clearly too late now for me to attempt to correct this regrettable trend. Indeed those who try—the purists who go so far as to write Korinth, and even Krete—look rather as if they are carrying on their own forlorn crusade. I feel it preferable to stick to what is perhaps wrong, but familiar. In any case names like Mycenae are firmly embedded now in our language. Unfortunately the practice of using the familiar form where there is one and other-wise using the correct one obstructs that most desirable of qualities, internal consistency. What I propose to do, therefore, is to use the form which seems to me most natural, and at the same time to point out its divergence, if any, from the Greek.

July 1977   M. S.

We shall not cease from exploration
And the end of all our exploring
Will be to arrive where we started
And know the place for the first time.

—T. S. Eliot, *Little Gidding*

GREECE AND ITS MYTHS

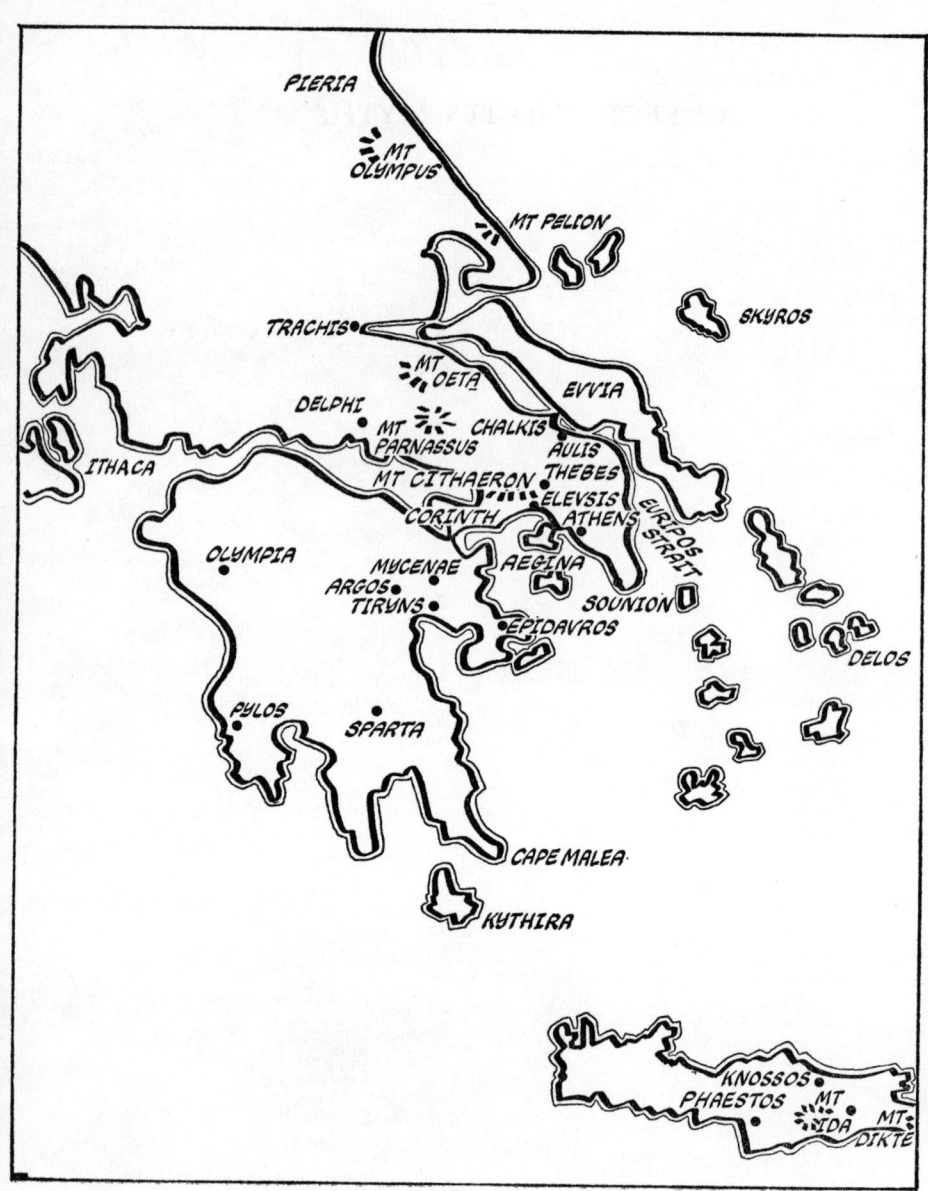

ONE

GREECE AND ITS MYTHS

THERE IS A PASSAGE in Erich Auerbach's highly enjoyable book *Mimesis* (a work of literary criticism so broad in its vision and analytical in its approach that it makes one see things in a different way), in the chapter about Homer, where the author makes the point, which once displayed seems eternally obvious: that there is a fundamental difference between the Homeric gods and the God of the Old Testament. This difference is that the former are the sort of beings of whom one might know where they are and where they have been. When God speaks to Abraham, on the other hand, in Genesis 22, where does the interview take place? 'Whence does he come, whence does he call to Abraham? We are not told. He does not come, like Zeus or Poseidon, from the Aethiopians, where he has been enjoying a sacrificial feast.'

It is this quality, so neatly identified by Auerbach, this fact that Zeus can be seen as having come from feasting with the Aethiopians, which underlies the subject matter of this book. It is as if in the clarity of the Greek light all things are seen as hard and salient, and the blurred outlines of abstractions are out of place. Of course there are various reasons for the phenomenon, and it is only fair to review them, however briefly. But it is really the result with which we are concerned: the location in space, and even to some extent in time, of what would otherwise have been nebulous events and figures.

This is not to say that the element of timelessness, so characteristic of myth, is absent. Much of the subject matter is timeless in the sense that the dimension of time is never properly applied to it, so that it has the same status in the present as it had in the past, however remote that is. It should not be thought that because it appears that something did indeed happen in Greece at some period to set this current flowing, Greek myths in any sense belong to a period, in that they lived and died then, like a human being. Least of all do I wish to be thought to say that myth and history are directly causally connected—that myth springs from history, or is itself a picturesque way of recording actual events. It does in a sense record something, the sense being that there is something there which is, in the process of the myth, recorded. It is rather as Constable's painting of Salisbury Cathedral could be said to be a record; but that was not its purpose. In those cases where myth and history deal with the same matter, for instance with the Trojan War, they do so as independent disciplines, not related in any direct way. Two quite different ways of viewing the same thing can co-exist. The student of geology and the student of geography may see quite different aspects of the same terrain; or the demographic statistician on the one hand and the anthropologist or sociologist on the other may deal with the same population, the very same people, but depict them as, respectively, a set of correlated data or a pattern of interconnecting relationships. This is not to say, either, that one of them, myth or history, is more basic, more fundamental, than the other.

Of course there are occasions when myth is on its own, when it concerns itself with areas which are not within the possible domain of other systems. One of my contentions is that the things we group together as myths are in fact fairly diverse, both in form and function. It happens that one of the uses they have been put to is what one might call genealogical, fulfilling the task of justifying the occupation of a position of power or a territory. Part of their role as apparent history is perhaps due to this use, the giving of respectability to leaders and kings, or a sense of righteousness to a people. Myths are often about kings for another reason, and that is that they are often about greatness. To some extent they need to be to serve one of the purposes which they do serve, and so, in fact, to have survived. This is a point of distinction between what we call myths and the related body of material which is better called folk-tale and legend. The latter tend to be about lesser beings, lesser deeds and lesser emotions. Myths refine and crystallize, set apart—almost, in fact, abstract from our common lives. They serve the same sort of function as the figure of the king himself serves.

In view of this it is perhaps not very surprising if we find them becoming located. They have to relate to certain selected features at the edges of people's experience. The fearsome and the unexplored attract them therefore, as for instance high mountains have always done, such as Olympus, Parnassus and, elsewhere, Sinai and Ararat. It is also quite understandable that things of great antiquity will provide a hook on which to hang them: ancient sites whose origins are too distant for early time scales and information channels to deal with. In this way in Britain one finds, for instance, King Arthur being associated with cromlechs and barrows, and other ancient British figures being identified with hill forts or tumuli. It was Merlin who built Stonehenge, simply for the reason that both Merlin and Stonehenge belong to a time before established memories.

The fact remains, however, that Greek myths are more specifically and more generally located than most. Welsh and Irish stories are close competitors, and in the Near East the doings of gods are related to the cities of which they were the special guardians. But almost every incident in Greek myth is given a place, almost every figure belongs somewhere, its movements chronicled with geographic preciseness in many cases not just to within a few miles but even a few feet. Demeter sat down on this stone beside this well, when she came to Elevsis. Zeus was born not just in a cave in Crete, but in this cave, and in fact right here, in this corner. Athena sat in judgement on Orestes not just in Athens, but on the Areopagus. Poseidon struck the rock with his trident here, and this spring burst out. Apollo lay in wait for the Python on the slopes of Parnassus, not somewhere on that vast and shapeless mountain but near the top of the gorge a short way outside the present village of Arachova. We know where Oedipus was said to be when the Corinthian shepherd found him, and where he was when he met and killed his father; we know the spots at which Heracles performed his labours. We can go and look at these places. In fact it is part of our concern here to do precisely that.

How does it happen that Greek myths have this extraordinary quality of preciseness? That, of course, is not the sort of question one can answer, making the assumptions which it does about the simple working of causality. Of course there are lots of factors, none of them, on their own, reasons. We can, however, come to understand a bit about the elements which go to make up the situation; and although this book as a whole will be doing that it may be helpful to sketch the outline of some of these factors now.

Something did happen. That is, not simply and concisely in the way that datable historic events happen, but over a vague and no doubt long period, during which something identifiable now as a European outlook came into existence. It seems that early movements, in the Near East and the Balkans, of people with differing interests and customs produced a synthesis of beliefs and religious ideas such that this amalgam could function and develop in a way that would not have been possible for the original parts of it in isolation. Perhaps integration is the key concept—not just integration of one religion with another, but increasing integration within the resultant synthesis itself. I have in mind the sort of process by which something originally external and remote can become absorbed into a way of life, personalized and related-to directly.

To the extent that Greek mythology is a religion (rather than, say, a body of folk legend) it is based on a number of cults which, though originally separate in function, have come to be related. They are, at that stage, not contradictory so much as complementary. From their separate and independent existence they have grown to be segments of a whole. And that is one facet of a process of integration: the combining of specialized items into a block in which they can work together. The growth of the body of mythology has brought together and related (this in fact quite explicitly) such specialized functions as that of the sky god, Zeus, and the corn goddess, Demeter. Dionysus the god of wine co-exists with the pastoral god Apollo. Artemis the huntress inhabits the same system as the love goddess Aphrodite. Yet although this situation contrasts strikingly with that in which these various functions would (as they presumably did at first) comprise separate religions, conflicting rather than combining with each other, the process of integration is not at this stage complete. Perhaps the identifiable segmental units represent a step just before the achievement of that total psychological integration which we (I think) would recognize as cultural maturity. Integration in that sense is a sort of wholeness; and perhaps that was what came next. If so, it would have been made possible by this great synthesizing process of the Greek myths. If this is right, again, the replacement of the Greek pantheon by a body of thought in which all the various functions were unified—the sun god, born at mid-winter, the shepherd god, sacrificed as a lamb, the wine god, whose blood is drunk, the harvest god, eaten as bread, the tree god, sacrificed by hanging on a tree, the god of vegetation, born again in the spring, and so on—would be the next stage in the development of culture and consciousness.

If we do in fact have, in the Greek myths, a stage in the development of religious and social ideas, then some at least of the slightly puzzling details in the stories can be explained in terms of an abhorrence of reversion, fear of slipping back to a previous phase. At any rate this possibility will seem, from time to time, to be a useful heuristic tool. The myths represent as shocking what is now forbidden—child sacrifice, eating the flesh of the sacrificial victim, succession by ritual killing, succession by marriage to the queen, and so on. It is forbidden, and so taboo, because it would tend to undermine a new order. Apostasy is therefore shown with something near to horror.

This is to suggest that a new ordering of life took place in Greece somewhere in the remote past; and such things of course can only be inferred, not proved. That too falls short of answering the question 'Why Greece?'—particularly as it can be shown that not only the themes and ideas but the population of early Greece itself originated elsewhere.

It is a truism that innovations and influence usually come, like daylight, from the east. Many of the themes we are to deal with seem to have had an eastern origin; and this in fact helps to explain, rather than confuse, the question of why it was in Greece that they became fully formed. Greece was at a critical time in a position to serve up such Middle Eastern ideas in a form which could eventually be digested by the rest of Europe. It acted as a medium, a go-between. (A long time later Christianity came to us by a similar route.) But the reason Greece could take up this role was perhaps not just geographical. It stemmed also from the fact that the country was, simply, a pleasant place to live in in an early agricultural age—even, no doubt, in its immediate prelude, the last period when man hunted rather than herded. But even herding involves an unsettled, rootless existence. Hunting presumably required almost continuous search as well. And that would not be conducive to imagination and to speculation, let alone to the formulation of complex systems of belief. It was not until sufficient leisure was achieved through farming, when people no longer had to keep on the move, governed by fear of hunger and unable to take risks with time, that anything approaching intellectual activity could take place. Consciousness, then, in the form in which we know it, must have been the fruit of a favourable climate.

Greece is a country undoubtedly blessed in many ways. It mostly has good soil and varied terrain, providing shelter in its valleys and space on its alluvial plains. Although warm throughout much of the year, indeed by comparison with the greater part of Europe positively hot, it is by no means as intemperate as much of Asia and Africa. A settled existence was possible there, in a way that it could not have been for the hunters of the forests of the north. And although it seems to have been the seed of a fruit from further east which put down roots in Greece, the flourishing of this shoot there, rather than elsewhere, into such a luxuriant plant must have been due to the fact that Greece is a much less harsh place than, say, Syria. There is a consequent relief from the pressures of mere survival. It is a country, simply, which allows space for purely human concerns.

Whether or not these generalizations approach a correct analysis, it is a fact that both the country and the myths exhibit strikingly human facets, the human concerns in the culture, history, social forms and attitudes of the one, and in the characters, events, the themes and preoccupations of the other, being perhaps the most conspicuous, certainly the most endearing, qualities of each.

It may have been, then, something about Greece which led to the merging of strands of thought there to produce a new type of awareness. If this appears to imply a claim to unity or cohesion, as it probably does, it must be qualified at once by a recognition of the multi-stratified, ramifying nature of the matter. To begin with, myths have quite diverse purposes or functions. That, of course, assumes to begin with that something describable as a function is involved. And this indeed I shall be inclined, from time to time, to suggest, if only on the grounds that it seems an acceptable principle that things with no benefit to offer do not prosper.

It is customary for books about myths to begin with an attempt by their authors to say what they take myths to be. Such a preliminary definition can have disastrous effects, and I propose to resist it firmly. 'Myths are sacred stories'; 'myths are derived from rituals'; or, alternatively, they are the conceptual basis of those rituals; myths are a type of decayed religion; on the other hand, they are an incipient religion; myths are the rationalizing of the subconscious; myths are 'only' a refined type of folk-tale; and so on. The danger in such an approach (apart from the fact that it tends to indulge excessively the proponent's preoccupations) is that it prevents an objective treatment of the subject. Once you have laid down the law, you cannot allow any item to transgress it. Moreover I do not believe that 'myth' (unlike, for instance, 'Greece') describes an area lying within distinct fixed and agreed boundaries. I think there is an ebb and flow, producing an inter-tidal zone where you may if you wish choose to say 'Yes, it's a myth', or 'No, it's just an old traditional tale'. Along with very much else, the area of myth has overlaps; at its edges it is vague, with disputed borders and perhaps sometimes allegiances to two territories at once.

Although the Greek myths do not belong precisely to any one

age, and do not seem to have time dimensions of the sort associated with human history, there are several points about early Greek history which are relevant to the mythology. There was a pre-Greek civilization which we know of in its Cretan manifestation as Minoan, and which no doubt had a parallel on the mainland before the coming of the Greek-speaking Achaeans. The survival of non-Greek place-names indicates that the country was once inhabited by a different group of people. Since the language of the Linear A tablets found in Crete has not been translated (though it has been established as being not Greek, unlike the slightly later Linear B language), we do not know much about them. But the evidence is that they worshipped a goddess connected with snakes, and that the gods which we know better, such as Zeus, were brought into Greece and later to Crete by the Achaeans, probably from the north-east. It is thought that these Achaeans came southwards *circa* 1800 B.C., or rather earlier—that is, during the archaeological period known as the Bronze Age. It was their coming that gave rise to the Mycenaean civilization, one of the first peaks of European development and no doubt one of the main causes of the expansion of Greek thought.

We now know quite a lot about these people, thanks to the patient and scholarly work of the archaeologists, and particularly thanks to the breakthrough made by Michael Ventris by decoding Linear B in 1952 and the long process of interpretation carried out by his colleague John Chadwick and others since. We know that many of the gods of the later Olympian pantheon were known to the people of that early time; the names of Zeus, Hera, Hermes, Poseidon, Dionysus and Artemis are found, among other less certainly identifiable ones, in connection with sacrifices and the apportionment of stores. There were deities too whose names we do not recognize, and some familiar figures, such as Aphrodite, are quite absent. Significantly there is no sign of any knowledge of the heroes, as opposed to the gods, although their names, as for instance recorded by Homer, seem to be authentically Mycenaean. But basically it seems that the foundation of what we think of now as Greek mythology was established by then.

The great civilization represented by the palaces at Pylos,

Tiryns and Mycenae collapsed in about 1200 B.C., and was followed by a long period of disintegration and disorder, known to us as the dark ages of Greece. This was still the state of affairs when Homer began to compose his epics, during the eighth century B.C.; that is, some five hundred years after the golden age to which he referred. To the later Greeks this period which preceded their time was regarded as archaic (and that is the term now used for the span from 700 to about 550 B.C.), but it did produce the beginnings of art and thought on which the classical Greeks built. Homer himself was the main influence on the poets and dramatists of the classical period, through whom we come to know the myths today. He was followed, sometime up to a hundred years later, by the poet Hesiod, who also recorded and put into its definitive form the history of the gods from the very beginnings of time. No doubt both these poets were dealing with material very much older than their period, and were in fact themselves probably part of an old tradition rather than in any way innovators. No doubt too it was the historical chance of the spread of writing into eastern Europe at about that time which has saved their work for us, unlike that of their predecessors—if such did, as one suspects, exist. Although semi-pictorial scripts such as cuneiform had been in continuous use in Asia, and in Greece itself the use of ideograms and signs had flourished for a time with the Minoan and Mycenaean civilizations, writing became common practice in Europe only after the dark ages had begun to wane, when the Egyptian ideographic script became developed into something resembling a Greek alphabet.

It is for this reason that we need not worry about the question of whether or not there were many proto-Homers, since it was from Homer onwards that the complex of myths entered litera-ture. Literature then, in fact, existed. And the works of Homer and Hesiod, no doubt at least partly elaborated and developed in the process of copying, and certainly subjected to a long process of polishing and refining, were available to Pindar and Aeschylus in the fifth century B.C., the high point of the classical age.

The period between the Achaeans and Homer had probably also made its own additions. Certainly there had been another invasion, this time by iron-using tribes, again from the north, known to the Greeks of later times as the Dorians. They came southwards into Greece during the twelfth century, and since they seem to have come from elsewhere than the earlier Achaeans they perhaps brought with them ideas and beliefs gained by contact with other more northern European tribes. Perhaps their contribution to the complex later fixed by Homer was the element of heroic saga, the family feuds and embattled leaders which by then had been added to the tradition. But that is only speculation, and one could probably as easily trace such influences to Mesopotamia or elsewhere.

The later writers saw in Homer the embodiment of a national ideal. Whether or not he had this image of himself is not so sure. The Greece of his time had not entirely begun to cohere into a nation. But at some point there must have emerged from the succession of invading and settling tribes a sense of national identity, and it is certainly not hard to read this into Homer. The rulers of what then became Greece were no doubt conscious that some of them at least had not always been there. They needed a history. The new country needed to put down roots into a sound past.

In this function—if it was so—Homer's production of the matter of Greece makes him a comparable figure to that, in our own much smaller and younger national tradition, of Geoffrey of Monmouth. By his time, in the twelfth century A.D., the Norman French had occupied the land of the Angles and Saxons, who themselves had subjugated the Iron Age Celts, in their turn invaders of a country inhabited by an early Bronze Age population. The current rulers had no natural background, and needed therefore to be provided with an apprehension of the identity of the country. Geoffrey of Monmouth's achievement was the consolidation of a disordered tradition. He, like Homer, was then followed by a number of writers doing the same job. Three hundred years later Malory built on this foundation, just as three hundred years after Homer the classical dramatists reworked the Homeric matter of Greece.

The myths of Greece, like indeed those of Britain, belong to a loosely linked body of European and Near Eastern tradition. Much effort has gone into trying to trace the paths of influence and the connections. To some extent I feel this is futile, and to some extent unnecessary. The position, however, is one which tends to be defended with some vigour, and in fact it often seems as if schools of thought, in this as in other disciplines, get themselves unnecessarily into a situation of antagonism, whereas it would be more useful to set about recognizing complementarities.

The school of thought in this case which would see the various instances of a mythic theme as being descendants of an extremely ancient Indo-European folk-tale does not, of course, attempt to explain how the story arose in the first place, let alone why it went on being told. The task it sets itself is not a rival to such an explanation, however, so much as simply a different task. One body of thought seeks to find functions and significance; the other looks for connections, paths, patterns and distributions. The two tasks are perhaps related rather in the manner of those of the psychologist and the neuro-physiologist, the one seeking to explain or understand the system as a working whole, the other taking it meticulously apart to investigate the mechanism. There are two sorts of approaches to understanding how things work. The chauffeur and the motor mechanic deal with cars in different ways.

There must be instances—in cultural habits and symbols as well as in myths—of forms which are inevitable, simply because that is the only form which could fulfil the required conditions. These, if they exist, would be such that one would have no difficulty in believing that they have arisen separately at separate places. Writing, for instance, came into being in different ways, but developed to look structurally roughly the same. An apparently complicated implement like the bow and arrow must in fact have come into existence wherever men hunted—and been improved wherever they fought. And so there is no particular difficulty in understanding why it arose in so many widespread places. Personally I find little difficulty in supposing that there is an equally fixed shape to the body of matter which men find to be significant or impressive, and to the form in which they will therefore depict it. In a way you do not have much choice. The shape of hands predetermines the shape of the glove.

This is in no way to deny that the movement of ideas has been as widespread in Europe as the movement of people, and indeed of languages. It seems at first amazing to think of the distances which must have been traversed; but in fact it is not really very far from the Danube basin to County Clare, as long as you have a thousand years to make the journey. We know that the various tribal groups which wandered into Greece have left their residues of culture, some of which have become absorbed and some left stranded like erratic boulders. The Celts, for instance, came southwards as they did throughout Europe, and they left the kilt and the bagpipes behind—as indeed they seem to have left either one or the other or both almost everywhere, where they turn up now as cherished and deep-rooted elements in the local folk culture. The sources of such things grow to be forgotten, and they become quite genuinely Gallician, Genoese, Macedonian, or whatever.

So it undoubtedly is with myths. In spite of their complexity and differing origins, they get an over-all unity simply through being for so long together. The country too becomes an entity, however diverse its features and form are to begin with. Greece certainly varies a great deal, from the crags of Delphi to the groves of Olympia, or, more strikingly still, from the tame land of Attica to the mountain wildernesses of Crete. Yet it possesses a distinctive over-all Greekness, a familiarity and even to some extent predictability. The people who live in this varied landscape too, though different from place to place in such things as shape and size, have a reliable familiarity, a concordance of habit and manner which binds them together as the climate, colour and vegetation unifies the land. 'Ethos' is a good word: originally meaning a custom or institution, later expressing the spirit, the sense of identity, of a people. It is part of the ethos of Greece that you get the same commoditities—*souvlaki* grilled on the same trays of charcoal, ouzo out of the same squat glasses, olives and goat's-milk cheese and lean fresh meat—wherever you go, from northern Macedonia to the Mani, from the Dodecanese to the plains of Boeotia. The same wistful music jangles, the same hawker peddles the same nuts with the same hoarse shout.

How Greece achieved such an ethos, such a unity, is another story. This is not a book about Greek history—although history does inevitably crop up in association with the subject matter we are dealing with, and when it does it will be mentioned to the extent that is necessary. Greece would probably not be of much interest to us, however, and the Greek myths would not be the coherent body of imaginative material they are, had it not been for the classical age, the remarkable upsurge of talent which took place in Athens during the sixth and fifth centuries B.C.

The myths come to us in the form of one golden age looking back on another. It is because they are presented to us as they were viewed from that high point of the development of civilization that they have the power and intellectual appeal they have. Greece in effect went through two periods, a thousand years apart, at which it was further advanced in artistry, in order and material circumstance, not only than any other European country of the time but even than most which have developed since. The first of these high waves had a very long span; its effects were widely spread in space, and we are only now coming to understand the sophistication of its standards. The second period was remarkably short, but all the more intense, and extremely well recorded.

Perhaps we can conveniently view the latter period as beginning with Solon, of whom we shall hear more in the next chapter. He set a standard of intellectual and artistic concern which must have been a paradigm for later politicians. He died as early as the middle of the sixth century, and so lies quite close to the gap which stretches between Hesiod and the classical dramatists. The fifth century then opened with war, with the two invasions of Greece by Persia, the first repulsed, the second more disastrous. In the meantime Pericles had risen to prominence, under whose authority much of the great flowering of culture was to take place. And by then Aeschylus and Sophocles, the tragic dramatists, and Pindar, the poet, had been born.

What was remarkable was that it was not (as would better befit an artistic and intellectual blossoming) a time of settled politics and peace. In fact the classical period both began and ended with Athens at war—and what is more, usually losing—and in between there was almost constant political tension. If there is a peak within the peak it must lie in that brief fifty years of peace sandwiched between the second Persian invasion, defeated in 479 B.C., and the outbreak of the Peloponnesian War in 431. Those two looming clouds overshadow the classical period at both ends, and much of it in fact lies within their territory. During the intervening span the plays of Aeschylus were performed, the poems of Pindar written, and the historical chronicles of Herodotus compiled. Sophocles' *Oedipus Rex* falls within that stretch, but towards its end. By the time the comedy writer Aristophanes reached the stage, during the period when Socrates was teaching and Plato beginning to formulate his philosophy, Athens was at war again.

The Peloponnesian War lasted twenty-seven years, during which time it drained Athens gradually of its wealth, confidence and self-respect. It is under the influence of this that Euripides wrote his tragedies, so that our final view backward towards the era of the myths is as if across a battlefield and fraught with corresponding disillusion. Within that period, during which the matter crystallized into the form it must always now have, a shift of outlook, a change of view, was taking place. The change from Aeschylus to Euripides (like that slightly later and more famous one from Plato to Aristotle) represents a form of bringing to earth, a humanizing, secularizing process, the process in which the gods are starting to become redundant.

We get the tension of these attitudes and partly conflicting concerns in the myths, and perhaps this helps to explain their richness. In this sense too they are what they are because Greece was what it was. Firstly there is that broad, sheer, daybreak view between high mountains, with Homer providing an intermediate ground of relation and perspective, from a resurgent Greece to a Greece perhaps even more golden and greater, the dizzying view across the thousand-year gap to a land of gods and heroes. That too relied on a sense of place, being so inspiring only because it was a view to this same land, to these very places. Then the tradition is, almost at the same time, infused with the feeling of change, the influence of reality encroaching, that same process of integration—bringing into the human being himself the previously external forces of significance—which seems to be part of the organic development of religions. Realism and humanism are allies, and in fact the gods of Greece were always such as would conform to human needs, and the heroes easily adaptable to the function of giving expression to essentially human interests. That too is perhaps connected with their having come together there, rather than elsewhere.

If this simplified model is anything like correct, it helps us to understand not only how the Greek myths gained their prominence in European thought, but how they have maintained it. It does indeed seem that they continue to possess the power to interest and please, to a considerably greater extent than do the myths of many other countries. Perhaps it would express this best to say that we find our interests and concerns do to some extent correspond with those of the myths; and if so then it could well be that it is because both we and they are political, in Aristotle's sense—in the sense, that is, of being about the business of living together in some sort of order and security.

It is a pity that the word 'myth' has acquired its secondary meaning, of something which is not real. The Greek gods have played such an important part in people's thinking and way of life that they deserve to be exempt from the sort of implications which that usage makes. In fact there is probably nothing more real, in a way, than such a neatly identified and packaged bundle of concepts. In that sense Greece is no more or less real than Zeus is. Greece is not something presented to us by nature; rather it is a cultural construct. It exists only so long as people talk and behave as if it exists. Indeed, viewed like that, there was a time when Zeus existed and Greece did not. And the process may be carried almost indefinitely downwards, seeing all our familiar concepts as having this sort of conventional, working-hypothesis existence —the difference between what is viewed as real and what is viewed as unreal being a matter of temporal or cultural position, or even simply a matter of degree. The great American logician Willard Quine puts this view succinctly, in his book *From a Logical Point of View*:

> Physical objects are conceptually imported into the situation as convenient intermediaries—not by definition in terms of experience, but simply as irreducible posits comparable, epistemologically, to the gods of Homer. For my part I do, *qua* lay physicist, believe in physical objects and not in Homer's gods; and I consider it a scientific error to believe otherwise. But in point of epistemological footing the physical objects and the gods differ only in degree and not in kind. Both sorts of entities enter our conception only as cultural posits. The myth of physical objects is epistemologically superior to most in that it has proved more efficacious than other myths as a device for working a manageable structure into the flux of experience.

Possibly one of the reasons for the success of the myths of the Greek gods and heroes is that they have helped to do such business: to work a manageable structure into the flux of experience.

	STONE AGE	
B.C. 1800		Achaeans enter Greece
	MINOAN PERIOD	
	(Early Bronze Age)	
1600	. . . .	
1550		
1500	MYCENEAN PERIOD	Eruption of Thera
1450		Greek invasion of Crete
1400	(Bronze Age)	Fall of Knossos
1350		
1300		
1250		Fall of Troy
1200		
1150		
1100	. . . .	'Dorian' invasion
1050		Fall of Mycenae
1000	'GEOMETRIC' PERIOD	
950	(Iron Age)	
900		
850		
800		Traditional first Olympics
750		Homer
700	. . . .	
650	'ARCHAIC' PERIOD	Hesiod
600		
550		Solon
500	. . . .	Persian invasion
	CLASSICAL PERIOD	

B

TWO

ATHENA AND THE CITY

OUT OF THE AFFECTION which comes from long familiarity, one is prepared to forgive it for its faults. This is not exactly the sort of fondness based on admiration. After all, there is no denying that it is an ugly, noisy city. One gets to like it accidentally, as part of the process of getting to know one's way around: knowing where to go to be left alone, where to go to get robbed. I think of it rather as one might think of an old friend, whom we might once, but would not now, have wished to be different. It shows that you do not have to respect your friends.

Looking from the Pnyx or the Acropolis you see the sprawl of it, the unabashed confusion of its hectic scramble towards the hills. Visually a shock—those undesigned square blocks merging into a cubist texture of nightmare complexity—that view evolves over the years into an understanding of its meaning, of the many facets and attitudes of the apparently simple city. The comfortable suburbanness of Kifissia, the sedate self-confidence of Maroussi, the haphazard practicality of the new housing around Imitos. And the Piraeus; and Glifada; and Kolonaki; and Monastiraki.

And, right below your feet as you stand on the edge of the Acropolis, Plaka. As in Naples and Lisbon, the old town crawls rather pitifully up the hill. It looks like what it is: the remnants of a previous, humbler Athens, become the quarter of cheap housing and the refuge of the vagabond industries and the poor, growing from its natural role as red-light district (into which all such old places with narrow streets inevitably develop) to become Nighttown; and hence, alas, moving to its present apotheosis, as the greatest, flashiest and most jangling tourist trap in the world, even including Bourbon Street.

The point that Plaka and Monastiraki make about the city is a valid one: its legacy is not pushed to its outskirts, but lies at its heart. And as it always has done, the Acropolis itself lies at the heart of that. To stand there looking out and down all around is to understand at once that the city has developed from that spot outwards—that the Acropolis is the hub, the nucleus, and the *raison d'être* for all that sprawling, raucous squalor. It has grown from the kernel outwards—indeed it is still doing so. It has grown in an organic and cellular way, but unlike most examples of that natural structure its peripheral development has not had the effect of draining the centre to the point of decay. The city is still quite firmly based on its original node.

It is inevitable, then, that Athena, patroness of this city, should dominate the Acropolis, its centre, which has from early times been her home. Her origins and those of the city in fact coincide, since the rock which bears such close associations with her in the myth formed also the citadel of the early settlements which grew into historic Athens. The latter had Stone Age origins, and no one considering the site would be surprised that from the time at which people began to group themselves into settlements this prominent view-point over the plain bounded by hills and sea would have been selected for the purpose. There is some reason to suppose that the other too, the myth, is decidedly ancient, and Athena may well have been worshipped at the Mycenaean settlement which grew up on this same spot.

Homer mentions her in connection with the list of troops attending the Trojan War. There he describes Athena as herself founding the residence of King Erechtheus, as a sort of proto-patroness of his city. This close association between the goddess and the legendary king is in fact basic to her story. And it is remarkable too that the other strand in the myth, the contest with Poseidon, is equally localized, and set in exactly the same place.

Athena, or, as she is often called, Athene, is, as originally presented to us by Homer, a figure worthy of respect. To him she clearly represented the heights of intellect and craftsmanship, the very qualities so admired and developed by his classical Athenian

successors. To them her possession of these qualities developed
into patronage of those who practised them, and she became not
only a goddess of wisdom but the patron goddess of several crafts,
of weaving and pot-making, and probably also of those metal-
working trades which still cluster around the base of the
Acropolis, where Plaka tails off into the chaos and din of
Monastiraki. In Monastiraki today the sound of the metal-
workers' hammers still competes with the general hubbub.

Perhaps it was the hint given in Homer of her unusual subtlety
of mind—the quality shared by her favourite among the heroes
(and we guess his favourite too), the wily Odysseus—that
endeared her to the later citizens of that complex city, where she
became, in classical times, so splendidly enthroned. Athens is
above all a city with a mind, a place where quick thinking often
pays, where things are not always as they appear to be on the
surface, just as the lines of the Parthenon are not the straight and
parallel lines they seem but have been carefully tempered to
match the eye's deceit. In this connection the contrast with Rome
is very striking, the comparison of these ruins with those and of
this city with that making the point that Athens has to be understood on a level other than the immediate one. It does not,
and did not intend to, present itself to you in all its glory just
as it is.

Possibly one of the reasons for Greece's pre-eminence in
intellectual history (and so one of the reasons for the status of its
myths) is that it was not entirely a materially based culture.
Certainly the period of expansion under the influence of Themistocles, the political chauvinism of Peisistratus or Pericles, have
strong imperialistic and economic overtones. But its values even
then were other than purely materialistic, and this fact is demonstrated sufficiently by a look at the remains. Pericles used the
wealth acquired by political domination to build temples. To
compare those two great cities, Rome and Athens, one has only
to compare the uses of their two main monuments: the Parthenon
for worship and celebration of an ideal, the Colosseum for
staging all those monstrous entertainments.

If Athena was influential in this, we have to thank her. Greece did not become the sort of military bureaucracy on which later empires have been modelled. By missing this it preserved a strand of concern with other matters, and to some extent, in spite of the emphasis on industrial development and the lure of the European Economic Community, it preserves this tradition of thought today. The Greeks remain an intelligent, subtle-minded people. They respect knowledge and thought, and even in their *embourgeoisement* they have not become severely vulgarized. What many Greeks value most about Greece is precisely the basic quality that we enjoy there: the air, the light, the warm nights and the clear sea. They have a sense of the value inherent in the nature of their surroundings.

Athena stands out in the Olympian pantheon for her specifically mental gifts; but in other respects she fits with the others into the spectrum of roles which they combine to fill. Like Artemis she represents womanhood in its non-sexual aspect: the rather aloof and impressive attitude of being womanly independent of sensuality. In this they are the counterpart of the other pair of major goddesses, Hera, the goddess of matrimony, and Aphrodite, goddess of love. But Athena quite lacks, in all her appearances in myth, Artemis' defiant masculinity. She remains a woman, doing women's tasks, an adept at the loom and a figure of comfort and affection.

She also remains, however, *parthenos*, the maid; and her story emphasizes the importance of her virginity. When wooed by Hephaestus, the craftsman god, she repulsed him and fled, with the result that he ejaculated accidentally on to Attica. In doing so he fertilized the earth, and a child resulted whom Athena (evidently feeling partly responsible) hid and arranged to have reared in secret. The story perhaps echoes a similar implied claim made by the Thebans, which we shall come across later, to the effect that the people of those places were indigenous, born from the earth itself.

Cecrops was the king of Athens at the time, the myth says, and it was to his daughters that Athena gave the basket containing the infant, Erichthonius, with the warning that the girls should not look inside. The sisters inevitably did so; in myth it seems to be sufficient to forbid something to ensure that it takes place. They went mad at what they saw and leapt from the Acropolis. Erichthonius was a monster, it seems: he had a serpent's tail.

In spite of that handicap the myth appears to see him as becoming king of Athens after Cecrops; his grandson Erechtheus, in these versions, is the legendary king who is worshipped on the Acropolis. Homer, however, speaks of these two as one and the same, names them both Erechtheus, and does not mention the serpent's tail. This certainly simplifies the matter. In other versions again Erichthonius/Erechtheus is not deformed, but merely accompanied in his basket by a serpent. That, however, hardly seems to present good cause for jumping off the Acropolis.

One of the main festivals of Athens in early recorded times, the Panathenaea, involved a reference to the myth which seems to indicate a cult of mystery and perhaps initiation similar to that of Demeter at Elevsis. Before the festival started a small procession of little girls carried containers on their heads down from the Acropolis to a temple below, and carried other receptacles back again. The connection with the myth resides in the fact that the contents of the containers was not known, and, it may be presumed, knowledge of it was forbidden.

Though there is much in all this that is obscure, due no doubt to the imposition of later on to earlier material, the Erechtheon is real enough, the complex Periclean temple covering the site where Athena was believed to have held her primordial contest with Poseidon for possession of the city—which in effect meant the whole of Attica. The Erechtheon incorporates the very spot where the trial was supposed to have taken place, and at the same time serves as a commemoration of the other strand of Athena's myth by acting as a shrine both to her and to Erechtheus.

The question of which of the deities should dominate Attica and Athens had apparently been smouldering for some time. That is—in translation of the symbolism—the choice which Attica had to make between a land-based culture and a seagoing one. The two immortals met to dispute it on the Acropolis, and there Poseidon struck the ground with his trident and brought forth a spring of salt water. In competition Athena caused an olive tree to sprout there, and the gods, through the mouth of Cecrops, judged this to be more useful. Athena became the patron goddess of the city, and olives the financial base of Attica.

The tree was still there when the Persians invaded in 480, and survived their attempts to burn it down. Indeed it seems that one supposed to be it was still there even in Roman times, when also the well of salt water was shown to the traveller Pausanias. Pericles constructed the present temple, the Erechtheon, around these sacred emblems, near the site of an old temple to Athena and Poseidon, in the course of his rebuilding and expansion in the early fourth century; and it is that interesting but slightly clumsy building which we can see today. The unique shape of it, which makes it seem quite unlike a classical temple, is due to the need to keep separate the cults which it housed. It is famous, of course, for what were at one time its six roof-bearing maidens, the caryatids, one of which has been in the British Museum and represented on site by a cast since its removal, at a time when only two of the figures remained in place, by Lord Elgin. The remaining originals were found in 1976 to need protection, since by then the poisonous fumes of the modern city had begun to eat into them. At that time many of the other statues on the Acropolis were removed to the museum and replaced by casts, and consequently even less now survives in its original place of the grand Periclean scheme.

Athena triumphed, at this spot on the edge of the rock, and the city became hers. She characteristically tends to pick the winning side. In her earlier form she is a warlike figure, and even when softened by gentler associations she is most often depicted with helmet and shield. Indeed the myths tell of her coming into being in this style, emerging fully armed from the head of Zeus, who had been suffering from an agonizing pre-natal headache.

Her love of battle and of the challenge of contest reveals itself from time to time, such as in the episodes of Perseus' fight against the Gorgons, in which she favoured and helped him to the extent of finally being given the severed Gorgon's head. This she is often shown as wearing hanging at the front of her aegis, that sort of leather breastplate which is characteristic of her dress—

although apparently it is regarded as being on loan from Zeus, to whom it belonged. In this case guile or wit again seem to have played their part in her warlike character, rather than sheer heroic might, since it was a question of finding a way for Perseus to cut off Medusa's head without having to look into the monster's terrible, stone-making face. Athena, the story says, guided the hero's hand, while he looked at the face of Medusa only as a reflection in his shield.

If her behaviour at Troy is anything to go by, we may indeed conclude that Athena's warriorship was rather a matter of love of politics and intrigue than a lust for fighting. She found herself on the Greek side not just as an Attic goddess but as the failed rival of Aphrodite, whom Paris had favoured in his award for the most beautiful and who therefore promoted the Trojan cause. In the *Iliad* we find Athena in disguise behind the enemy lines, inciting provocative actions, diverting arrows, and exhorting her troops once battle is joined. She has a special role as the spirit which inspires heroes, and it is in this that she shines in the *Odyssey*, where, from the opening council onwards, she dedicates herself completely to the long and demanding process of steering her favourite hero, wise Odysseus, through his torments and trials towards home.

This human concern, coupled with a love of complication, seems to me to be very Greek. It is as if they have instilled into her, their home goddess, some of the features in their own make-up which perhaps they themselves would never recognize. On the one hand they display those qualities which combine to distinguish human beings from both machines and animals; and on the other they have a sort of restless, interfering spirit which will not let them live peacefully. The latter quality it is, perhaps, which makes them ungovernable, even after every form of government yet devised has been tried. If no one can govern the Greeks, it is perhaps because they are simply too interested in political ideas.

This sort of questioning awareness was very much at the back of the classical crescendo, the time when Athena came into her own. The age which built the Parthenon was that which then condemned the pacific Socrates, for heresy and for holding anti-government opinions, and which, perhaps most tellingly, gave rise to the iconoclastic and rebellious works of Aristophanes. It is the close political concern, the almost obsessive refusal to leave anything unquestioned, which makes plays like the *Wasps* seem so poignantly Greek. Scurrilous, irreverent, lewd: but mentally independent.

When the Parthenon was built, in the 440s B.C., Athens had reached some sort of a conclusion to a period of quite remarkable political variation. Since the early seventh century, by which time monarchy had been abandoned, almost every form of government had been tried and rejected in Attica. Oligarchy turned to aristocracy, which became, with the rise of trade and the invention of coinage, plutocracy. Solon for a time gained complete personal power, but his benevolent autocracy was replaced by the tyranny of Peisistratus. After that there was a spell of such frequent change that it must at times have resembled anarchy, which had been replaced shortly before the Persian invasion by the new democracy of Cleisthenes, which Pericles was to stablilize, and which later became so famous and influential throughout the world. Yet it is ironic that it is often said that democracy originated in Athens, when so did every other form of political rule. In the long spell of ding-dong politics, from Solon, in about 600, to the first Persian invasion, in 492, and the subsequent rise of military power, almost every form of control for which the Greeks have a word can be identified.

The democracy of Cleisthenes, Cimon and Pericles was itself the child of the reforms introduced by Solon. He in turn was the product of his time, the result of even earlier political experiments and complications. Greek politics is not so much a series of new starts as a continuous flow, in which each mistake may be seen as an attempt, itself, to put right the previous mistake. Solon's self-imposed task was to bring Athens back from the edge of a near-crisis, the result of the accelerating effect of the social and economic measures embodied in the Draconian code.

Like so many of the major figures in early Greek history, Solon had not set out to become a politician. He was influential by birth, but his rise to power was largely a consequence of the situation. The people recognized him as a suitable arbitrator in the conflict of interests between the increasingly estranged social classes. By Draco's laws it was possible to lose one's freedom if one got into debt, and with the coming into being of a new economic system more and more people found themselves in the power of the owners of property. With no capital or security, the relatively poor were open to exploitation, at this time when trade had replaced barter and circumstances favoured the few who could control the market outlets.

Solon was appointed archon (a type of magistrate) in 594 B.C., and asked for, and received, the power to legislate. The choice and confidence of the people were not misplaced, since he then produced a set of laws which led to a new kind of state, and on which the future leaders were able to build. What is remarkable about him is that this was not all he did; he was known and revered as a philosopher, wrote poetry which stood comparison with the greatest, and travelled abroad, being received with honour at the courts of the Egyptians.

Perhaps no less a person could have undertaken the crucial reformation of the social order which his laws amounted to. As a result of his new code, the classes found themselves both clearly identified and given reasonable security, their imbalance removed, with a role in public affairs for even the most humble citizen. This was the foundation built on by Cleisthenes, who established the first thing actually labelled a democracy, in 507 B.C.

That way of putting it is perhaps more accurate than it would be to say of it, as is often said, that it *was* the first democracy. What originated in Athens was rather the use of the word as a sort of euphemism for something else. In fact true democracy, the rule by the *demos*, the people as a whole, is probably impossible, and can hardly have been tried. At first sight the Athenian form looks remarkably like a possibly unique example of the real thing. The Council, which had the executive power, was chosen by lot from the whole of the citizenship. It was responsible to the Assembly, which every citizen was entitled to attend, to speak and vote and (to make this not just the sort of right enjoyed by those who could afford it) to claim attendance pay. The President of the Council was chosen in the same way, by lot, and to ensure even further that this position would not put power into the hands of one man, he stood for a single day. Any citizen of Athens could thus become President; but not for long.

This procedure of appointing officials not by election but by drawing lots clearly has much to recommend it. It provides a truly equal chance for all, while the winning of elections too often depends not just on the ability to tell popular lies and be believed, but on the possession of sufficient funds and friends for an effective campaign. The qualities required to win elections are in fact not those which go with integrity, sincerity and the sort of altruistic dedication to one's fellow men which ideal politicians might have. Votes favour the specious and the rich. Through the strenuous campaigning required to win them they promote the ruthless and the ambitious. Drawing lots has the advantage that it favours no one. In the Athens of the first democracies every citizen really had an equal chance to share in governing.

Every citizen. The catch comes when we consider that the right to citizenship was, to put it mildly, somewhat exclusive. Living in a 'democracy' was no particular benefit if you were a slave, as more than a hundred thousand of the small population of Attica were at the time. In fact the exercise of such a complete 'democracy' probably depends on the possession by the ordinary citizen of sufficient leisure to take an interest in politics; and so it is perhaps essentially a slave-based system which the Greeks invented under that name. Only a minute proportion of the total population would actually have had both the right, as adult male citizens, and the opportunity, living within reach of the place of assembly, to take part—perhaps in fact less than a tenth of the people then living in the territory which they directly governed. Resident foreigners were not citizens, nor were women and children. The idea of democracy in the end turns on a matter of definition.

In the meantime Athens had begun to flourish as a cultural and political centre. Under the tyranny of Peisistratus, in the 540s, those great institutions had come into being which were the ground of the artistic flowering of the next century. He it was who promoted the tales of Homer as a national expression of identity, encouraging dramatic performances of them and even the first proper publication. He reformed the great Panathenaic festival, to make it a sort of Athenian advertisement. He founded another festival, later to become of even more importance, the Great Dionysia, centred in later times and no doubt then on the theatre of Dionysus below the Acropolis, where the birth of drama took place and, in the course of the festival's expansion, many of the world's best plays came to be written and performed.

Peisistratus, as part of his policy for the aggrandisement of Athens, started the building of great temples, and instituted by doing so a sort of official Olympian religion. There is no doubt that from then on the Athenian version, those gods ranked high by being honoured in Athens, became the official religion of the Greeks. What is remarkable, however, is that although Zeus and others had their place in this renewal of Athens, when Pericles came to give it its finished form Athena remained triumphant in her city. All three of the temples on the Acropolis are dedicated to her.

The layout of the Acropolis is similar to that of many other Greek religious sanctuaries, only grander. It makes the most of its advantage of being, from the start, above you. You enter the area up broad marble steps, a steep climb in the heat, having already wound your way upwards for some distance along the processional way. The great gateway itself, the Propylaea, provides a suitably imposing formal entrance, still impressively noble and tall, much of it still fortunately standing. It is interesting that this elaborate gateway was designed in close relationship to the Parthenon itself, in its alignment and proportion, so that its function seems to have been that of preparation and introduction. It is as one steps out of the Propylaea the other side that one gets a first uninterrupted view of the Parthenon, seeing it now, due to the Propylaea's position, at a diagonal angle, and from a slightly lower level. Thus it reveals, at this first view, many of its best achievements to their best advantage. Both the length and the breadth can be seen at once, a side and an end, and its height and size are emphasized by its position at the top of a gently rising open slope.

Since one usually passes through the Propylaea merely eager to get that view, it is easy to overlook the point that it is at least partly to the careful siting of the approach that the view owes its impact. The building itself, moreover, the massive gateway—though the Peloponnesian War prevented its completion—is remarkable enough to be enjoyed in its own right. When roofed and with gilded ceilings it must have served the function of inducing a suitably reverential mood in those who passed upward through it.

The area enclosed on the flat top of this hill contained then, as it does now, the remnants of several ages of use. Pericles' architects seem to have wanted to preserve the relics of the work of their ancestors, since for instance the south wing of the Propylaea carefully avoids a section of Mycenaean walling, still to be seen on the uphill side of the temple of Athena Nike. All over the Acropolis small remnants of pre-Periclean buildings can be found; and the classical age itself added a spread of small structures to the main design. The Periclean plan itself was spacious and simple, consisting of three great buildings, the temples of the Parthenon and the Erechtheon, and the entrance-way by which they must be approached. To these the delightful Athena Nike was added in the 420s, in belated celebration of the defeat of Persia, to house a statue of Athena in her warlike role of Nike, bringer of victory. From early times confusion with a separate embodiment of this idea, a goddess usually shown as winged, gave the statue the nickname of 'the wingless Victory', a description of this version of Athena which, for all its antiquity, is totally incorrect. The temple juts out almost vertiginously to the edge of its bastion, and this edge then provides a high and wide view towards the sea—none other (says the characteristically specific myth) than the view which Theseus' father Aegeus had when, seeing the black-sailed ship returning from Crete, he wrongly thought his son to have been killed by the Minotaur, and leapt from this view-point to his death on the rocks below.

While the Erechtheon was built (as we have seen) to cover the

sacred sites of the Acropolis and house their cults, the Parthenon—
which gets its name, 'place of the virgin', from the chastity of the
goddess who lived in its inner cell—was clearly a central showpiece from the start, a place which one would come to to be
awed and made to gasp. It took some nine years to build, a band
of master craftsmen supervised by the sculptor Pheidias working
all at once on its various components. Though Pheidias himself
concentrated on the cult statue which it housed, he no doubt
planned and oversaw the making of the other statuary. All the
highly developed architectural expertise of the age was brought
into play in the construction of what was clearly intended to be
(as it probably in fact is) the best building ever made. Geometrical
accuracy was combined with a highly advanced study of optics
to give us those well-known architectural tricks: the rise towards
the centre of the base lines, by which a curved line comes to
look horizontal where a straight one would, over this length,
appear to sag; the swollen middles of the columns which make
them appear to taper evenly, where even ones would look
pinched; the corner columns fatter than the central ones, and the
distances between them correspondingly wider; the columns
moreover all leaning slightly inwards, so as not to seem to be
leaning out. These were not new or exclusively Athenian tricks,
but the great size of the Parthenon increased their importance and
emphazises the extraordinary precision required in their application. Roofed in wood with marble tiling, the finished temple
was then painted in such a way as to emphasize its shadows and
highlight its reliefs. Nobody could ever have failed to be
impressed.

Plutarch, looking back with some awe from the Athens of the
early decades of our own era, tells the story of how Pericles came
to be able to carry out his astonishing scheme. It was not, it
seems, without is shifty aspects, since Athens had somehow
succeeded in taking charge of the contributions of money which
all the Greek states had made to fund protection against the
Persian invasion, a treasure formerly stored on the sacred island
of Delos. The Athenians moved this to the Acropolis, 'for its
greater safety'; and it was thus that it came to be used by Pericles

to finance his grand design, with the argument that in doing so he was providing employment.

It is sad, but perhaps in the style of things, that this time of prosperity, the golden age of the rule of Pericles, was succeeded in his own lifetime by the catastrophe of the Peloponnesian War.

It seems to have been a sort of self-destructive will that drove Athens to war. As Thucydides reports it, it looks like a matter of pride as much as necessity: as if the Athenians had to believe that they could withstand anything, even the threatening Spartan invasion, rather than come to terms. The imaginative report he gives of Pericles' oration bears the message that all they stood for, as Athenians, was superior to the institutions of their enemies. Their attitude to work, their use of leisure, their training and education . . . 'Our love of what is beautiful does not lead us to extravagance; our love of the things of the mind does not make us soft.' It is a statement both of what it was they believed they were defending and of Pericles' own ideals, but particularly of what it meant to regard oneself as an Athenian at that climactic time. 'Mighty indeed are the marks and monuments of our empire which we have left. Future ages will wonder at us, as the present age wonders at us now.'

We are lucky, of course, to have Thucydides to record these impressions for us, to enable us better to understand what sort of thing it was that took place, just as we are lucky to have Herodotus to do the same for the earlier period of the Persian war. The two great historians span the classical age, each in his own way bringing his qualities to bear on the slightly different times and circumstances. As a historian Thucydides is the more careful, level-headed and reliable, but he lacks the personal touch which makes Herodotus so readable, the liveliness of mind and flashes of insight, the highly lit, almost glamorous, depiction, and the sharpness of style which lifts the works out of the often wooden spirit of serious academic history, and places them among works of art. As with Ruskin's *Modern Painters*, or the books of Gilbert White and Isaak Walton, one reads Herodotus not just for the subject matter but because the mind and attitudes of the man are accidentally revealed.

The war gave rise to political change, and when the Spartans eventually won they imposed on Athens the brief but unpopular rule of a militaristic junta known as the Thirty Tyrants. This was a time worthy indeed of the sarcasm and bitterness of Aristophanes and Euripides. It was also the period of the brief involvement with politics of the philosopher Socrates.

Though he remained as far as he could politically aloof and independent, circumstances conspired to ensnare Socrates at a particularly difficult time. He had by chance found himself President of the Assembly on a day when a controversial motion was proposed, which he ruled to be illegal and refused to put, thus making himself seem biased. But what most lay behind his political unpopularity was his friendship with some of the dictators in earlier days, perhaps associated in the public eye with his known distrust of the arbitrariness of democracy.

Democracy came back—it all seems rather familiar—and an amnesty was declared; and it was during the amnesty that Socrates was put on trial. As a consequence he could not be accused of any political crime, such as his suspected involvement with the dictators. Instead the new leaders accused him of corrupting the young, and of not believing in the gods recognized by the state but in other deities. With a stubbornness which seems to mirror the self-destructive impulse of his city in those years, he mocked his accusers rather than answering the charges, and, though given many opportunities to save himself, was duly condemned to death.

Perhaps he felt it was time to go. Athens was suddenly past its best. Perhaps he felt that the farce of his trial and condemnation was itself a fitting memorial, guessing rightly that it would never be forgotten or forgiven.

Such a dedication to a mental standpoint is exceptional, but in its combination of obtuseness and wisdom it seems peculiarly Athenian, a part of that drive which leads the Greeks to continue to destroy their own ease and peace of mind. Perhaps it was true that Socrates did not believe in those fixed, bounded deities; to him probably the gods were an unknown quantity. If so, this too is a traditional sort of reaction, an unwillingness to accept the packaged official form, the state-approved way of thinking. 'Men of Athens,' said St Paul, 'I see that in everything that concerns religion you are uncommonly scrupulous. For as I was going round looking at the objects of your worship, I noticed among other things an altar bearing the inscription "To an Unknown God".'

The idea perhaps seems absurd, and certainly it is in conflict with what one sees when one stands now on that rock, the Areopagus, above the plate bearing the text with those numinous, suggestive words—*Agnosto Theo*—and looks out from there across the small hollow to those rearing emblems of the gods who were, so very clearly, known. You do not build such temples to provide a dwelling for, or to mark the site of the deeds of, a god who is not known. Everything about the Parthenon suggests definition, precision, delimitation, reification in a comprehensible form. The gulf between the ways of thought obtrudes itself, seen from the Areopagus, the separation of the abstract from the real. Even the unconstructed naturalness of these bare smooth heaps of rock, where one comes in the evenings to savour the glow which falls across the city, as the lights begin to assert themselves across the miles of rattling urbanness below, and the Parthenon begins to crumble warmly into the dusk. The wildness of the Areopagus, the formal articulateness of the Acropolis: a contrast like the two moods which the two places, and their functions, induce. Amongst the mathematical precision of the temples you come to understand, to conceive in terms of fixed forms, of firm ideas and ideals. You come up on the Areopagus in the evening to be influenced by a mood, to contemplate and consider.

It is a contrast too to leave either place then and descend to the haphazard, jostling streets of Athena's very human city. In many ways the centre of it has a small-town feel, and as in any small town one sees the same people again and again. The durability and persistence of it impress one too, the way it goes on and on; day and night, year by year. Every night at about the same time the frail flower-seller comes down the taverna steps to walk around the tables with her red and white carnations, her white face and her red shawl; year after year. The old man sits for decades behind the same desk, counting the perpetual receipts. You go back to places years later and you find the same waiters cleaning the same tables. Durable, intransigent, familiar city.

How can you really love it, people wonder: how can one love a place so dirty and disordered? Chickens turning in cheap restaurants behind Omonia? Whores in the doorways of Athinas Street? The smell of *souvlaki* grilling in the windows of Ermou? Sordid and uncouth, one thinks, particularly on those suffocating days of car-fumed airlessness; not recognizably lovable at all.

And certainly there is much that is not, even seen through the rosy haze of nostalgia and old associations (memories of the dawn coming up over Kolonaki, and walking home through empty streets). That sound from the Acropolis at dusk, for instance: the despairing wail of a thousand amplified bouzoukis, each competitively playing a different tune. Those steps up which one struggles constantly concussed by the vulgarity and self-destruction of Plaka, now a cruel caricature of its one-time self. But every aspect of it seems to throw to you, if you persevere, the reward of an unexpected compensation. And Plaka even at its worst is to some extent saved by the fact that once you have at last struggled up those nightmare steps, fighting off the touts and importunate waiters, maddened by the electronic din, you come out on to open hillside under the Acropolis, the remnants of old strata of Athens, where the hovels dotting Plaka's fringe almost merge into the stone of the slope. There chickens scratch and goats bleat and old women carry bundles across the worn ground of a perennial Greek hillside village.

Its quirks redeem it. They also reveal its latent nature, the sort of palimpsest of ages in which you can even now observe the old under the gloss of the new. Although the modern city is largely undistinguished, featureless and free of any depth of history, Plaka and Monastiraki seem like the remnants of older places, which they are—the fortified area of the pre-classical city, the area of retreat from invasion specified by Thucydides and, later, the humble village to which Athens had shrunk during the long span between the end of the Roman Empire and its restoration to eminence in the 1830s.

We have to remember that Athens had, by then, nearly disappeared. The Acropolis itself was in even greater ruins than it is at present. One of the temples—that charming, delicate Ionic temple of Athena Nike, 'Victory' Athena—has been completely rebuilt. The Ottoman Empire treated the Acropolis as a garrison fortress, and from 1456 until the War of Independence in the 1820s and '30s it was badly mistreated. But even before the Turks came, as Roman power faded and Christianity developed, Athens had become a small town.

The Parthenon consequently has seen a very varied life. Since its initial success as the principal feature of Pericles' grand plan for the reconstruction of Athens after its sack by the Persians, it has undergone various uses. It became a Christian church as early as A.D. 450, and later attained the status of a cathedral. Under the Turks it was a mosque, complete with hastily erected minaret. In spite of this continued sacredness the Parthenon was being used as a store for gunpowder in the siege of 1687, when on 26 September the Venetian artillery landed a mortar shell into it and blew it up.

Until 1976 you could walk freely through the ruins that are left, and lean against those carefully carved pillars, come and go up those precipitous steps, treading the sacred floor, touching the walls. It gave a special sense of location; leaning against the pillars of the Parthenon you know exactly where you are. This is curtailed now, by small forbidding notices, the whole thing having become afflicted not just by time but by exponential growth. Too many people come now, a horde of increasing thousands, rubbing the enduring pavings with twice as many feet.

If you can dodge the cameras and the posing wives—Shall I stand here? Are you close enough? Is the focus right? And shall I smile?—and get away from the guided tours and the herded, packaged parties, it still looks confidently majestic. Battered and eroded, but with a sense of being indestructibly sublime. Not in the flat light of the afternoon, when most people see it, when the stone sits lifelessly in the shadowless glare. But for instance in the early evenings when it throws long shadows, when the light coming from over Phaleron takes on a glow of colour, and the thing starts to stir to life in the process of its gradual change towards that rich warmth with which the stone glows at sunset. But most of all it comes into its own on the nights of full moon, when the size and sheer audacity of the concept impose themselves, the ruin becoming again the complete idea which it was in daylight when it had its roof and corners, since in this sheer white light it shines as a whole and single object, like a large and pure quartz crystal. Few things in fact have that completeness, that self-identity, as when in a clear night it rises from the rock in brilliant command and precision.

Perhaps with all its trappings and decorations it would even have seemed less sublime. It was certainly a very elaborate building. After the explosion many of the statues of Pheidias and the friezes were lying cracked and broken, and the few that remained in place suffered later. The Venetian general Morosini tried to lower one remaining group from the west pediment with inadequate tackle, which broke while the statues were in mid-air and smashed them to the ground. For a hundred years then nobody cared. Lord Elgin was the British Ambassador to Turkey at the turn of the eighteenth century, and in 1801 sought permission to make drawings and casts of the remaining fragments and specimens of the ancient statuary. By then it was almost too late, since bits and pieces had been sold arbitrarily and had spread all over Europe—as a result of which we now find a large number of enormous torsos, and very few heads. Elgin decided that what was left on the Acropolis was not in safe hands, and in the years 1802–4 he set about removing what he could to safety. Transporting them to Britain cost him over £75,000, drawn from his personal fortune, for which he was awarded by a grateful nation by the purchase of the marbles for £35,000. A special room was built for them at the British Museum, where they may now be seen in almost ideal conditions.

Of course it would have been preferable if they could have stayed where they were, and no doubt there is an argument for returning them to a site on the Acropolis itself should space there be available. But when they were removed they were no longer in position, and would not have stayed for long among the rubble of the ruins. And those statues which remained on the Parthenon have themselves now been taken down, after having suffered considerably in the meantime from erosion by the filthy Athens air.

The Elgin Marbles, as they are always called, are in fact sadly fragmentary and much damaged. Many of the heads of the best pieces are in museums in other cities, having presumably been picked up by amateur collectors or souvenir hunters of various nations. From the south side of the Parthenon we can see the dramatic depiction of the battle of the Lapiths and the centaurs, referring to the occasion when at a wedding feast the centaurs got drunk and abducted the bride. Pheidias seems to have enjoyed shaping horses, and these struggling human/horse forms have a special power. They have human heads and hands, and incidentally human sexual organs, and also human expressions of anguish. Unfortunately the statues of the west pediment are badly incomplete, and give us only a suggestion of the power and pomp which the group must have possessed, since this is the story of the contest of Athena and Poseidon, in which he produced a spring of salt water, she an olive tree.

A processional scene of horses and youths ran round the north and south friezes, with, on the east end of the south one, a religious procession of maidens and cows flowing to join it; the whole culminates on the eastern side with groups of waiting gods. This is the Panathenaic procession, when the people brought to the goddess a new sacred robe to cover her cult statue on the Acropolis.

The scene on the east pediment is also dramatic, with the head of a braying horse of the chariot of the moon sinking into the sea on the right, as the horses of the chariot of the sun burst from the waves on the left. The care and detail can be seen at the close quarters permitted by the British Museum display, although one can only imagine the effect which this vast arrangement must have had on the equally grand end of the Parthenon. That their detail stands up to close inspection under museum conditions is amazing enough, but most remarkably these figures, designed to be seen from a distance and from below against the roof of the temple, are as finely and carefully carved at the back, where they could never have been seen at all had they stayed where they were intended to be.

The great gold and ivory statue of the goddess which formed the central feature of the Parthenon's interior has not survived, but we do on the whole know what the goddess was thought to look like. In the National Museum, for instance, we find a bronze statue of the fourth century B.C., showing her wearing her helmet but otherwise dressed in gentle female costume. The eyes of the statue give to the face a look of sympathy, almost of pity. Her aspects of wisdom and righteousness, rather than the cunning, are being displayed.

In the Acropolis museum there are further fragments of frieze and broken statuary, left behind by Elgin. There are statues there as well from other parts of the Acropolis and from other periods. It is interesting to see on many of these the remains of the colouring with which they were originally covered. The red tresses of the women and the key-patterned costumes are picked out. We can see from an example in the Agora museum that even the capitals of the columns were painted. Now and then one begins to suspect that the statue-crowded, highly decorated Acropolis, with its dense elaboration of ornament and its clutter of minor monuments, would have seemed to us much less impressive than these existing ruins.

This sort of ambivalence too is probably characteristic, the feeling that a fair amount of human error may have occurred along with the examples of perfection. It is doubtful, in fact, if perfection would have expressed them adequately, the multi-faceted, complex Athenians, and their warlike but womanly patroness. Homer perhaps reveals his opinion of them when he makes Athena, in the *Odyssey*, praise (and yet at the same time criticize) Odysseus for those very qualities of deviousness which, she admits, or boasts, she shares with him. We are both, she says, experts in trickery. You in the world of men are peerless in politics and oratory; among the gods I am foremost for invention and resourcefulness. So devious you are, she says, lover of lying and intrigue. And yet so civilized, intelligent and self-possessed. Homer intended Athena to express there the qualities with which she sympathized. Perhaps in doing so she accidentally summarized the character of her own home city.

Dates mostly approximate:

– 600
–   Pericles born 590
–
–
–

      Solon died 558
– 550
–
–

      Aeschylus born 525

–   Pindar born 518

–
– 500
–

      Euripides and Herodotus born 484
–   Persian invasion 480–479
–

      Socrates born 469
–   Thucydides born 460
      Aeschylus' trilogy 458; dies 456
– 450
      Aristophanes born 445
      Sophocles' *Antigone* 442
–   Pindar dies 440
      Peloponnesian War begins 431
–   Herodotus dies 430
      Pericles dies 429
      Plato born 427
–   Sophocles' *Oedipus Rex* 420
      Plays of Aristophanes 423, 422, 414; *Frogs* 405

–   Euripides' *Orestes* 408; dies 407
      Sophocles dies 406
      Peloponnesian War ends 404

- 400   Thucydides dies 400
         Socrates executed 399

-
         Athens Academy founded 386
         Aristophanes dies 385
         Aristotle born 384

-
-
-
         Alexander born 356
- 350
         Plato dies 347

THREE

DEMETER AT ELEVSIS

IN ONE OF THE ODES he composed when he was a young man
at the start of a promising career, in the heroic Greece of 498 B.C.,
Pindar wrote that to be without an anguish in the heart is to be a
god, not a man. It is a theme which underlies much human art
and thinking both before and since, the knowledge of the sadness
at the heart of things, crystallized for instance a thousand years
before in the agony which tormented Gilgamesh in the Mesopotamian epic, or later in those curt words of a monkish Latin
epigram which somehow found their way into the Book of
Common Prayer, words which Martin Luther built into a central
feature of his thought, to the effect that in the midst of life we are
in death. The pleasanter things are around us, the more we feel
the pang of our mortality.

It is both a recognition of this state of affairs and an attempt to
overcome it that seems to be involved in the cult of Demeter at
Elevsis.

Elevsis lies on the shore of a plain, backed by distant hills,
looking across a completely land-surrounded gulf to Salamis, at
somewhere near the point at which the traditional geographical
area of the Isthmus, Boeotia and Attica conjoin, and only about
eleven miles from Athens. It is a well-favoured position, low-
lying, with a small limestone hill marking its ancient site. Perhaps
it is something about the lack of outlook, in fact, which gives it an
overlay of depression. It is not a bright or cheerful sort of place
at all.

It would be hard to overstate the importance to the Greek
world in the classical period and its before and after, of the cult of
Demeter at Elevsis. It is characterized, in the writings of the time,

by an almost intimidating atmosphere of secrecy and awe. The secrecy, perhaps, augmented the awe. There is nothing like forbidding people to know something for making them think it must be worth knowing. Perhaps it was the secrecy of the mysteries, the esotericism of the idea of initiation, which boosted its reputation to an international scale. What was kept in those containers, themselves kept in the holy of holies which only the Hierophant was ever to enter? What took place at the ceremony of initiation, in the enclosed and forbidden temple? It is not surprising that non-initiates, particularly the later Christian propagandists, assumed that the whole thing must be somehow obscene. The fact of its being forbidden knowledge automatically gave it overtones of sex.

One thing we must bear in mind is that the cult and shrine seem likely to have been extremely ancient. Possibly even more than with any other sacred site in Greece, this goddess and her cult have been fixed together at this point at the coastal edge of the Thriasian plain since the very beginning. To the Greeks it must have seemed as if it had always been there, since, indeed, the time when gods and goddesses really walked the land of Attica. And although so many of the myths of Greece are local, in that they have attached themselves to a place or an area, perhaps no other deity is so firmly identified with a place as Demeter is with Elevsis. They are so entwined, in fact, that in this instance the myth could not be separated from the place.

Demeter was the daughter of Cronus and Rhea, and as such the full sister of Zeus. In origin she seems to have been another aspect of the earth goddess, and became connected, in the wide areas in which she was worshipped, with the earth in its role as provider, the cultivated, fertile aspects of the earth. Of the two parts of her name the meaning of the first, 'de', is disputed, but commonly thought to be 'earth'. The second half is not in doubt at all, though it may indeed have been changed to the form it has for the reason that its bearer grew increasingly to have maternal connections. 'Meter' is the Indo-European root word from which all our 'mother' words come, such as German *Mutter* and Latin *mater*, and it seems indeed to have meant literally 'meter', provider in the sense of one who metes or measures out, as in 'gas meter' or 'parking meter': an interesting reflection on the social role of being mother.

As earth mother, then, as we may confidently regard her, Demeter had been the object of probably universal worship, though under different names reflecting different language groups. Her more highly personalized form in pre-classical Greek, from which she emerged into the dazzling light of archaeology and written sources, coincides with the discovery and spread of agricultural practices. To that extent she embodies the most ancient and primitive of all religions in its first civilized form, appearing on the border of transition from the very ancient, the priestess-dominated earth cults such as we find in Crete, to the more developed deities, more male-dominated and specialized, such as the descendants of Cronus are, with all their separate functions.

Demeter is traditionally associated with horses: in an episode of her story she hides from Poseidon, who is wooing her, by becoming a horse and grazing among the herds of King Oncus; the incident presumably came to be thought of as an attempt to hide, but probably stemmed originally from her role as a horse goddess. And in the representations of her at several of her cult centres, for instance in Arcadia, she is depicted as having a mare's head. Her daughter Persephone was the result of a seduction by her amorous brother Zeus—a theme of brother–sister incest which seems to have archaic overtones. It is, of course, this daughter whose story forms the main thread of the myth.

Cronus had three sons, Zeus, Poseidon and Hades. After dethroning their father they divided among them the ruling of the world. The earth itself, the dry land, they shared jointly. Zeus became lord of the sky, Poseidon of the sea. The third brother Hades, later known as Pluto, was allotted the less enviable kingdom of the underworld, where he ruled over a land populated by the souls of the dead.

The myth of the abduction of Persephone by Hades had an official form, the so-called *Homeric Hymn* to Demeter, a work in fact probably much later than Homer, and tentatively dated at about 600 B.C. It undoubtedly records old and authentic traditional material, and its detail has the familiar Homeric air of reference to a real but idealized period long since past.

It was a time when gods and goddesses were to be found walking the countryside of those lands. Demeter's daughter Persephone was gathering flowers in a meadow; the hymn, naming the flowers, identified the time as spring. She stooped to try to reach one even more lovely than the rest, and at that moment the earth gaped at her feet. Hades in his chariot appeared out of the ground, swept her up and carried her back down. Her mother heard her cry for help, and set off in a state of dismay to look for her. She searched the earth for nine days, without eating or drinking, until she was told by Helios, the sun, what had happened. Zeus had connived at the rape, it seemed, and Demeter avoided his court on Olympus in her anger. Instead she went to live among men, disguised as an old woman. In this form she eventually came to the city of Elevsis, and sat there on a rock beside a well, where the women came to collect water. The daughters of the king, Celeus, found her there and took her back to the palace, where she was hospitably received by the queen.

The royal family of Elevsis succeeded in cheering the goddess a little, and persuaded her to take some nourishment. She was given the job of minding their infant Demophon, who grew unnaturally fast under her divine care. Through this it became known that she was an immortal goddess, and when she had disclosed her identity she ordered a temple for her to be built below the citadel wall, beside the well where she had rested when she arrived. The king did as she instructed, and the goddess at once went to live in the temple.

She was, however, still disconsolate. Because of her seclusion, her keeping apart from other gods, the earth became barren. Crops failed and no seed sprouted, and a terrible famine resulted throughout the earth. The gods on Olympus could foresee that if this continued the race of man would be extinguished, with consequent loss of worship to themselves. They therefore came to Demeter in Elevsis to beg her to rejoin them. But she informed them that the famine would continue until her daughter was returned to her.

Since there was no alternative Zeus sent Hermes, messenger of the gods, to bring back Persephone from the realm of Hades. They burst out into the light, riding in the chariot in which she had been taken away, and drew to a halt in Elevsis outside the temple. Demeter ran out and an emotional reunion took place. But it was a peculiarity of the kingdom of Hades that all who had taken food there must return; and although Persephone had abstained from eating during her stay, she had lapsed in this to the extent of swallowing (apparently through a trick on the part of Hades) the seeds of a pomegranate; and this was enough to ensure that she was never to be free of the place. It was consequently arranged that she should spend a third of the year below, as queen of the dead, and the remainder with her mother on Mount Olympus. The flowers blossomed again and the trees grew leaves, and the land became rich and fertile, as the two goddesses set off to rejoin the other gods.

Before she left Elevsis (the *Hymn* concludes) Demeter showed the king and the leaders the rites and mysteries which they were to practise there. These were to be secret, and interestingly it is said not only that no one may, but that no one could, divulge them; so great is the awe of the gods which they induce that it silences the voice.

One other deed attributed to Demeter before her departure from the world of men was the introduction of agriculture. She taught the practice of cultivation to one of the Elevsinian princes, who was told to travel the world teaching it. The origin in Attica of the cultivation of grain became traditional for the Greeks, even being mentioned by Plato.

The myth as a whole has close parallels in other cultures, and particularly in the Near East, where many of the ancient Asiatic cycles are concerned with the fertility of the land and even occasionally feature famines resulting from the withdrawal of a god. For this reason, and because such total long-term famine resulting from drought is a common experience in western Asia but not likely ever to occur in Greece, it is thought by some (for instance by an expert on the subject of Greek and Near Eastern mythology, G. S. Kirk) that this myth has an Asian origin, and arrived from Mesopotamia at a later date to become combined with a local fertility cult at Elevsis. It is clear, however, that there is much more to the story which is being symbolically told than simply the memory of one devastating famine. Perhaps the near-fatal lapse of fertility in the myth can even better be regarded as a sort of summary of the droughts and famines of many ages, the tendency for bad years to occur, for the fruit to fail, and for people to have to go hungry from time to time. It seems to be suggested that husbandry is in some measure a remedy for this: a precaution which needs to be taken. And this is the more necessary, perhaps, because of Persephone's annual retreat from the earth's surface, and the consequent withdrawal of nature. Certainly the myth can be read as dealing with this other aspect of the land's fertility as well: the barren winter period when all we can do is prepare and wait for Persephone's joyful bursting forth again, bringing the shooting and sprouting of the earth; one of our few certainties, the certain spring.

There is of course much food for thought in these rather basic matters, and needless to say it has not been ignored. The whole business of the mother goddess, the descent into the underworld (which may so easily be equated with the unconscious), the period of infertility, and the emergence from this in the form of a rebirth bringing general renewal, has such a distinctly Jungian ring that it seems almost that it must have been devised by Jung himself. Frazer, too, has much use to make of these themes. To him the re-emergence of Persephone represents not so much a psychological experience as a socio-ritualistic one, being an expression of the practices surrounding the figures of the corn mother and the corn maiden in widely dispersed European customs, by means of which mankind tries to grasp, smooth and ensure the annual passage of the seasons.

It is true that Greece is not subject to the severe conditions of places further east, having a relatively high annual rainfall, and that there are large parts of it (such as much of Attica and in particular the coastal plain around Elevsis and towards the

Isthmus, where strips of oats and barley are gold and ready for harvest from early June), where the land is fertile and good and the harvest fairly easily won. Much of the country on the other hand is steep and rocky, and the summers can be viciously hot. If one has seen the hard-got harvest being gathered from the thin soil of terraced mountainsides, practically stalk by stalk, hand-cut by sickle, bound in sheaves and loaded on to mules, the perilous fragility of such a livelihood is apparent, and the resulting importance of its success. Over much of Greece, not just because of lack of progress but as an unavoidable result of terrain, the corn is still gathered in by hand, in a slow and meticulous process, the women leading the heaped mules, like moving straw stacks, down precipitous paths. And that, of course, is how it must always have been. The fact that so much effort is involved helps towards an understanding of how an aura of supreme importance could attach itself to a cult concerned with fertility and the good-will of the corn goddess.

Many aspects of the myth strike chords in other cycles, as for instance the connection of Demeter with horses, and her occasionally being depicted, in fact, as mare-headed. Frazer, in *The Golden Bough*, gives instances from parts of Europe, including England, where the corn spirit is viewed as having the form of a mare. The Welsh story of Rhiannon has close connections here, since not only is Rhiannon clearly a mother figure, but at one stage of her story she appears to become a horse: as a penance for losing her child she has to sit by a horse block at the gate and carry people on her back to the court. Rhiannon, moreover, is connected with another of our themes, the abduction to the other world and the barrenness of the land. This part of her story, in fact, bears some striking similarities to that of Demeter.

Rhiannon and her husband Pwyll, who himself in an earlier episode has swapped kingdoms for a period with the king of the underworld, find themselves with two companions in a country suddenly emptied of its crops and flocks. In this apparent reversion to a pre-agricultural state they inevitably take to hunting. One day they come across a newly built castle in the waste land, where

Above
Athens: the
Acropolis

Right Plaka

Athens: a street in Monastiraki

Elevsis

Getting in the corn harvest

Corinth

Corinth: the Peirene fountain

Mycenae: Lion Gate from inside   Mycenae: Lion Gate from outside

Mycenae today

Oak trees near the Diktean Cave

Mouth of the Diktean Cave

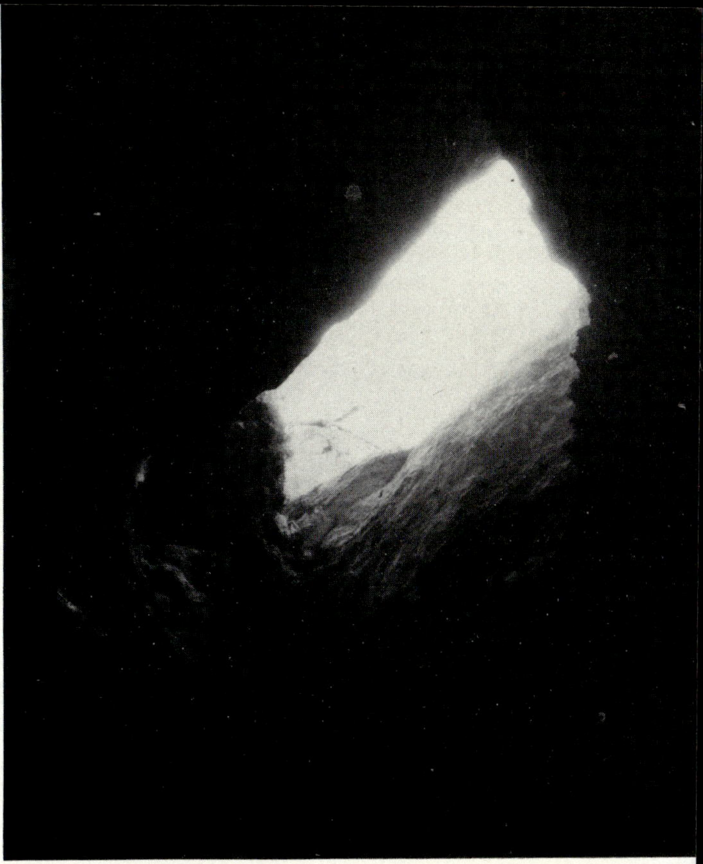

right The Diktean Cave from inside

below The cave on Mount Ida

Right
Tiryns

Below
Nemea

nothing stood before. Pwyll goes in, and finds in its centre a fountain and a bowl, which, when he grasps it, renders him unable to speak. Rhiannon following him does the same, and is also struck dumb. (These cases of apparent spellbinding, and others which occur in Celtic myth, remind us of what the Hymn implies, that initiates at Elevsis are also mystically silenced.) They and the castle then disappear, and only much later in the story are they released from the spell, at which the enchantment on the land is also raised, and it becomes clothed and populated again. The significant element in this is that in the meantime the companions they were with have introduced to the waste land the practice of tilling and cultivating corn, and it is in the course of their agricultural activities that they bring about the release of Pwyll and Rhiannon and the restoration of the land. Although—as often happens in myth—the items appear in a slightly different sequence, we have the same set of elements here as in the story of Demeter: a visit to the other-world kingdom, an abduction, a period of barrenness and infertility of the land, the discovery of agriculture, the release and return, and the recovery of the land. Rhiannon is seen by some authorities to embody both the European mother goddess, Rigantona, 'the great queen', and the major Celtic horse goddess, Epona. As such she is clearly a relative of Demeter.

There is nothing unique to Elevsis, either, about the journey to the realm of Hades. We have seen that Pwyll in the Welsh story exchanged his kingdom, for a year, with the other-world king. A Babylonian character, Ishtar, who suffered a period of imprisonment below, during which time the earth was barren, is a direct counterpart of Persephone. Persephone herself was not the only character to enter the kingdom of Hades and return, even in Greek myth. An obvious comparison is the story of Orpheus, who by the power of his music persuades Hades and his queen Persephone to release his dead wife Eurydice; the condition that he shall not look back while leading her out of the underworld is of course broken, and he loses her for ever. Odysseus too visits the realm of the dead, by following directions given to him by Circe, in order to consult the prophet Teiresias who alone can

C

advise him on his future. The hero Theseus also paid a visit to the underworld, and after some adventures succeeded in returning. There are instances of coming and going between the two realms also in Mesopotamian mythology, some of which may well have influenced the European examples; and of course the idea is clearly preserved in the story of Christ, who, in the words of the Apostle's Creed, 'descended into hell,' and 'rose again from the dead'.

Another theme which this concentrated and rich story of Demeter provides is that of the Waste Land, the theme of a country being made desolate through some equivalent state occurring to a king or deity. This too has very wide application, and probably therefore some general importance as the vehicle of an idea. We have seen it occurring in the Welsh examples, and of course the best-known cases of it are those of the Grail legends, from which the title of T. S. Eliot's poem is derived. In these it appears that the waste land through which the hero passes in his search for the Grail is in that state as a result of a debility on the part of the king, the ruler of the land and keeper of the Grail; on his recovery (in some versions as the result of being asked about the Grail and its associated emblems by the hero) the land becomes fertile again. Such an association of the health of the land with the health of its ruler (sometimes in his role as personification of the relevant god) is not uncommon in myth, and in fact—Frazer gives examples—is known to have been a part of the beliefs and customs of some primitive peoples.

These medieval stories of the Grail are thought by some to embody the vestiges of an initiation ritual, and certainly they involve both ritualistic talismans, such as a lance and a bowl, and the performance of specified actions, such as the need to ask a certain question. In fact in at least one there is a reference to the 'mysteries' of Grail Castle, which, as the tale puts it, no one returned to tell about. Of course there were many secret cults involving mysteries of initiation, and in several cases their secrecy may have been due to their contravention of the established religion, as for instance in cases of paganism surviving the advent of Christianity.

Symbolically the infertility of the land can be seen as the projection of the inner state which Demeter's desolation represents. Call it regression of libido, *la nausée*, accidie, anomie, or whatever: the world has gone grey, everything has lost its meaning and any action seems futile. It is a sort of moral infertility, a withdrawal of the values with which, without knowing it, we normally invest the world. Demeter is surrounded by potential friends, but refuses attempts even by the gods to console her. Rather, she is simply inconsolable. She has fallen into the abyss which renders her absolutely alone—alone in the sense of being bereft of the only company she wants. That hollowness of the spirit which the myth shows her as experiencing at Elevsis carries over even into the sequel, as if once it had occurred its possible return is a constant threat. So that even the harvest might seem to carry implications of sadness, because it marks the ending of Persephone's sojourn with her mother in the over-world. Only the spring itself is happy, free of overtones of parting, because only that has a time in front of it. Perhaps one of the strengths of the story is the thought that this knowledge of mortality, of temporality, should occur as well in the supposedly timeless lives of the deities. For Demeter the ultimate and inevitable departure of Persephone back again into the underworld is, though in a sense only temporary, from now on a permanent condition of life. The state of things presented to us by the Elevsinian myth is the understanding that even an endless cycle of rebirth does not remove the fact that to die is to be parted.

We cannot but be curious as to the form which these potent abstractions gave rise to in the physical world during the two thousand years or so of their involvement with Elevsis. But as might be expected with a place in use, and indeed of great importance, for so long a period, the site of the worship of Demeter is today to say the least confusing. The centuries of construction overlying one another have been revealed by the analytical, dissecting work of the archaeologist, and lie around us now like an incomplete and scattered jigsaw, almost entirely impossible to interpret.

The remains of what must have been a very large and stately

temple are clear enough, ledged and terraced into a limestone slope, at the focus of the broad approach which was, in fact, the Sacred Way. What is not clear is that this was only the latest of a long series of temples on exactly the same spot, each one larger and more elaborate than its predecessor, as the importance of the cult spread and the size of the territory able to communicate with Elevsis increased. The first of these temples—of which some slight traces can be seen—was Mycenaean. This, if anything, must have been the one supposed to have been erected at the command of the goddess herself. It dates from about 1500 to 100 B.C., and its small scale indicates that whatever cult there was here at that early date was such as to involve only a limited number of participants. Its existence evidently had the one significant effect of making the spot particularly holy, since in each succeeding rebuilding and enlargement that same place seems to have been retained as the focal point of the religion. The remains of that original temple can now be seen just below floor-level slightly on the downhill side of the centre of the terraced area.

Around this area later buildings, though still early, were constructed. They take their final form with that large square area flanked by step seats which, at the back, are cut into the rock of the hillside. The bases of the pillars which held the roof can still be seen. This, the greatest of the temples, the one which forms the bulk of what we can see now stretching around us on this levelled terrace, was of the time of Pericles, the fifth century B.C., contemporary with the buildings of the Acropolis in Athens. It was in fact a major reconstruction following the disasters of the Persian war, when, in 480 B.C., the invaders committed the ultimate sacrilege of burning down the whole of the sacred site at Elevsis, including the holy of holies itself. This Periclean building, the one now most easily visible, bears considerable embellishments of the Roman period, when the site continued to expand, buildings were enlarged and many of the present features such as platforms, steps and terraces were added to the area of the sanctuary.

Before one reaches this temple, known throughout the ages as the Telesterion, one has already passed a rather more conspicuous feature, a mouth-like natural cavern gaping blackly in the pale stone of the hill. This was the site of the Plutonion, the temple dedicated to the god of the underworld, who apparently had become reconciled with Demeter and been accepted at Elevsis. The remains of the triangular base of a fourth-century B.C. temple may be seen in front of the cave. Since the rites almost certainly included a re-enactment of Persephone's descent and return, the black mouth of the cave no doubt served as the entrance of the abyss into which she sank, so that a part of the annual ritual must (if this is so) have taken place here, perhaps as a preliminary to the initiation ceremony in the central secrecy of the temple. The Sacred Way curves past the Plutonion on its way up the hill to the temple.

Between the Plutonion and the entrance lie the remnants of temples and gateways of the Roman period; but among these an object of some interest is the well, a simple circular structure, which seems to have been that shown to Pausanias, in Roman times, as the well by which the goddess sat down on her arrival at Elevsis, and may also be the place referred to in the *Hymn* as one of the landmarks for the original temple which the king was to construct: it was to be beneath the citadel, on a small hill, and above the 'Kallichoron', which is thought to be the name of the well. This construction is dated by its style to between 550 and 500 B.C.

Without a detailed map, or even with one, it is nearly impossible to pick out other buildings of significance, among the jumble of so many superimposed ages of construction. The overall effect is one of confusion, giving no clear view of what the whole complex looked like at any one stage. It is of interest that there are remnants of Mycenaean buildings on the outskirts of the site, indicating a fairly large early settlement, and some of these may be found on the seaward slope of the hill, beyond the museum. Perhaps more of this original town lies on top of the plateau, among the present scrub, a probable position since it could be fortified there by a surrounding wall. Certainly we feel that something is missing; that under the soil and scrub of the hill itself lies more of Elevsis, in fact perhaps the first authentic one of which these steps and pillars were a subsidiary accretion. As a result an element of mystery, almost of diffidence, remains.

In the small museum are a number of fragmented marbles found around the site. Among these some reliefs show the two goddesses, though not very satisfactorily since in the best of them the heads are missing. One of them, however, shows Demeter in full, seated, holding a staff in one hand and in the other some corn stalks. She is facing a maiden carrying torches, a motif which occurs in other depictions and which seems to indicate an important part played by torches in the rituals. Undoubtedly the most striking object in the museum is the impressive and finely-worked caryatid, a large sculpture of the first century A.D. which was one of a pair supporting a pediment of one of the entrance buildings, the 'Lesser Propylaea'—evidently a highly decorated Roman building at the edge of the sanctuary. The partner to this figure was removed by an English traveller in 1801, and is now in a museum in Cambridge. The maidens carry on their heads baskets decorated with flowers and stalks of wheat, and evidently represent the priestesses bearing the Hiera, the sacred, and secret, objects, on the occasion of the ceremonial processions to and from Athens.

The legendary origins of Elevsis—formerly, but misleadingly, spelt 'Eleusis', but now spelt as pronounced—which the myth represents as being a substantial place even before the coming of Demeter, seem to connect it with Thebes, of which it may therefore have been the seaport. Certainly that important inland city would have required an outlet, in a time when seagoing trade was expanding. Legend also indicates rivalry and war with Athens, the city's other neighbour. We find that Elevsis became subjected to Athenian rule in still-legendary times, and by the time of Solon, ruler of Athens in the early sixth century B.C., it was clearly under the established rule of the Athenians. The Mysteries were of course important and well known by then, and in fact ancient sources indicate a date for the start of the cult as early as about 1400 B.C. If this is right, and if the Mycenaean remains were centred on the worship of Demeter, then the rituals at Elevsis had been in existence for nearly a thousand years before they entered history.

Athenian expansion certainly further promoted the cult's fame. The periodic enlargement of the temple reflects this, and the spread of Athenian influence is strikingly paralleled by the spread of the buildings and the site at Elevsis. Athens made a remarkably swift recovery, under Pericles, from the devastation of the Persian invasion in 480 B.C., when not only Elevsis but the Acropolis itself was plundered, ransacked and burnt. We have to remember that this apparent defeat was in fact the immediate prelude to an Athenian victory, in which Elevsis and its goddess were inevitably concerned.

The battle of Salamis, fought in the left-hand entrance to the bay at Elevsis as one looks out at it from the town, was the culmination of a traumatic period of Greek history. The expansion of the Persian Empire under Darius had been temporarily checked by his defeat, on a first attempt to subjugate Greece, at Marathon in 491 B.C. It seemed, however, to be destined to continue. Darius had already conquered the surrounding states, such as Lydia and Babylon, and even Egypt. The Ionian Greeks of the eastern Aegean were under his rule. Marathon strengthened rather than undermined Persia's determination to advance into Greece.

A second expedition was duly launched, led by one of Darius' sons, Xerxes, who had now succeeded to the kingdom. They scored an intial success at Thermopylae, where perhaps nearly two thousand Persians defeated a mere three hundred Spartans; and the Persian army swept through into the Greek heartland. An inconclusive battle at sea off the north coast of Evvia, in the strait between Artemission and Trikeri, allowed the Persian fleet to continue southwards in support of the army.

The Persian fleet and the Greek fleet were almost evenly matched, and found themselves facing each other in the Saronic Gulf, the defenders drawn up behind a headland of the island of Salamis, the invaders off the headland of Phaleron, opposite the island. Many of the leaders wanted to retreat to their various cities; but Themistocles, a forceful leader although not the commander-in-chief, realized that that course of action would at once have turned the war into a rout. Some of the Athenians' families had taken refuge on the island of Salamis, and this perhaps strengthened their determination when they decided to stay and fight.

Themistocles supported his argument by his interpretation of the Delphic oracle's reply to the Athenians, when, at the approach of the invading masses, they had asked about their future. The oracle had at first given them no good news, appearing to foretell only defeat and death. When pressed to say how Athens might be saved, the priestess had delivered the god's message to the effect that only 'the wooden walls' would stand. Salamis was also mentioned, though obscurely, in this connection. Themistocles, then an almost unknown politician, persuaded the Athenian leaders that the oracle advised them to make a last stand at sea.

Herodotus tells the story which, at this point in the preparations, relates the battle off the shores of Elevsis to the shrine of Demeter near by. An Athenian who had been in exile in Persia and had returned with Xerxes, was walking through the countryside of the Thriasian plain just before the battle, when he saw a cloud of dust on the road to Elevsis, as if a vast army was on the march. Coming nearer he heard singing, and recognized the sacred chant of the procession at the annual festival of the Mysteries. There was no one left in Attica who could have been making the noise, since the country had been devastated and abandoned. It was the god of the festivities himself, the impersonation of them known as Iacchus (later confused with the other god of revelry, Dionysus). The invisible crowd of singers went out from Elevsis towards the Greek camp on Salamis, and by this the witness knew that the Persians would be defeated.

The Greeks used the stratagem of dividing the opposing fleet by allowing them to think that they intended to escape through the channels behind Salamis. They managed to draw the enemy ships into the congested waters of the strait, and then unexpectedly attacked them on both sides. The Persians suffered from confusion and disorder, the leaders turning back and colliding with those still coming in, and they lost more than two hundred ships. Xerxes himself watched the battle from a vantage point on the mainland, from where he must have seen the remnants of the fleet scuttling back to the protection of the army at Phaleron.

After this warning the king felt himself to be unsafely far from home, and he despatched the remains of his fleet to the Hellespont to secure his means of retreat. Leaving his right-hand man with an army still ravaging Greece, he himself with the bulk of his troops set off back to Asia. The invasion had come and gone.

The road out of Elevsis on which the Athenian heard the procession singing was the Sacred Way, the end of which, curving past the Plutonion and round the hill towards the temple of Demeter, can still be walked. This is simply the termination of the road connecting Athens and Elevsis, which formed an important feature in the annual celebrations surrounding the Mysteries and initiation.

It was because Elevsis, as a city, became subject at an early date to Athens, and in turn because Athens became the leading Greek city-state, that the cult spread throughout Greece, and later throughout the Roman Empire. Athens consequently took part in the festivities; indeed it seems almost as if they were regarded as Athenian festivities. It was an autumn festival, taking place over several weeks in September and October, at the start of which period heralds went out from Elevsis to all the Greek states, proclaiming a holy truce and inviting delegations to be sent for initiation. The festival actually started with a procession from Elevsis to Athens, taking the Hiera, the sacred objects in their casks. These and the Elevsinian priesthood then stayed in Athens for five days of ceremonies, after which a great and colourful procession of priests, officials and would-be initiates set off on the fourteen-mile road to Elevsis. Some idea of the size and exuberance of this can be gained from the fact that the later versions of the Telesterion, the temple of Demeter, were expanded to take rather more than three thousand people. In a central episode of his comedy the *Frogs*, Aristophanes parodies the rowdy procession, singing and dancing their way to Elevsis, and manages to catch, in spite of his humorous intent, something of the thrill and the sense of occasion.

The Sacred Way ran, almost inevitably, along the same track as the modern road from Athens to Elevsis, keeping close to the coastline. When the procession reached its goal, having been on the road all day, it entered the outer court of the sanctuary by torchlight, and the participants probably held dances and performances there for much of that night.

It was the following night that the Mysteries of the initiation began. The penalty of death, and considerable public moral feeling, ensured the total secrecy of what took place. We know that when the popular dramatist Aeschylus, himself born in Elevsis in 525 B.C., was suspected of revealing some of the secrets of the cult in a play (unfortunately a lost one), he was stoned in the theatre and was lucky to escape with his life. The great and famous were not exempt from the strong moral prohibition surrounding the secrets. The politician and general Alcibiades (a favourite of Socrates), who had the unfortunate habit of behaving badly when drunk, was accused by his enemies of having parodied the Mysteries during one of his rowdy parties. Popular feeling against him was so strong that in spite of his eminence he had his lands and property confiscated in his absence during the Sicilian campaigns of the Peloponnesian War. This had fatal consequences for Athens, since it caused the capable and flamboyant general to change sides.

We do not know whether those accused of it ever actually did utter the forbidden words in front of non-initiates, but the strength of feeling surrounding the possibility is unmistakable. Believers, it seemed, were not willing, perhaps for their own religious reasons, to risk contravening this. It was therefore the Christian writers of the second century A.D. who were the first to put on record what took place. And they, by the nature of the situation, are unreliable. Firstly, what they were engaged in was manifestly propaganda, aimed at discrediting pagan practices. Secondly, none of them had any first-hand knowledge of the rites, nor made use of accounts of people who had. Probably an initiate simply would not have revealed the secrets, even then.

George Mylonas, a distinguished Greek archaeologist who has done much work at Elevsis, who speaks with the authority of a lifetime's study of the matter, shows the early Christian accounts to have been incompatible with what little we do know, and to be concoctions based on the more accessible Orphic rites and on speculation. He concludes his book *Eleusis and the Eleusinian Mysteries* with what seems like a cry of pain, the bitter conclusion that the last of the high priests of Demeter carried the secrets to his grave, that the work of scholars and archaeologists has not revealed them, and that the Mysteries of Elevsis will now never be known.

Most authorities are agreed that some sort of re-enactment of the myth must have been involved, and that the *Hymn to Demeter* therefore gives us a clue about its elements. We know also that the climax of the ritual was the revelation of the Hiera, those items which it was forbidden for anyone up to that moment to see, which were shown to the new initiates by the Hierophant— literally 'he who shows the Hiera'—in the inner part of the sanctuary, the holy of holies, which only he could ever enter, where the Hiera were kept. That occasion was accompanied, it seems from the slight accounts which we have, by a dazzling light—again a quality shared by the Grail. The rest of the performance, being at night, took place by the light of the torches held by the initiates. All this we know, or may reasonably surmise, because it was not really secret. What was secret were the words which the Hierophant spoke, and the identity of the Hiera themselves. We know that these were not large: they were kept in baskets, which were carried to and from Athens in the annual procession. Whatever they were the sight of them, with the presumably explanatory words, had a powerful effect on those who experienced it.

The theorists of the matter have viewed the initiation, in this case as in others, as being most probably a dramatized, or at least symbolized, enactment of the death and rebirth of the initiates. All are agreed that the experience provoked deep and enriching emotions of hope and joy; we have that on first-hand authority, since many writers, such as Cicero, speak about their own experience of it. It is not easy to imagine how anything which could have been in the baskets could produce this effect, and no doubt the effect was induced rather by the whole occasion. Whatever it was that took place, it somehow satisfied a deep longing. It was found to be a sustaining and ennobling force for some two thousand years. And it only became obsolete when it had been replaced by another religion, Christianity, which has now lasted for about the same length of time.

There are of course crucial differences between the two. Though the Elevsinian cult was not elitist—it was, for instance, open to slaves—one of the prerequisites was a knowledge of Greek, presumably so that what was said by the Hierophant would be understood. The only other qualification was freedom from the taint of having shed blood. By contrast Christianity was for everybody, and has often been categorized as a religion for sinners. The secrecy at Elevsis was again a major difference. Presumably its basis was the conviction that enlightenment should be achieved only through the proper form of initiation, which excluded the unworthy. There remains in Christianity, of course, a similar need to undertake a form of initiation in order to be saved, and the uninitiated are excluded from the most sacred sacraments.

Nevertheless we do know that what was provided at Elevsis was something such that its place in European spiritual life could be filled by Christianity, so that it is not unreasonable to think that it may have fulfilled a form of the same function. A father-and-son religion has replaced a mother-and-daughter one. It might be that we can therefore learn something of the latter from the former, and if so it is not inconsistent with what we do know of Elevsis to think that the message was that the kingdom of death had been overcome in the person of Persephone, in that she descended into hell, and rose again from the dead.

The connection with corn seems to strengthen such a hypothesis, since corn has often been viewed as an apt symbol of regeneration, the grain put into the ground in winter reproducing its living form in the spring. Perhaps it was not just for convenience, but rather on this model, that even the earliest people seem to have buried their dead in the ground. As Frazer remarks, in one of the characteristic asides which make *The Golden Bough* (for all its faults) so enjoyable,

> No doubt it is easy for us to discern the flimsiness of the logical foundation on which such high hopes were built. But drowning men clutch at straws, and we need not wonder that the Greeks like ourselves, with death before them and a great love of life in their hearts, should not have stopped to weigh with too nice a hand the arguments that told for and against the prospect of human immortality.

The heyday of the cult came near its end, when the whole of the Roman Empire looked towards Elevsis for inspiration, when emperors themselves and prominent citizens came to Greece to be initiated. Already by then, however, Greece was under pressure from raiding barbarians. When Marcus Aurelius was initiated in A.D. 176, it was in a temple which had been repaired after a destructive attack six years earlier. The spiritual force of Christianity was at the same time growing. A sort of death-fling of paganism took place during the short reign of Julian, known as the Apostate, who gave Elevsis its last years of importance in the 360s. The sanctuary was definitively destroyed by Alaric and his Visigoths in 395, and what they left the Christians levelled. It disappeared almost completely then until the eighteenth century.

Excavations began in 1822, and have continued year by year since. The area of the sanctuary is now completely cleared, and little more can be expected in the way of discoveries in the central area. Today it forms an isolated clearing in a world of shipyards and oil refineries, the sea black with cargo boats and tankers moored, waiting, between that shore where old Elevsis occupies the side of a hill on the seaward side of the town and the low bulk of Salamis across the strait. From the top of the hill above the sanctuary one looks out towards Salamis, and sees a bay crowded with shipping.

The past magnificence of the place has, in fact, gone completely. The present town of Elevsis is one of the world's less charming places, a flat and featureless succession of utilitarian buildings, with something of the feeling of being a suburb, as if it were waiting for those already extensive outer suburbs of Athens to spread out yet further and absorb it into their anonymity. The functional squareness of ordinary Greek buildings can sometimes be made inconspicuous by the surroundings. But at Elevsis, on the plain from which the hills towards Thebes and Corinth are withdrawn to a distance, they are all there is. Their inbuilt soullessness and lack of grace come over strongly there. Beyond the site of the ruins the town becomes a port, with a cluster of decaying seamen's bars, where a few tired girls patiently await the return of the Sixth Fleet.

FOUR

OEDIPUS AT THEBES

THEBES, NOW CALLED THIVE, is the main town in the largely
rural and not much populated area called Boeotia. It lies on the old
road north from Athens, which separates at that point to take you
alternatively to Chalkis and Evvia, or to Levadia and Lamia.
Nowadays the new toll motorway sweeps past to the north,
looping around the central mountain area of Boeotia, pronounced
Bee-oh-sha, which is the whole of that land to the immediate
north of the Attica peninsula, lying between Athens and the gulf
of Evvia. In the old days one had to go through Thebes, since it
lay in the way of almost all journeys. Now it is much quieter, or
rather, since it has been remarkably quiet for many centuries,
even quieter. Those of us who still prefer to take the old and
winding road occasionally pause there for a *souvlaki*, and find
ourselves stared at.

It hardly needs to be said that this is in striking contrast to the
Thebes that was. The history of the place is quite formidable,
rivalling that of Athens; and the great city of Laius which the
myth envisages undoubtedly had its counterpart not only in
classical but in Mycenaean times. In fact the first of the cities on
this site seems to have come to an abrupt end as early as the middle
of the thirteenth century B.C. It is that one, presumably, the
Mycenaean one, which we have to imagine as the one which the
myth intended to refer to.

One gets as good a feeling of the area as any, at present, coming
towards Thebes along the Delphi road. Oedipus was apparently
travelling in that direction when he met his father. Laius was
going the other way, along the level road which later rises towards
Delphi. Before he reached Levadia he would have started to catch

glimpses of Parnassus, glimpses at first and then extended views of that impressively massive and beautiful bulk. On the way to Delphi from Thebes it gives you a sense of direction. You can see where you are going, and what it is like. Much of the year the higher gullies are streaked with snow, a silky shine decorating its great height.

The road which the myth says Oedipus' father Laius travelled on that fatal journey runs across much good level farmland, open cultivated fields. From Levadia it becomes involved with hills, which close in to surround it, giving a foretaste of the mountainous country into which it is heading. It is at Levadia itself that the roads now split, the one going north to Lamia, the other westerly towards Delphi. The village itself—a rural sort of place, with old buildings and trees along its streets—seems in fact to have grown up around this junction of ways. The road from Lamia comes down into it sharply to join the straight way from Thebes, while the third road snakes away up to Delphi through the shadows of the hills. It was here or somewhere near here, in a countryside which has changed remarkably slowly, if at all, that the meeting between unwitting father and son supposedly took place. At the place where three ways meet, Sophocles says. When Oedipus begins to wonder what is happening, much later, he gets the queen to describe again where the survivor of the fight said that it occurred: at the place where three roads meet, on the road between Thebes and Delphi. He remembers in the same phrase where it was that he met and killed an old man on his journey here: 'Where the road divides, leading to Delphi and to Daulia.'

It cannot but be somewhere on that level stretch beside Levadia. Laius was setting out to consult the Delphic oracle, to seek its help in ridding Thebes of the plague of the sphinx, which was at that time threatening the city. Oedipus was coming away from the same oracle, having heard from it that he would kill his father, and having decided—with that frail determination which mortals show in the face of the inevitable—to go elsewhere and not return to Corinth, where Polybus, the man he took to be his father, was king. To add to the sense of the inevitability of it all, the quarrel between the strangers, in which the fatal killing occurred, was trivial. They disagreed about who had the right of way.

To get to that stage of the story, however, we must really go back to its beginning. Like Oedipus in the later part of the same story, his parents Laius and Jocasta had attempted to outwit the god. Apollo had foretold of their son, when he was born, that he would kill his father and marry his mother. Though no hope occurred to them that the child might be reared without this dreadful result, they thought they saw a way of preventing it from becoming possible. The child must die. In myth, and in some ancient customs, it is conventional for unwanted children to be abandoned on a near-by mountain. Presumably that way the parents are not guilty of the murder of kin. In this case— mindful, perhaps, of instances where infants manage to survive even this ordeal—the parents attempted to be absolutely sure of it by piercing their child's feet with an iron pin. The detail seems designed to explain the name he eventually acquired, Oedipus meaning 'swollen-footed'; but it meshes awkwardly with the supposition that the infant was newly born, since the pin must have been thought to be to prevent him crawling back to some- where where he would be found. Perhaps two stories have become merged, in which the same thing happened to children of different ages.

In any case it was of course all in vain. The king and queen did not take the child to the wilderness themselves, but entrusted the job to a shepherd. He had his flocks on that mountain, Mount Cithaeron, now called by the same name, Kithairon, which lies in the background of the Theban plain. The long bulk of it is visible in the distance, to the south, from most parts of the plateau on which the town of Thebes itself sits, on its series of small rises. It is a broad, scrub-covered mountain, blue with distance and haze against the normally dazzling sky.

Mount Cithaeron forms a long and smooth-flanked watershed between this part of inland Boeotia and the neck of land which runs down towards the isthmus and the city of Corinth. Thus it was that the Theban shepherd grazed his flocks up one side, and a Corinthian shepherd pastured the other; and they met at the top, old friends, apparently, in the loneliness of the large mountain.

That at any rate is the picture which we have from Sophocles, and it has the credibility of naturalness to support it. The force of such a tale as that of Oedipus is that, oracles apart, every episode in it could really happen. It was natural that the shepherd should have preferred to dispose of the child far away and out of harm, as he thought, rather than kill it; and that Oedipus should come in such a way to be brought up in the court of the king of Corinth, who adopted him as his own son. Thus he thought that Polybus and his queen were his parents, and had he not heard from the oracle at Delphi about his destiny he would have lived contentedly as prince of Corinth. It was in fact his effort to avoid it which led to the oracle's prediction coming true.

Thebes and Corinth were, historically, neighbouring kingdoms. Both were extremely old foundations, 'Corinth' in fact being a pre-Greek name of uncertain origin. It seems quite certain that a town had dominated the isthmus in the same position since as early as the Neolithic Age, that is perhaps about 4000 B.C. One of its early kings was said to have been Sisyphus, who lived such a generally wicked life that he was condemned to a most poignant punishment in Hades. Precisely what he did wrong is not quite clear; but his punishment is much better known, largely through its having caught the imagination of Albert Camus, who compared it in his book *The Myth of Sisyphus* with the human lot. Condemned to roll a vast block of stone up a steep slope, Sisyphus never quite succeeded in getting it over the top. Just as he reached the summit the weight of the rock overcame him, and it rolled back down to the bottom. And this went on for ever. It is not the frustration, the sweat and effort, or even the sense of futility that Camus points to. It is the feeling of brief pause on the walk back down: 'That hour like a breathing-space which returns as surely as his suffering, that is the hour of consciousness.'

Sisyphus seems to have been regarded as the founder of the dynasty at Corinth, which emerges gradually from myth into history at about the time Homer was composing his epics.

Thucydides mentions Corinth supplying ships for other forces at about 700 B.C., and records a battle in which the city took part, the first sea battle on record, forty years later. The city reached an early peak under the dictatorship of Periander, during the early sixth century B.C. Always a powerful and wealthy place, it expanded continuously through the classical period, and became a Roman port of some importance. The isthmus has evidently widened since, and we now find an area of very substantial ruins some way inland, surrounding a magnificent temple.

A glance is enough to make one realize at once that this was a very notable place for a long time. What is visible now, however, is almost entirely Roman, the great Greek city having been conquered and destroyed by the Roman general Mummius in 146 B.C. Almost the only Greek construction still to be seen is the great temple of Apollo, seven monolithic pillars of which have survived the city's various catastrophes. Until the excavations began in 1896, this noble Doric structure of the mid-sixth century B.C. stood alone among the fields which covered the rest of the ancient site. The Roman buildings are fine in their way, and include the long stoa, in the middle of which St Paul was accused and acquitted of inciting illegal worship, in A.D. 52. This, one of the longest buildings in Greece, is a Roman restoration of a much older Greek foundation on the same spot. Archaeological Corinth in fact has this form almost throughout: the grandiose Roman overlay on the base of an old and sumptuous Greek city. The justly famous Peirene fountain is, as it now stands, a Roman construction, but something of the sort must always, it seems, have been a feature of the original ancient city; one of the well-known assets of Corinth was its sweet water. The fountain, with its six arched basins, is still quite beautiful, in spite of its crumbled grandeur.

While Corinth was continuing its expansion into Roman times, its neighbour Thebes had long before declined. To go back to its origins we have inevitably to cross the blurred line between pre-history and myth. Thebes was founded, the story says, by Cadmus, a descendant of Poseidon, who was wandering the world at the time searching for his lost sister, Europa, who had been abducted by Zeus in the form of a bull. In the course of his travels he came to Delphi, where the oracular priestess realistically advised him to stop looking. Instead, she said, he should follow a young cow which he would find grazing near by. Eventually the cow would lie down, and where it did so Cadmus was to found a city.

Not far from the Delphic groves he found the animal, and followed it on to the plains of Boeotia, where it stopped and, according to Ovid's charming version, mooed loudly, before reclining in the fresh spring grass. It was in that way that Thebes came to be where it is.

In the process of founding the city Cadmus and his attendants encountered a serpent which was guarding the nearest convenient spring. It killed the men who came to draw water, and Cadmus, after a heroic fight, in turn killed the serpent. On the instructions of Athena he then sowed the serpent's teeth in the ground, and almost at once a crop of warriors emerged, already fighting one another. When a number of them had been killed the five who remained formed the nucleus of the new population of Thebes and Boeotia, and because of their origin are known as the 'Sown Men'. It is assumed that the people of that part of Greece believed that, unlike the wandering tribes which moved into their country from the north, they were truly indigenous, born from the land itself.

Laius was the great-grandson of Cadmus. After Laius' death at the crossroads Oedipus ruled Thebes for more than a dozen years. He had succeeded to the throne immediately on his arrival, since he there and then rid the city of the sphinx which was plaguing it, the trouble which had been the cause of Laius' journey. This monster was, like the Egyptian sphinxes, a hybrid: it had a woman's head on an animal's body and, in the early Greek representations of it, wings as well.

The manner of the sphinx's attack on Thebes is somewhat curious, since it took up its position outside the city and asked all those coming and going a riddle. This was the one to which, fortunately for us, we now all know the answer: what is it that has four legs at first, then two, and ends with three? Those who failed to answer the riddle got eaten, and Oedipus alone among the Thebans guessed the solution. This is of course that it is Man that is referred to: he crawls when an infant, walks on two feet as an adult, and uses a stick when old. The sphinx was discountenanced, and leapt to its death from a near-by hill. The people, saved from being eaten one by one and also from having to rack their brains in the meantime for the solution, in their relief proclaimed the newcomer king, and offered him the hand of the recently widowed queen. This, it seems, went with the crown, as we shall see that it appeared to do in several other cases.

In the years that followed Jocasta bore Oedipus four children. After the passage of those years, in which the gods but no one else knew of Oedipus' shameful state, an outbreak of infertility and pestilence descended on the city and country; and when Sophocles' great play opens we learn that Creon, Jocasta's brother, has been sent to ask the Delphic oracle what can be done. At the start of the play we await his return.

Of course the oracle says that the murderer of Laius must be found, and like the active and determined king he is Oedipus sets about discovering who this is. The oracle had added that the murderer was still in the city, giving rise to a truly tense detective-story situation, with the added seasoning of irony since we know, though no one else does, that the king is looking for himself. It is in his own interest to find the killer, he says, since he, whoever he was, 'might think to turn his hand against *me*'.

Another of the intriguing characters of myth enters the story at this point. The citizens suggest sending for Teiresias, a mortal prophet who, however, is closest of any human to having Apollo's power of foreknowledge. The old man is blind, a result of having upset a goddess in some earlier episode of his story; but he has been compensated for this by Zeus with the gift of second sight. His knowledge indeed exceeds that of most, since he has been both a woman and a man, having undergone these changes for the rather mystical reason, in some versions of the story, that he had struck a pair of serpents while they were copulating. What rites or arcane thoughts are being referred to here we do not know, except that snakes are obviously phallic and are also associated with the cult of the earth goddess. However, the result was that Teiresias, having experienced sex in the form both of a woman and a man, was able to answer the question which puzzled even Zeus and his wife Hera, and has indeed been broached by many theorists since: which of the sexes gets more pleasure from the sex act, man or woman? He was the only valid authority available, and when they found themselves arguing about it the gods sent for him. We have to take his word for the result, though the matter is fraught with overtones of envy and propaganda, and any answer was likely to be unpopular. It would not have been surprising in the circumstances if the wise Teiresias had come up with an equivocal reply. But he did not. He gave the answer firmly and confidently: women get the more pleasure, by a clear margin. This is of course, and was taken to be by Zeus, a justification for male philandering. We have to try to catch up.

When sent for now by Oedipus the prophet is obliged to tell the truth; but Oedipus does not at first grasp its import, and is merely angry. It is only later, and bit by bit, that the possibility of the truth of what Teiresias has said—that he himself was the man—begins to occur to him. At first he thinks that Creon is plotting against him, and has put the prophet up to spreading false rumours, intending in the end to get the throne himself. The king in the meantime sends for the sole survivor of Laius' party, and we await him with the more suspense since it is implied that this man had not, at the time, told the full story. While we are all waiting a messenger comes from Corinth to say that the king is dead, thus apparently making void the prophecy that Oedipus would kill his father. But the word of the gods is not so direct; and it is this same Corinthian who, intending to relieve the king's fears still further, reveals that Oedipus was not, after all, Polybus' child. It was he himself, formerly a shepherd on Mount Cithaeron, who brought him as an infant to the court.

All is becoming clear to them, and there can be no escape from the sudden rush of the recognition of the truth. When the survivor of the fight which killed Laius turns out to be also the shepherd who took the child to the mountain, his arrival and revelations complete the understanding of the past, as it is now, which matches so precisely the future which the oracle long ago foretold.

The Theban plays of Sophocles are, like those by Aeschylus, about the events at Argos, three in number; but it is (in both cases) the first in the sequence which bears the main burden of the myth, the catastrophe happening to the king of which the remaining two are the consequences. At the end of *Oedipus the King* we are left with Jocasta dead, having hanged herself, and Oedipus blind, being led away to exile. He has blinded himself with the queen's brooches, a strange, though potent, expression of his previous inability, when sighted, to see the truth. The atmosphere of sexual guilt which hangs heavily and explicitly over the end of the play accords with the psychologists' claim that blindness is symbolic of impotence, fear of being blinded equated with fear of castration, and so on; and this seems particularly apt, as symbolism, having been introduced already in the figure of Teiresias, who was blinded in connection with an apparently sexual transgression (in one version it is for having seen Athena naked) and in whom a complex sexual past is now replaced by an enlightened present.

In the second of the Theban plays (the one actually written last) we deal with Oedipus' state of exile, at Colonus near Athens. He has been replaced at Thebes by his mother's brother, Creon, and now wanders homeless in the company of his two daughters. The play was written much later than the others, in fact towards the end of both the playwright's life and the fifth century B.C., and its tale of family intrigue is told with some subtlety and pathos. It lacks, however, the central role as purveyor of myth which characterizes the first, *Oedipus the King*. It is not even certain in fact that it records an authentic version of the myth, rather than a fancy on the part of the playwright. Homer tells the story up to that point: how Oedipus had killed his father, married his mother, and how this had afterwards been discovered. In that first version, briefly told in the *Odyssey*, he remains king of Thebes, and suffers all the more remorse by staying in his home town, a suffering increased by the curses of Jocasta (in Homer, Epicaste) who, as in the play, has hanged herself out of guilt. It is not made clear whether or not the shameful marriage had been undertaken wittingly or unwittingly; the attribution of guilt and remorse seems to imply the former, the gods merely making the truth of the situation become public.

The third play is the poignant political drama *Antigone*, and tells the sequel to the story taking place in Thebes itself. This play, however, is thought to have been written first, so that it cannot have been intended that the three should be performed in sequence—and indeed there is no formal continuity, and even some instances of inconsistency. Probably some forty years in fact separate the writing of the first of them from that of the last. Sophocles, who lived to be about ninety, had an exceptionally long working life. The dilemma of political and moral opposition, of two sorts of right and wrong, which this earlier play works out, has proved to have continuous application; and it is not surprising to find it played from time to time in modern dress and idiom, and even rewritten in modern form, as in the French version by Jean Anouilh. It tells how Creon, now king of Thebes, has forbidden the burial of intending invaders who have fallen in battle outside the walls, among whom is one of the sons of Oedipus, Polynices. The latter's sister Antigone, however, finds the ties of blood stronger than those of loyalty to the king and city. She buries Polynices and is accordingly condemned to death. Creon, by acting the part of the strong king, finds himself embroiled in a pitiful family tangle in which he loses his own son (who was to have married Antigone, and who kills himself when she must die) and, as a further result of that, his wife. We cannot but pity him, particularly as his course of action initially seemed to be right and reasonable.

The story of Antigone is not a sequel to that of Oedipus, but rather to a further episode which comes between them, the event known as 'the Seven against Thebes'. One of Oedipus' sons, Polynices, had gone into exile in Argos, having quarrelled with the other, Eteocles, who stayed in Thebes. Polynices eventually invaded Thebes with an army led by seven champions, corresponding, apparently, to the seven gates which are usually mentioned as characterizing the city, 'Seven-gated Thebes'. Here we may feel that we have something rather more approaching a historical reference, since doubtless Argos and Thebes, at times two of the main cities of Greece, felt some sense of rivalry. The story of the Seven against Thebes is told in a play of that name by Aeschylus. The invasion eventually failed, ending with a hand-to-hand combat between the two brothers, both of whom died of their wounds; it was then that Creon, their mother's brother, who was acting as regent when Oedipus first arrived, became king in his own right. We have seen how Sophocles dealt with the immediate result.

There is a further sequel, which in a way seems to take us even further into history, describing how the sons of those who had died invading Thebes, in their turn invaded again from Argos, this time with more success. What seems certain is that other Greek states from time to time did invade Thebes; and reading between the lines of Herodotus and Thucydides we do not feel that we can really blame them. The Thebans appear as not exactly a peace-loving people.

During the war with the Persians they sided with the foreigners, giving Xerxes and his invading army an advance base for their campaign against Athens and the allied states. Thebes had a fierce traditional rivalry with Athens, and in fact actually started the Peloponnesian War by attacking Plataea, a Boeotian city allied to Athens, thus definitely breaking the truce which was the only thing that kept the Greek states from getting embroiled in conflict. When it was realized what had happened everybody sighed and resigned themselves to the long and bitter course of that seemingly inevitable war. The Thebans remained allied to the Spartans, for no other reason, apparently, than that like the Spartans they were enemies of Athens. They proved a danger and a trouble to Athens through the war, in which they seem to have fielded a powerful cavalry as well as the heavy infantry for which they had become well known.

The first city on the site of Thebes was traditionally a Phoeni-cian foundation—Cadmus and his company were said, in the myth, to be Phoenicians—a point which has some slight archaeo-logical support; that there were at least Asiatic connections is demonstrated by the discovery of Anatolian cylinder seals, now

in the museum. Like most of the Mycenaean settlements throughout Greece this one came to an abrupt end perhaps shortly before
1200 B.C., having apparently been destroyed once a little earlier
and rebuilt. Perhaps these two destructions are the parallels in the
archaeological record to the two Argive attacks in the mythical
one. The second seems to have marked the end, in any case, of the
powerful early city.

Most of the evidence of that civilization was only to be understood much later, in fact during the second half of the present
century, when the tablets found at Thebes and elsewhere have at
last been deciphered. The area of Mycenaean Thebes has by no
means been fully investigated, and probably never can be for the
simple reason that the modern town is on top of it. But what has
been found is of considerable interest, indicating a settlement of
some prosperity which imported jars, probably of oil, from Crete,
and was apparently ruled, like the other palace-cities, by a king.

A classical city arose on the site of the Mycenaean one, and it
was during the prelude to the most stormy period of its history,
the Persian invasion, that it gave birth to its most eminent
historical (as opposed to mythical) citizen, the poet Pindar, who
was born there in 518 B.C. He thus found himself a man of the
same city as Heracles, and appropriately devoted his life to a
celebration of the aristocratic and heroic ideals. It is Pindar's
Odes—commissioned works which in theory celebrate victories
by young noblemen at the games of Delphi, Nemea, Corinth and
Olympia—that we owe much of our understanding of the classical
view of the Greek myths. The Odes usually follow a pattern of
incorporating, within the format of praise of the victor and his
city, a more or less complete story of a god or hero, subtly woven
into the eulogy by means of an allusion or simile. In spite of a
distinctly elitist set of values, which no doubt were essential to
success in his chosen role as the subject of patronage, Pindar
comes over as a poet of great understanding and thoughtfulness,
rich in incisive phrases and compelling truths. He did not, of
course, stay in the embattled Thebes of the early fifth century, but
travelled throughout the Greek lands of his time, doing much of
his work for the ruler of Syracuse in Sicily.

Ancient Thebes did not, like other cities, go on accreting and evolving into Roman times, into the era when it could be regarded as something surviving from the past in the eyes of people thinking of themselves as modern, as representatives of the new age. It was destroyed, in its antique form, by the troops of Alexander in 335 B.C., when the Macedonians swept down into the heart of Greece. Although there was undoubtedly some rebuilding, it was nevertheless, unlike several of the other important sites, simply not there in its original form to be looked at and described by Pausanias. In his time it was, he says, nothing but a fortified rock with a tiny population.

It may be partly for this reason that there is so little to see there now. The ancient city was evidently so levelled that it could be almost completely built over. Consequently not much remains to be seen of it, except some marbles in the small museum, and a few fragments of stone by the roadside, including some parts of its once-famous gates; the base of the pillars of at least one of these can be clearly seen. A strange sandstone hill hollowed by caverns and tunnels, known as 'the tomb of the sons of Oedipus', lies near the outskirts of the town. There is the base of part of the Mycenaean palace, but that is about all. It seems at first that Thebes still awaits its Schliemann, though in this case further uncovering is necessarily restricted to the occasional incidence of building sites. But work has been, is being and will be done, and more discoveries may be expected.

What we may see clearly is that the old town is in this case well represented by its successor, sitting around those same small hills, now quite a substantial modern Greek town, with sprawling residential outskirts.

The story of Oedipus too has found a sort of modern counterpart existence, taking up a central role in that corpus of thought which perhaps comes closest, in our time, to fulfilling the role which myth once occupied. If Freud had been content to point to a pattern of relationships across the wide range of those occurring in human situations, then he might have made a valid, but admittedly inconspicuous, scientific point. Instead he made a claim for the centrality of the conflict between father and son, the 'ambivalent emotional attitude' which governs their related behaviour, which can hardly stand up to the generality he imposed on it. And in doing so, in being so categoric, even simplistic, in his insistence, he somehow caught the popular imagination.

We find in much myth—it will occur again—the sort of ambivalent emotional attitude with which Freud was concerned. It crops up when a man has both a rivalry and a duty towards another, as for instance when Paris has fallen in love with Helen, under the influence of the scheming Aphrodite, yet as Menelaus' guest should not behave as he unavoidably does. In so far as it is a dilemma, it is the stuff of narrative, and therefore common in folk-tale; but dilemmas of this sort pose a moral or social problem, and in their capacity as contradictions or tensions of opposites too they are the proper subject of myth. 'The hatred of his father that arises in a boy from rivalry for his mother is not able to achieve uninhibited sway over his mind; it has come to contend against his old established affection and admiration for the very same person,' Freud explains. It might be an interesting point if he had chosen to stop there.

Unfortunately he was tempted to offer an explanation for this situation, and to do so in his characteristically reductionist terms. There is no doubt that the essay in which he does it, 'The Return of Totemism in Childhood', is gripping and intellectually exciting; in the end, however, it itself destroys as effectively as any criticism could the whole idea of what he there names the 'Oedipus complex'. Freud cites Darwin as describing primal man as living in family hordes, in which the young males would have, in the end, to contest with the older ones for mastery, the strongest eventually establishing himself as the head of the community. The ones who were driven out, Freud hypothesizes, would eventually gang up on the horde-father, whom they would then kill and eat. This primal crime gave rise to remorse and guilt, and so strong was its impression that it then formed the basis for a permanent prohibition of incest. Indeed he sees in the resulting emotional state the whole foundation of religion and morality.

Apart from the absurdity of attributing feelings of affection, admiration, remorse and guilt to people who, he says, were capable of killing and eating their fathers, Freud provides no mechanism for the transmission of the memory of this event through so many thousands of years. (Such mechanisms as those posited by Jung, the 'collective unconscious', or the engraving on the mind, and subsequent inheritance, of 'archetypal' forms, would of course have been totally rejected by Freud.) Perhaps this can be overcome in some way, but the whole base of his thesis is weakened by its anthropological assumption of universal patriarchy. It is thought by some authorities that at least some, if not all, early communities were matriarchal. This would indeed seem probable, since there is evidence from primitive peoples studied in relatively modern times that the role of intercourse in procreation is not always understood. As a result there is no place for the idea of fatherhood, and hence for its particular apparatus of inheritance.

This is of interest to us here because the possible tension in such a society—or indeed in any society which practised matriarchy and matrilinear inheritance—cannot be between a man and his son. In so far as kinship between brothers and sisters would inevitably be recognized—both being reared by the same mother —the natural method of inheritance, and therefore the natural relationship of conflict between generations, would be between a man and his sister's son. One of the results of this would be that with the change from matriliny to patriliny there would be a whole class of people, sisters' sons, who would feel traditionally entitled to rights from which they were now debarred. Moreover it is not hard to see how at about this point, during the transition, rights (to a kingship, for instance) would best be acquired by a man by marrying the female inheritor of them, the widowed queen, which is precisely what was done by Oedipus at Thebes and by Aegisthus at Argos; or the daughter, as in the case of Menelaus at Sparta.

It is doubly unfortunate that Freud should have burdened the work of Sophocles with overtones of these theories. His argument meshes badly, to put it mildly, with *Oedipus the King*.

That play, and the myth, are in no way about the struggle between a man and his son for dominance, arising out of their sexual rivalry for the mother. In so far as there is any struggle for dominance in the play it can hardly be thought to be between Oedipus and his father Laius, who has been dead for many years before the play begins. In fact as father and son Oedipus and Laius never really meet. The only trace of a struggle in the myth between two males of different generations is that between Oedipus and Creon. Moreover, it is between these two only that there is anything which might be called an ambivalent emotional attitude. Oedipus at first blames Creon for his plight, and there is a further violent scene between them in which he accuses him outright of plotting to take the crown. At the end of the play his feelings revert to friendship, and he entrusts his children to Creon with the words 'You are their only father'. It seems then that the only equivalent to a Freudian 'father complex' (as he calls it) in *Oedipus the King* is concerned with Creon. And Creon is Oedipus' uncle, his mother's brother. Oedipus is in the critical position of the sister's son.

Have we, then, a record of a change in the method of succession to the Theban throne? Have we here a way of describing the coming of a new order, a patriarchal tradition which first of all removes the woman-dominated religion, represented (as evil, of course) by the sphinx, and then somehow, in spite of tension, occupies the seat of royalty depicted as held, under the old order, by the queen and her brother? Certainly it is remarkable that it is that very factor—the complication of matrilinear inheritance—which spoils the Freudian description of the origin of the Oedipal relationship, which also helps to explain elements which might otherwise be puzzling in this and other myths. And if it were the case that something of lasting importance to the social order, the transition from one type of inheritance to another, were being recorded here, then this way—the crystallization of the situation and its tensions in the kingship—would be an appropriate way of doing it. The difficulty of synthesizing the customs, the super-imposition of one system on the other, could conveniently be encapsulated in this way. The heavy atmosphere of sexual guilt, present even in the brief summary of the story in the *Odyssey*, while it seems to point to a psychological, rather than a social, function, could itself result from a previous custom (for instance, the new king marrying the wife of the previous one) becoming forbidden, and so regarded with horror, on the accession of a new order.

Unfortunately the ultimate origins of the story are lost to us, but the experts are agreed that it is old, and probably of folk-tale origin, coming into prominence in Greece along with many others not in Mycenaean times but nearer to Homer's age. Certainly between Homer's telling of it and the full development available to Sophocles elements had been added, perhaps from other tales. In that form it had acquired its local connotations—the part played by shepherds, and the insistence on topographical features such as Mount Cithaeron. And in fact it relied by then specifically on the geographical location of the road to Delphi, the comings and goings between there and Thebes having become crucial elements of the tale.

FIVE

APOLLO AT DELPHI

───────────────

SOME MORNINGS THE MIST lies both above you and below you, muffling the outline of the slopes which rise above the town, lying in imitation of the sea across the gulf which falls below the town. Delphi is suspended until about midday, its cliff-top nature and its mountain-foot nature both in operation at the same time.

You feel either one or the other of these things most of the time there, moving about the town and the temples. But the thing falls into place as part of a complex massive mountain country when seen (and only then) from those slopes which rise towards Parnassus, reached by the primal pathways built for pack mules of past eras, used by pack mules of today: those long sloping steps which rise, twisting and snaking, gaining height without the use of effort, as if they had conquered gravity.

Up such a path behind the town one rises towards the mountain, reaching, in time, a high, spacious plateau from which can be seen, and felt, the bulk of Mount Parnassus. Except when the thunder comes down or as it grows dark this is not wild, but simply empty, country. There is in fact at times a peaceful pastoralness about it, emphasized by the bells of goats grazing among the herbs and thistles, by the slow lope of a farmer with a donkey descending, by the basking of lizards on warm stones, and the sweet vacuousness of the mountain air.

In spite of the dominance of the elements of pitch and fall, and in spite of the scale and surprise of its cliffs and gorges, Delphi is not intimidating at all. There is nothing foreboding or archaic about it, as there is about Mycenae and Olympia, even nothing inexplicable, nothing which baffles as Knossos does, lying a little beyond our conceptual reach. There is a mood of civilization

about it, in the restrained architectural proportions of its monuments, decorating rather than trying to dominate the lovely
hanging valley of their setting. It is not chance, of course, that it
bears Apollo's qualities, the rational and ordered air of the
dragon-slayer. This is the form the delight of Delphi takes:
sweetness and light.

The dominance of these qualities testifies to their strength, to
the very brightness of the air and the sharpness of the shadows, the
softening effect of the trees, the almost delicate complexity with
which it all fits into its enormous surroundings. It might not have
been so, in a cliff-hung place bounded by terrible chasms and
overhangings crags.

The main approach along the road from Thebes has brought us
through pleasant mountain country, the foothills of Boeotia, with
glimpses down on to the Gulf of Corinth, one of Greece's many
sheltered arms of sea. Delphi begins (at any rate for me) at the
small town of Arachova near by, a name, probably for that
reason, with a special resonance and power. Say it with a soft
rasp, with dark a's, a stretched stressed second syllable and a soft
ch—Araachova. It is an ordinary quiet, quite natural Greek place,
on to which now the seeds of tourism from its famous neighbour
have begun to blow—the gift shops and the occasional hotel. In
appearance reminiscent of a Tuscan hill town, its old brown roofs
held down by stones, the sweet mountain air and view of hills and
valleys give it, and the area as a whole, a sort of enchantment.
Peacefulness still settles on it heavily, like a cloud, in the evening.
But the modern town of Delphi itself, which lies round the corner
from the historic sites, is now given over to tourism almost
completely.

It seems that in its ancient origins Delphi was really established
twice, once by tribes from the south and from the sea, out of
whose various cults and worships emerged the figure of Apollo,
a god already worshipped in Crete and perhaps brought to Delphi
by travelling Cretans. The second main wave of occupancy came
by constrast from the far north-east, from Thrace, and with it
came, as we shall see, a different worship and a different myth.

As so often (indeed, some would say, as always) the details of

D

the myths of Delphi, with their conflicts and defeats, reflect the comings and goings of tribes. It would be a rash mythologist who would claim that that was all they have to say—that Joseph's sojourn with the Pharaohs, for instance, is reducible to proto-history and nothing more; but that an element in their construc-tion is this encapsulated recollection of the movements of peoples is so likely that it cannot wisely be ignored.

There seems moreover to have been some basically physical source of the trance and inspiration which the place induced, which, along with the beauty and majesty of its setting, made the site sacred in the eyes of the ancients. The area is subject to earth-quakes, perhaps as a result of which the cavern from which the intoxicating vapours issued—in the mouth of which the priestess, according to all descriptions, used to sit and become, in a very literal sense, inspired—has been obliterated. We do not know, consequently, what sort of vapours they were; but we may perhaps conclude (though some geologists, it must be said, dissent from this) that the mists had some volcanic origin.

Since the cavern and its gift of hypnotic prophecy formed the original cause of Delphi's sacredness, the deity worshipped there at first was almost certainly the earth goddess herself. It was this cult which was ousted by Apollo, the god brought perhaps by the Cretans; at that point the site, probably already ancient, changed its name from the original Pytho to that, from Apollo's Cretan symbol the dolphin, which it still has. Since the Pytho goddess in the myth became the serpent-dragon Python, the indication is that worship there, before Apollo, may have incorporated sacred snakes like those which the Cretan statue of the earth goddess holds in her hands. It is these same snakes which, in enlarged form, so many early Christian heroes (such as Sir Gawayne and St George) are represented as destroying, which legend presents St Patrick as banishing from Ireland, and which may be metaphors for (or alternatively depicted by) those primal double spirals which decorate, throughout the world, the sites of the oldest religions—occurring (among many other places) at the earth goddess's shrine in Malta and the burial mounds in the Boyne valley. It is interesting that the theme of the prophetic serpent occurs also in connection with Eve, the mother of mankind, in the Genesis story of the origin of moral knowledge.

Apollo, when established at Delphi, took over the prophetic function. The priestess now spoke for the god, and it is in that form that the oracle entered the corpus of mythology. Later the coming of the new cult of Dionysus did not change this; Delphi has always been a place of prophecy.

There is no doubt that the history of this shrine is very ancient indeed. Certainly Mycenaean ruins and artefacts have been found in parts of the *temenos*, the sacred enclosure. Thanks to Pausanias, who described the layout as it was when he visited Delphi during the second century A.D., we can be fairly clear about the identity of what we see today. Earthquakes and time had in the interim covered it all over, and the village of Castri grew up on top of it during the Middle Ages. The first proper excavations took place between 1892 and 1900, though tentative efforts had been made earlier in that century. The village of Castri, which had itself been destroyed in an earthquake in 1870, was removed, and gradually the sacred centre came back into view.

One thing the ruins tell us is that the centre of the worship of Apollo was a rich as well as an important place. The treasure houses in which the offerings were stored form a significant part of the constructions. Many of the buildings one sees around one now, moving up the slope of the site, were built by various cities and states of Greece to form, and to house, offerings to the god. It was the custom to commemorate in this way any significant victory, with the resulting irony that we have the Athenian victory over the Persians being celebrated in stone only a short distance from that of the Spartans over the Athenians. The Athenian treasury, built to form a setting for the display of the spoils gained at Marathon, which they dedicated to Apollo, is a small and graceful building with a Doric-pillared pediment, which was reconstructed in the early years of this century. At the spot of the oracular seat itself, a little further up, the rock of the Sibyl rears, primitive and unformed, among these well-dressed ruins. It was there that the offerings were placed, and from there, in return, that the messages of the god were delivered.

In the area of the Sibyl's rock, remains of offering-buildings crowd each other confusingly, and only when one gets a little higher does the plan of the site become clear again.

At this point we reach the most sacred and esteemed of the main buildings. This, the temple of Apollo itself, superbly sited on an outlooking shelf, is, like so much else about both Delphi and Apollo, clear and comprehensible, and not grandiose at all. The temple rests on a base of Cyclopean walling, which is covered with the minute patterning of script, forming important and informative commemorative inscriptions. It was in this temple that the priestess presided over the adoration of the god, this being Apollo's main shrine in the Greek world. Here too was the centre of the earth, and the place where the slaughtered dragon was entombed. What is more, it was a centre of the reverence for wisdom which is so well represented by the famous dicta carved on its vestibule walls.

Of the other main buildings of the site, both the theatre and, much higher up, the stadium, are in an excellent state of repair. But it is without doubt the Rotunda (a tall-pillared circular construction of such delicacy that it seems quite small) which best presents the sweet delightfulness of Delphi. Now normally referred to as the Tholos, which simply means 'dome', its precise function remains in some doubt. It lies apart from all the rest of the site, down a steep path below the road, a monument very much in a secluded and delightful world of its own.

The crags which rise above the *temenos*, the Phaedrian Rocks, shelter, to their east, the gorge through which flows the Castalian spring. This is best reached from the corner of the road from Arachova, before one comes within sight of Delphi itself, and it runs very suitably, clear and cheerful, down its rocky course. The so-called fountain there, a kind of dam and culvert, the main pool of which is now drained, was a place of worship as well as of refreshment. The water, which indeed tastes pure and sweet, was thought to be a source of divine inspiration.

That inspiration of various sorts was evidently not lacking in ancient Greece is clear from the artefacts in the museum. Everybody knows of its star piece, that steady-eyed, attentive figure of

the Charioteer, standing in the eternal upright, balanced pose of
horse drivers, gaze fixed on the near distance, on the centre of his
concern, the control of his team. The reins are still balanced in his
hand. Balance, in fact, the feeling of the careful disposition of
weight, influences his whole stance. His stillness is the motion-
lessness of tension, the stress and alertness of it running right
through him, even down to his toes. He was one among many
valuable statues found during the excavations, this particular one
lying near the top of the *temenos*, above the temple. Probably
it, like other treasures, was a votive offering brought by an
important pilgrim to the shrine—symbol both of its wealth and
of his—sometime, it is thought, during the fifth century B.C.

   Fine too, in their way, are the statues of the dancers, and the
winged sphinx brought by the citizens of Naxos. These and other
works possess a skilfulness, a delicacy of touch and manner suited
to their destination. In another room is a later marble of Antinous,
the favourite of the emperor Hadrian, whose rather childish and
plump face decorated many sanctuaries and cities during the
Roman occupation of Greece. Perhaps it is perverse, with so much
beauty, to devote what will seem to many to be undue enthusiasm
to the omphalos, the navel-stone of the earth. Round and almost, in
its proportions, gross, it bears no decoration other than the simple
pattern of a net. Is it the concept which intrigues, something
in the idea, the thought of marking thus the centre of the earth?
Perhaps what lures me, with the repeated visits of passing years,
to let it buttonhole my thought and attention more than the
fine-featured Charioteer or the maidenly dancers is the air which
it bears of manifesting a mystery, of presenting itself without
further explanation as a simple entity, not something to be further
analysed; perhaps it is, simply, a form and an idea combined, as
near as a physical image can get to materializing an abstraction.

   Apollo was not at all a god of mystery, except in so far as he
carried with him the earlier cult of the earth mother and her gift
of prophecy. The omphalos is not a typical element of Apollonian
Delphi, and that is one of the reasons it stands out. Apollo was a
clear-headed god, orderly rather than vague. It is after all in the
first room of his temple that we find those most telling of graffiti,

the one commending moderation and, most noteworthy of all, the one commanding simply 'Know yourself'.

It would perhaps be hard to overstate the importance of this dictum in the history of European thought. It came to us chiefly through Socrates, for whom it formed one of the principal elements of ethical thinking. More than that, it represented Socrates' philosophical attitude, the leaning away from metaphysics towards analysis of what is, which has characterized several of the milestone figures in later philosophy. After the Renaissance the new sciences, as well as the intellectual attitudes, turned away from such matters as biblical exegesis towards the practice of the Delphic maxim, the quest for knowledge from the source nearest at hand. In Pope's words, 'the proper study of mankind is man'.

Perhaps this Socratic attitude led in the end to the reductionism of Darwin and Freud. Perhaps, on the other hand, it has not yet achieved its apotheosis. What is of interest here, however, is that the carved letters on the wall of the temple of Apollo bear a message which is essentially humanistic. You would not find such thoughts occurring in the presence of Zeus or Poseidon. Apollo in fact took a surprisingly human form.

Basically, it is agreed, he was a sun god, a god of light. From this came probably the connection which he had with crops and fruits. His other attributes, however, seem more likely to be due to the merging in him of several gods: Apollo the huntsman, Apollo the healer, Apollo the god of prophecy. These seem to be too diverse to have belonged originally to the single figure. They are the product, one feels, of amalgamation.

At Delphi, we have seen, his oracular function was dominant. His shrine in the deep cave from which vapours rose was presided over by a priestess, who replied to questions in a gibberish language which would then be further interpreted by Apollo's priesthood. The theory was that the god spoke through her; in effect she was in some sort of hypnotic trance, and those who do not go along with the supposition that it was really induced by the vapours from the earth attribute it to the effect of the rituals and ceremonies. The Greeks over a long period set much store by these mutterings. Many of the most important myths (such as those of Agamemnon, Oedipus, Orestes) involve a visit to the oracle at Delphi, thus testifying to the ancientness of its acknowledged importance.

The other major role which Apollo, this most complex of gods, possessed was that of shepherd god, protector of the flocks. In this his nature is rural, his worship coming clearly from the country people. A further attribute of his, that of musician, one which results in his being so often depicted holding a lyre, may well be due to a traditional connection between flock-watching and certain musical instruments. We shall find, when we come to the pastoral myths of Arcadia in a later chapter, that other shepherd gods as well played instruments.

Apollo was the son of Zeus by Leto, who seems to have been viewed by Homer as being the sky god's wife before his marriage to Hera, and by later sources as the subject of one of his affairs. Probably both mother and son were in origin Asiatic deities, since otherwise we have no explanation for finding them, in the *Iliad*, supporting the wrong side in the Trojan War. The birth of Zeus' children was never a simple matter, threatened as it was by the jealousy of other relatives, in this case and in that of Heracles by Hera's anger. Leto, with Poseidon's help, found a sanctuary on the island of Delos, where, as we shall see, the births of both Apollo and his twin sister Artemis took place.

Apollo's first adventure took place near to Delphi, where the serpent-monster called Python lived among the crags below Parnassus. The god journeyed there by a characteristically specific route from Olympus, across Pieria, Evvia and Boeotia, arriving at the coast below Delphi from the sea, at Crissa. From Crissa the gorge winds up, becoming, with greater height, more savage and dark. It was on the lip of this abyss, below Arachova—so we gather from the Homeric-style *Hymn to Apollo*—that he waited for the dragon with his bow, arrow in hand.

The episode of the death of the monster is known to us, not only because recounted in detail in the *Hymn*, but because it formed the basis of the rituals at the four-yearly ceremonial gatherings at Delphi, which are described for us by Pausanias, who evidently attended them. These seem to have been a matter of ritual song and dance, the songs being poems describing the battle and the dragon's death, the 'Pythian Songs'. They took the form of five separate sections, the first being a prelude concerned with Apollo in waiting for the dragon, the second describing the preparation for the battle. The third section was an account of the battle itself, and the fourth a celebration of the victory. The last one is described as representing the dragon's hissing as it died. Games and competitions surrounded these rather mystical central ceremonies, and the whole event seems to have become increasingly important up to the time of Delphi's rather sudden decline under the Romans, at the dawn of the Christian era.

The story of the Python is evidently partly an explanation of the origin of the sanctuary and the foundation of the cult, in this unproductive landscape at the top of the precipitous gorge. It is typical of the realism of the myth that it provides its explanation in terms of these identifiable physical features, firmly binding together the physical and the supernatural. The *Hymn to Apollo*, an anonymous work of the seventh century B.C. which has occasionally been mistakenly attributed to Homer, is so carefully specific about the details of the foundation of Delphi that we sense that it was felt there were things in need of being explained. Why is Apollo worshipped in Crete in the form of a dolphin? Because when he needed priests to serve his newly formed temple at Delphi he approached a Cretan ship in the shape of a dolphin and diverted it to Crissa. How did the priests live, in a land where nothing would grow? It became the custom for worshippers to bring offerings when they came to the shrine, off which the priests could live.

From these intimations we can perhaps get the gist of what happened. A first wave of settlers came, bringing their god, from the south, from the sea. We know that the Thracian tribes came down through Boeotia and Attica, and in the process occupied Delphi, at some early, though not precisely identifiable, time. With them they too brought their god, this time Dionysus, the god of wine. Since Dionysus is represented, in friezes and statues, as being attended by goat-men, such as the satyrs and Pan, and since we have authentic testimony, including that of Virgil, that goats were the animals most commonly sacrificed to him, it is not hard to see the Thracians as being goat-herding people, moving south perhaps because their animals had stripped and destroyed, as goats do, their home pastures. Prehistory presents us with few things more comprehensible than the clash of goat-herding and sheep-herding cultures; the one more voracious and destructive than the other, both needing space and mobility.

We shall find Apollo again having to come to terms with a goat god, Pan, who not only is often depicted as one of Dionysus' followers but may well have been, in origin, a version of the same god. The effect of the movement of goat-herding tribes in early times is, interestingly, probably still recognizable today. Goats, unlike sheep, kill the vegetation of the areas they pass through. They do this by eating the foliage of the trees, which then die. It is not uncommon in Greece to see a goat actually up a tree, a strange sight but one which helps to explain their drastic effect. When the trees have gone the land becomes eroded, and the climate in turn becomes less conducive to new growth. One may see in many parts of Greece this barren, arid land, a contrast to the lush and idyllic 'Arcadian' landscape of the more temperate country of the myths.

Dionysus was, of course, the prototype of Bacchus, a god of wine and drunkenness, whose festivities not surprisingly took a notably rowdy form. Ecstasy and raving seem to have character-ized his worship, a style at first quite foreign to Greek religion but, with the spread of the cult, quickly accepted. Frazer, in *The Golden Bough*, explains this success by reference to 'that love of mystery and that proneness to revert to savagery which seem to be innate in most men'. Certainly some explanation is required for the success of the cult, not least at Delphi. But there, however, the trances of Dionysus' followers were more clearly a reversion, a return to the pre-Apollonian religion of the earth and its mystic messages from the realm beyond consciousness, which had in fact never been displaced.

Towards the end of the eighth century B.C., it is said, the two cults at Delphi had found some sort of *modus vivendi*. Apollo, as a sun god, retained the realm of the daytime and the things done under the sun; Dionysus took over the dark and the knowledge of the secrets of the underworld.

It is not hard, of course, to see in this dichotomy a parallel to our modern preoccupation with the conscious and the sub-conscious realms of mind. Jung developed the theme in the third chapter ('The Apollonian and the Dionysian') of his influential book *Psychological Types*. It was almost certainly Nietzsche who first saw the possibilities of the Apollo–Dionysus pair as metaphors for more general ideas, for instance for the controlled and the emotional in art, the classical and the romantic. In *The Birth of Tragedy* he says: 'These two so different tendencies run side by side, for the most part in open conflict with each other, ever mutually rousing the other to new and mightier births in which to perpetuate the warring antagonism that is only seemingly bridged by their common term "art".' The duality, he says, thus leads to the continuous development of art.

How seriously one should take such applications of the Delphic situation is open to debate. It illustrates the point, however, that a myth is something more than just a story. Myths have a sort of usefulness, as ways of dealing with otherwise rather ungovern-able ideas, or as images in which thoughts of various sorts can be safely stored. And in the cases of the best of them they fulfil this function in multiple form, operating on, as it were, several levels at once, or meaning perhaps one thing to one person while meaning something slightly different to another.

Returning, however, to the more substantial matter of the place itself, we find the oracle emerging from myth and entering history some time during the sixth century B.C. Croesus, the archetypally rich king of Lydia, apparently bought the Delphic priesthood's support during his expansion in Ionia. An oracle which can be bought is a historical oracle, and we have plenty of evidence from the treasuries at Delphi for this sort of involvement in politics. Herodotus shows us a delicate situation arising when the Persian invasion of Lydia appeared to be successful. The Athenians were at first given no words of hope by the Pythian priestess:

Dead men, dead men, why do you sit there? Leave
Your country far behind, leave the high walls
That circle your city.

On asking Apollo again for advice as to how Athens might be
saved, they received from the shrine a baffling and ambiguous
message: 'Zeus allows Athena to save the wooden walls; they
alone will stand.' Some thought, Herodotus says, that it was the
thorn fence around the Acropolis that was being referred to;
others, however, got it right. The wooden walls in the coded
message meant the fleet, and the battle of Salamis produced the
desired result.

That was in 480 B.C. The period of internal unrest in Greece
which followed gradually undermined the influence of Delphi.
In 373 B.C. a major earthquake toppled the temple of Apollo. At
great expense (the money being raised by collections for the cause,
all over the civilized world) a new temple was built, being completed by 330. But more wars followed, and the shrine never
regained its prominence. In 279 B.C. Delphi suffered the indignity
of being invaded by Celtic tribes which over a long period swept
south through Europe. The Roman Empire in the meantime had
of course expanded through most of Greece, and the oracle does
not seem to have got on well with the emperors. Nero carried off
over five hundred statues, and by the time Plutarch came to
Delphi this relic of the old religion was something of a curiosity,
visited by tourists. People said that Apollo had gone. When
Julian the Apostate, in the third century A.D., approached the
priestess, he received the last reply: the oracle had nothing more
to say.

Apollo himself comes down to us, like the other gods, partly
through Homer, where incidents of his career are mentioned in
passing when he occurs as a participant in the matters of the
Iliad. This is certainly our oldest source. But details of his bio-
graphy are mostly to be found elsewhere—in Pindar's Odes and
in the later writers such as Pliny and Pausanias, as well, of course,
as in the valuable *Hymn to Apollo* itself. Euripides, who shows
general disapproval both of the mindless habit of reliance on

oracles and of the sort of savage behaviour sometimes justified by Apollo's instructions, gives a rather unfavourable picture of him in his play, the *Ion*—a result, presumably, of the attitude taken by Delphi, favouring Sparta rather than Athens, in the Peloponnesian War.

As visualized, as one can see in several instances in the museum at Delphi, Apollo was heroic in the classical Greek style, a little too idealized, perhaps, for modern eyes—his features somewhat smugly godlike, his stance elegant and superior. An early bronze (about 500 B.C.) in the National Museum in Athens shows a sharp-faced young man with long plaited hair, a strong chin giving him a determined and incisive look. The best example of him is to be found not in Greece at all—though probably it is a copy of a sculpture which once was there: the Apollo Belvedere, called after the Belvedere gallery in the Vatican Museum, where it may now be seen. It was found in the excavation of Roman ruins in 1495, and purchased by Pope Julius II for his Vatican collection; hence, incidentally, it must have been an important influence on Michelangelo, who first went to Rome in 1496 and whose 'David', begun five years later, bears much of the Apollo's classical perfection. Probably a Roman copy of an original at Delphi, the Apollo Belvedere gives us perhaps our best clue as to what, in the view of those who worshipped him, the god Apollo looked like.

Beauty is the overriding attribute both of the god and his sanctuary. Beauty and clarity, as of the light falling through the trees. The music he played on his lyre would need to have sharpness of definition and measured proportion to be properly Delphic. The place is not given to ominous undercurrents of emotion. The sort of pleasure it gives is that of a high place with a clear outlook.

SIX

AGAMEMNON AT AULIS

EUBOEA, OR, TO SPELL IT as it is now spelt and pronounced, Evvia: Italianate with little hills and cypress trees, it stretches towards the northern sea. From its eastern coast, at Kymi, one takes the boats for the Sporades. The sedate resort of Edipsos, much loved by Greeks and almost unknown to tourists, is the main feature of its western end. In the south, where it is largely fertile and empty, frequent crossings go from its tiny ports to the Attic coast at Rafina. And in between the straits which separate it from Attica form a deep, land-dominated gulf, called in ancient times and now the Euripos Strait. It runs up to a neck at Chalkis, where a swing-bridge joins the island Evvia to the mainland. Just near by on the mainland coast is Aulis.

Perhaps that puts it in perspective. It is not really far away. One can drive from Athens to Chalkis in a morning, and Aulis is slightly nearer. But the grove in which the Greeks sacrificed before their journey to Troy lay on a shingle shoreline which is, and was, remote in feeling, as if essentially isolated from other places and times.

There is something specially intimidating about the events which were said to have occurred at Aulis. One feels they are on a higher and perhaps more serious plane than we are accustomed to, even in myth. It is almost as if Agamemnon's choice was between acting as human or as divine. The episode is loaded with large ideas: of the duty of kings, of the need of the nation, of the will of the deities.

Why did these things become associated with this harmless place? The assumption is that it was not just for convenience that the fleet gathered there, though certainly at first sight it looks as if no better gulf could have been found in which to moor or beach the galleys, the assembled sea power of Greece, before that north-easterly crossing. But the land-locked position turned out to be not so ideal as a departure point as it might have seemed, since the story says that the fleet was penned there either, as it appears from Euripides, by a lack of wind, or (more likely since the boats were manned by oarsmen as well as sails) by contrary winds. Some state of the weather, anyway, prevented them from sailing; they did not get the wind they needed.

Probably in any case the site was sacred even before those times. Certainly it became so later, but the temple of Artemis may have arisen after the event, in commemoration of the supposition that it was to Artemis that Agamemnon was finally obliged to sacrifice. It was to Zeus, and perhaps to other gods, that the Achaeans first sacrificed at Aulis when they assembled. The gods were so much involved with the whole expedition that it is likely that there would be something divine about each feature of it, including this meeting place.

Homer puts the ships at rather more than a thousand, and the list he gives of the places represented, in Book II of the *Iliad*, shows them as coming from all parts of Greece, from Rhodes, Corinth, Samos, Pylos, Elis and Arcadia, from the cities of the Peloponnese and the distant islands, from Crete, Athens and Epidaurus. Why were all these diverse people said to have come, on that occasion, to Aulis?

It is a rich and varied story, or, on its different levels, several rich stories. The ebb and flow of trouble on the frontier of Europe and Asia Minor is of course at the root of it—a theme we meet everywhere in subsequent Greek history, from Darius and Xerxes to the present day. This is one of the abiding preoccupations of Greek politics, almost as constant a source of trouble as the Greeks' own problems of internal government. Probably long before Agamemnon there had been raids and counter-raids across the Aegean. Even in the story the abduction of Helen is not the first; there is a clue in Priam's reaction to Menelaus' demand for her return that he, Priam, had as good a case for complaint. His own sister, Hesione, had been taken away to Greece, and his

patient requests on that matter had met with no satisfaction. Even
in the story, then, the trouble goes back a long way, an old saga
of expropriation between uneasy neighbours. On one level,
certainly, this mustering at Aulis, with its preludes and sequel, is a
summarizing expression of the territorial and power-balance
rivalries between Greece and its eastern counterparts.

Herodotus shows us how a similar unity of all the separate
Greek states was achieved on a later occasion, when the border
territory of the Aegean came under another dispute. The power
across the water that time was the mighty kingdom of Persia,
which extended by then to what is now the Aegean coast of
Turkey, formerly the independent kingdom of Lydia and the
Greek Ionian colony, including that same area of Troy. Then, in
spite of an earlier victory at Marathon (which itself followed a
Persian punitive expedition in turn the result of a rebellion by the
Ionian cities), the states of Greece were confronted by the vast
army of Xerxes, which had crossed the Hellespont and was into
Thrace, supported by their fleet, before the threatened nations
combined and mobilized. Cunningly Herodotus tells us the first
part of the story from the other side, from the point of view of the
apparently invincible invaders, who were, we know of course, to
be the losers in the end. He shows their might, dignity, ambitions
and value; presenting their thoughts with apparent sympathy, he
depicts them moving confidently forward. Then he shows them
systematically destroyed by the sheer determination of the Greeks.
Just as on that later (though still ancient) occasion it was, in the
end, the fleet which saved them, and just as Thucydides many
years later was to take up again this theme of sea power and its
influence on the history of Greece, so the gathering at Aulis, being
nautical and directed against the eastern enemy, seems to summarize some essential elements in eastern European political
history. Herodotus tells how the various states stopped fighting
each other, in their sudden realization of their danger, and united:
bearing out, perhaps, one's continuing impression that the Greeks
can only be distracted from their internal political disputes by the
threat of trouble from Turkey. It was something of that sort
which seems to have occurred on the occasion of the gathering at

Aulis. In the terms of the tale, in its simplified, personalized form, a common bond or treaty brought them all together against a single enemy.

To see how this is presented in the myth, we must go back to an earlier point of the story.

If anything was ever foredoomed, it was the war with Troy. Events had started to combine to make it inevitable even before the birth of the participants. In fact the story says that it was at the wedding of the parents of Achilles, when Peleus married Thetis, that the first step towards the destruction of Troy was taken. The goddess of discord, Eris, threw down in front of the distinguished guests assembled there the golden apple bearing the words 'To the fairest'.

Perhaps, in the resulting claims to the prize, influence counted for something as well as beauty. One would not like to say specifically that the competition was rigged, but it certainly reduced itself very quickly to a short list of three, who happened to be the three major goddesses. Zeus refused to arbitrate, and it was at that point that Paris became involved.

Paris, the son of Priam, king of Troy, should himself have been killed at birth, since it was prophesied that he would bring about the ruin of his country. Instead the shepherd who was to kill him adopted him, and reared him as a herdsman. We are inevitably reminded of how Oedipus' destiny occurred, despite his parents' efforts, in the same way. The events in the Paris story took place on a mountain called Ida, south of Troy, on the Turkish coast near the island of Lesbos. And it was there that he was visited by the three goddesses demanding the award of the disputed apple.

Quite why Paris got the job of judge in this contest is not clear, but one reason evidently was that nobody else wanted to do it. It was, on the face of it, an unenviable position to be in, and perhaps acceptance of the post required a certain level of political innocence. Anybody who knew how these things turn out could have foreseen that regardless of who won the contest there would be one certain loser: the referee. Competition among the goddesses was bitter and ruthless; we shall see later how Artemis and

Aphrodite regarded themselves as rivals for the attention of Hippolytus. On this occasion the competitors were Hera, wife of Zeus, the wise Athena, and the love goddess Aphrodite. Paris really had no chance.

A bronze statue which probably represents him and, if so, shows him in the act of awarding the apple, stands in the National Museum in Athens. It presents a well-built, open-faced young man, with a calm, untense expression. Perhaps—we guess, looking at that untroubled face—he failed to comprehend the implications of what he was doing. Perhaps that mild look is one of innocence. Perhaps, in the end, he was simply not too bright.

One can see, in the story, that from the moment he gave the prize to Aphrodite, Troy was as good as in ruins. He earned by doing so the enmity of both Hera and Athena, and at the same time the equally problematic friendship of Aphrodite. He chose her because she bribed him. Yet they all did that. Hera offered wealth, Athena wisdom. What Aphrodite offered was a bride as beautiful as she was, and it happened that one existed in the form of Helen, though—a minor inconvenience—she was someone else's wife.

Helen was the daughter of Zeus by Leda. As such she was the daughter of Zeus in his swan form, and no doubt that accounted for her unmatchable loveliness. Aphrodite arranged for her to fall in love with Paris, and he with her. As the story progresses we feel more and more that he chose the wrong goddess. Wisdom would have been a better gift for him, from everybody's point of view; but things are not like that.

In any case, the judgement had predestined the considerable trouble which followed. It was because of the friendship of Aphrodite that he eloped with Helen, and because of the enmity of Hera and Athena that the act was not to go unpunished.

Like so many deceived husbands, Menelaus was away on business when Paris came. The trusting and otherwise-occupied husband is a stock figure in myths of *amour courtois* down the epochs. Often in such tales a bond of duty between the lover and the husband adds to the tension and dilemma, and in this case that bond was the duty of a guest to his host. This time, exceptionally, it was a bond which was not adhered to.

When Menelaus came back from Crete and found both Paris and Helen gone, he and his brother Agamemnon set about raising a force to pursue them. They were in a good position to do so, for several reasons. First, as king of Sparta Menelaus had considerable power in his own right. Sparta it seems was already set on its historic course, destined to become the first and most mighty city of the Peloponnese. At that time, however, it was overshadowed by its northern neighbour Argos, which, together with the citadel of Mycenae, formed the province of the High King. It is noteworthy that in the Trojan expedition Agamemnon commanded a hundred ships, more than any other of the leaders, and Menelaus sixty, as compared with the normal fleet of thirty or forty which Homer attributes to most of the other local forces. Indeed Thucydides gives as his opinion that fear was a greater power than loyalty in the raising of the army against Troy.

But the reason given by the myth for the success in raising so large a force is again couched in personal terms. Because of her beauty Helen had been courted by many suitors. They came to her father's palace at Sparta, of which city he was at the time king. It was Odysseus (who was among the suitors) who suggested to the king a means by which he might avoid trouble among the disappointed applicants when the princess eventually chose her husband. In accordance with this subtle scheme the king made each suitor swear an oath, made more potent by being sworn on the severed pieces of a sacrificed horse (an animal sacred to Poseidon), to the effect that he would join with all the others to defend Helen and her husband, whichever of them it would be, against any attack or injury. The horse was then buried on the spot; and many centuries later Pausanias, leaving Sparta on the road towards Arcadia, saw the site, called 'the Horse's Grave', with an ancient monument near by.

Helen chose Menelaus, who in due course succeeded her father as king of Sparta, which was evidently then ruled by succession through the female line—a factor which would have made the contest for the hand of the princess rather more pressing, perhaps, than would her beauty on its own. We gather from other evidence that this had always been the custom there, since Lacedaemon, legendary founder of the city, called it after his wife, Sparta, having attained the kingship of the area by marrying her, the daughter of a previous king.

The Sparta of history was the capital of Laconia, originally a Dorian town, the Dorians having moved down into the Peloponnese during the eleventh century B.C. The town they founded there expanded by means of a type of feudal system, the previous inhabitants of the area being enslaved, and in this way came to occupy sufficient territory to be self-providing. By about 730 B.C. we find it attacking its neighbours. Argos, at a later period, was its traditional enemy, being its major rival for territory in the Peloponnese.

We have from Plutarch, writing in Greece at the end of the first century A.D., a picture of a distant past in which Sparta represented some sort of ideal. Certainly Aristotle, in his *Politics*, gives what seems to be a more realistic and much less favourable view, at a time when the golden age of Sparta was only recently over. The view of it as a state of Nietzschean supermen, however, seems to have influenced not just later schools of thought but even the Greeks themselves. In spite of its apparent unattractiveness, it appears to have been an ideal for some, for instance Plato, whose Republic would have incorporated many Spartan aspirations and values and excluded those which the Spartans disdained. Thucydides, speaking of his own time, the mid-fifth century, contrasts the old extravagance and flamboyance of Athenian fashion with the simplicity which the Spartans first adopted, which, he says, is more in accordance 'with our modern taste'.

The effect of the rise to power of Athens under the stable democracy of the time of Pericles (which coincided with that great upsurge of philosophy and the arts), posed for Sparta not just a challenge but a threat. Greece was not big enough for both of them. We thus see how it came about that after a series of indecisive skirmishes the Greek states became embroiled in or encumbered by the great Peloponnesian War, which lasted from

431 to 404, during which time Athens and Sparta duelled for supremacy.

It was a clash of more than rival powers. We can see in retrospect that a conflict of ideals and cultural attitudes was added, when the civilized democracy of Pericles confronted military totalitarianism in its harshest form. Not surprisingly, perhaps, Sparta eventually won, after a complex series of defeats and recoveries, truces, negotiations, broken pacts, insurrections, retreats and alliances which must, at the time, have seemed endless. No doubt there is much scope here for thoughts of what might have been; but Sparta won, and in so doing checked the further expansion at that time of Athens and its talents and values, perhaps thereby facilitating the domination of Greece by later militaristic powers such as that of Alexander and, shortly afterwards, the Roman Empire.

The power of Sparta rose and fell quite swiftly. For a time at the turn of the fifth to the fourth centuries B.C. that Peloponnesian city-state ruled Greece; but its power dwindled throughout the fourth century, when it was defeated first by Thebes and later by the forces of Alexander.

Thucydides himself unintentionally prophesied what would become of the city, in describing the comparatively unimpressive remains of Mycenae, a place which gave little evidence by then of its once supreme importance. Imagine, he said, what would happen if Sparta itself became deserted, and all that was left for future generations to see were the temples and the foundations of buildings. They would find it very difficult to believe it was once as important as they were told. And this is exactly the state of affairs which we find. Yet, he said, the Spartans once controlled the whole of the Peloponnese, themselves occupied two-fifths of it, and moreover led allied nations outside their borders. Thucydides adds that Sparta was anyway badly planned and had few distinguished buildings. In any case now we have nothing, or almost nothing, of it to see.

When Pausanias came, in the second century A.D., things were rather different. The town and its buildings seem still to have been in good shape, lived in and run on traditional lines; he identified many of the monuments he saw as being from the original ancient city, but of course much else there in his time would have been of Roman rather than classical Greek construction. It is mainly the sparse remnants of that later city which one can see today, the bulk of it having gone some centuries ago for use as building stone in the surrounding country.

The modern town of Sparta, or rather Sparti, as it is called, was founded near the site of the former one in 1834, by which time the ruins had been thoroughly stripped and flattened. It is a medium-sized town, a little dull in character, less haphazard and unruly than the average Greek provincial town. The ruins, such as they are, lie outside the present town, and are in fact quite overshadowed by the Byzantine fortress-city of Mistras, which climbs the hill above them to the west. Perched up on one of those brittle, sparsely clad Greek hills, where lizards and snakes lie on the warm rocks and no shade breaks the almost unbearable daytime, Mistras is ghost-ridden, heavy with the presence of the past, something ominous, perhaps even depressing, clinging to its clutter of complex Byzantine buildings. Most people who come to Sparta now do so in order to see the medieval art of the churches of Mistras, merely passing through the tidy, unpretentious country town which bears, though rather sheepishly, its great predecessor's name.

Sparta enters the complex of mythology with the wooing of Helen, the episode which lies at the root of the explanation for the gathering at Aulis. Another suitor found a bride there in the process, since Odysseus, after he had brought about the oath which bound the suitors to support the winner of Helen's hand, himself married Penelope, her cousin. Pausanias, on his way out of Sparta, passed a statue commemorating the departure of that bridal couple. Penelope's father had attempted to persuade her to remain in Sparta (in accordance, perhaps, with the practice as adhered to by Menelaus, of the husband moving to the bride's property rather than vice versa) but Odysseus, whose fondness for his island became proverbial, insisted on returning to Ithaca. Her father followed them for four miles, to the spot where Pausanias saw the statue, at which point Odysseus insisted his wife should either come with him voluntarily or choose to remain in Sparta. She replied simply by hiding her face in her veil, and her father let her go. He raised on the spot a statue dedicated to Modesty.

Since Odysseus had been among the suitors, when Helen and Paris eloped Menelaus and his brother Agamemnon went to Ithaca to fetch him. The whole prelude to the war is loaded with foreboding, and Odysseus was aware of the long struggle to return which lay ahead of him, if he went. He pretended to be mad, and the envoys found him ploughing, with the ill-assorted team of an ox and a horse, a furrow which he sowed with salt. Doubtless these features of the story are symbolic, but in any case the visitors soon proved his sanity by placing his infant son in the way of the plough and forcing him to stop. He joined the expedition.

Achilles also had been warned of what would befall him in Troy. His mother Thetis, the sea nymph, knew that he would not come back. She had in his infancy rendered him practically immortal by immersing him in the Styx, but as a result he had a mortal portion, the heel by which she held him.

It is the fate of heroes whose death is almost impossible that the almost impossible shall take place. The Welsh hero Lleu Llaw Gyffes, in the *Mabinogion* tale (who will form the subject of comparison for us again), could not die on horseback or on foot, inside a house or out of doors, nor, apparently, on water or dry land. How then could he die, he was asked? There was one way— but, as his deceitful wife said, 'that can be avoided easily'—and that was for him to stand half in and half out of a bathtub, under a canopy, with one foot on the back of a goat; and needless to say these remarkable circumstances came about. Similarly in Norse mythology it seems that when everything on earth swore not to harm Balder, Odin's son, they did so by categories: trees, plants, stones and so on. The result was that the mistletoe was left out, presumably as not having the qualifying characteristics of a plant, so that Balder could be killed by that; and of course he was. The Irish hero Diarmait could only be killed in contradictory circumstances which he rightly thought unlikely to occur, but which then did. Shakespeare, of course, makes use of the same motif in the witches' prophecy of the apparently impossible circumstances of the death of Macbeth. The theme is universal, and results in the Indian demon Namuci being slain by Indra at twilight with the froth of water, and also perhaps in Samson suddenly losing his formerly secret invulnerability.

Achilles therefore had, from the start, no chance. Possessing a mortal heel he would be killed, while many who were mortal all over could escape. The tension between the improbable and the actual runs, a strand of fatalism and a feeling of powerlessness, through all myth. Nor could Achilles avoid going to Troy, precisely because to go there was destined to be his downfall. But his mother the goddess Thetis tried, with a foolishness more suited to a mortal, to outwit this fate. She had him disguised as a woman and hidden among the maidens at the court of the king of Skyros, that remote and rocky island of the Northern Sporades, off the coast of Evvia, where, some time earlier in the mythic chronology, Theseus the Athenian leader and, a greater deal later, the English poet Rupert Brooke both met their deaths.

Ironically it was Odysseus, himself prevented from evading the conscription, who went to Skyros and found Achilles out. He did it by means of a particularly Odyssean trick, laying before the ladies of the court, our hero among them, an assortment of trinkets and ornaments with a shield and a spear mixed with them. Achilles revealed his identity by choosing those, and found himself drafted.

Very probably the story derives from a misunderstanding, at some early stage, of a depiction of some forgotten ritual in which men dressed as women. Though not unique (it is mirrored by episodes in the stories of Heracles and Dionysus), it seems to need some such explanation. The notion of Achilles in drag is to say the least somewhat unheroic. But actually he is always presented by Homer (and hence by subsequent authors such as Euripides) in a rather unfavourable light, as arrogant and conceited, ill-tempered and disposed to take any thwarting of his will as a personal insult.

One of the many remarkable things about the *Iliad* and the

Odyssey is that few of the participants come out of it with un-stained characters. Homer, however, seems to have had an entirely favourable view of Nestor, the old and wise king of Pylos, a coastal kingdom in the extreme south-west of the Peloponnese. His position is thus that of Menelaus' western neighbour in that area, Messenia, which was later brought under Spartan domination. Pylos is a rocky, cove-dotted area, a place of cliffs, beaches and clear water, remote and uncrowded because of its distance. Near the modern village of Chora, some way from the position of the place now called Pylos, ruins of Mycenaean date were found in modern times, and inevitably christened the Palace of Nestor. Homer calls it 'sandy Pylos', and indeed the bay of Navarino, protected by the island of Sphactiria, is skirted by sand hills; and on the western side of the neck of the isthmus where the old castle of Pylos is, across the bay from the present Pylos, a crescent of sand forms a secluded, private-feeling bay. Cliffs rise around it on either side, in one wall of which is the cave to which Hermes brought the stolen cattle of Apollo, the subject of an episode in another chapter. The ruins of 'Nestor's Palace' occupy the top of a hillock overlooking the flat land which sinks, with one or two lumpy outcrops, to the sea on the one hand and the sandy bay of Navarino on the other. There is a lot to see now of the extensive, well-planned palace, which seems to have been burnt in about 1200 B.C. It has yielded a fair quantity of artefacts, some of which, including pieces of fresco, are in the museum near by. Clay tablets which the fire hardened rather than destroyed revealed that Nestor's historical counterpart, like Agamemnon's, wrote Greek in Linear B.

Nestor is represented as being already old when Menelaus fetched him from Pylos to come to Aulis, the two of them making their way across land to collect the other forces. He had, Homer says, seen two generations of his people come and go, ruling now over the third. Nevertheless he was to endure the nine years of war, and, unlike some of his colleagues, to return home in peace. At Aulis he commanded ninety ships, indicating the power attributed to the early kingdom of Pylos.

The course of the war was fully prophesied, like the fate of most of the participants, from the start. Soon after they first gathered they sacrificed to Zeus, and were surprised by the sudden appearance of a serpent which climbed a plane tree near the place of sacrifice and ate a nestful of birds, nine in all, that was at its top. Calchas, the prophet who accompanied the army, interpreted this strange event. Troy would fall, but only after nine years of war. The story mentions that the snake was turned to stone; evidently there was an otherwise puzzling emblem of a climbing snake on one of the altars which were apparently around the grove at Aulis in later times.

Most effective of the versions of what happened then, and probably the best-known, the one in which the human and ritualistic situations combine in their most poignant, inescapable form, is the play by Euripides, *Iphigenia at Aulis*, written mainly by the elder Euripides shortly before his death in 406 B.C., and apparently finished by his son. The play starts with a brilliant piece of mood-setting, the tension of a windless dawn over the Strait. Nearby Chalkis is mentioned, apparently already an established port. The Chorus in this case is a party of sightseers from Chalkis who have come across in boats to see the assembled fleet and the Achaean camp on the shore, competing in spotting the famous heroes there. One of them actually saw the great Achilles running on the shingle beach. The play, and indeed all versions of the myth, provide a strong sense of Aulis as the site of great events. This is the more surprising when one knows it, as it is physically quite undistinguished.

It is a low-lying, mild-tempered place, looking straight out from a long shore across the calm waters to the mountains of Evvia. A dozing village a little way inland now preserves the name—now spelt Avlis, and pronounced with the emphasis on a long second syllable: Avleess. On the left one can see the outskirts of Chalkis itself, at the end of the enclosed bay. There is little vegetation now, apart from the olive trees near the shore, to soften the light which pours over the level land. An occasional clump of cypress trees on the landward hillsides, or a pine-covered hilltop, give us a clue as to what it may have been like in more fully vegetated times.

The foundations of a temple of Artemis were indeed found there in 1941, and excavated during the 1950s; but there is probably more still to be found. What we may now see is a classical-period foundation with embellishments of a later date. Both these signs and Pausanias' description suggest that the temple was in use into Roman times, which makes it all the more puzzling that it should have disappeared for such a long period, especially as everybody knew roughly where it must be. There may well have been, of course, an earlier use of the same site, and perhaps archaeology may yet reveal one. But it seems equally possible, as suggested earlier, that this temple (which is shown by an inscription to be definitely dedicated to Artemis) was built in commemoration of the story of the sacrifice of Iphigenia. The building which we have is anyway clearly post-Homeric.

When Euripides' play opens Iphigenia has already been sent for, and we then learn the reason. Calchas the seer had prophesied that the fleet could not leave Aulis, where they were windbound, unless Agamemnon sacrificed his daughter to Artemis. It is perhaps implied by Euripides that this was in accordance with a local custom, since he makes ominous references to the altar of Artemis even before Iphigenia's arrival. The theme of child sacrifice (echoed in the story of Abraham and Isaac in the Old Testament) is not uncommon in universal myth, and it seems at least credible that it could refer to some ritual required of sacred kings. A similar story is that of Idomeneus, the king who led the Cretan force at Troy, who was caught in a storm during his return after the war and vowed that if Poseidon spared him he would sacrifice the first person whom he met when he landed— which of course turned out to be his son. It is ironic, in this instance, that Priam, king of Troy, had refused to kill his son, Paris, although instructed to do so, for the sake of Troy, by the priests of Apollo.

Frazer has a whole chapter in The Golden Bough, called 'Sacrifice of the King's Son' (with examples from Sweden, Greece and western Asia), in which he suggests that in ancient cultures the king died for his people in his capacity as representative of the god, rather in the way that the god's sacred animal, his emblematic form, was put to death in later cults; it is part of Frazer's over-all theme that these sacrificial deaths were a means of ensuring renewal, or of preventing decay; he goes on to argue that the sacrifice of the king's son, of which he gives instances in myth and custom, was the first step towards the provision of a substitute, a means by which the king could continue to reign beyond the fixed period of his sacred term.

We know in any case that the New Testament assumes an understanding of the symbolic meaning of a father sacrificing his son for the good of the people, the gift of his first-born, his representative or successor, being a sort of ransom or expiation, ensuring renewal and the perpetual continuity of the bond between him and his people. And if this theme is in fact foreshadowed in the words of the Old Testament prophets, then the sacrifice of the human representative of the god may be a very ancient Judaic tradition. Perhaps it is this that is referred to in the story of Jephthah, in the eleventh chapter of Judges, where the king sacrifices his only child, in this case too a virgin daughter, as an offering after a battle. Such a theme is far from unknown elsewhere. CuChulain, for instance, the Irish hero, killed his only son Conlair, and carried the dead boy to the king and the people, saying, 'Here is my son for you, men of Ulster.'

Whether or not Frazer's is an accurate explanation, this occasion at Aulis is distinguished by it being the daughter, not (as in most cases) the son, who is sacrificed. This would be neatly explained if, as appears to have been the case, the kingship of some early communities, such as those at Sparta and Argos, were passed on through the female line.

Iphigenia was sent for, and she and her mother Clytemnestra made the journey across the northern Peloponnese, through Attica and Boeotia, to Aulis. Euripides creates a tense state of dramatic irony when we, the audience, know why she has come, but the army and the other characters become excited and emotional at the reunion of father and daughter. Iphigenia eventually goes to her death voluntarily, for the sake of Greece. The idea of Greece becomes a strong force in the play, as indeed it was in the original story, in Homer, in which the Achaeans (the people equivalent to the archaeologists' Mycenaeans) seem to possess an ultimate sense of joint identity. Iphigenia sees herself, in dying, as being the conqueror of Troy. This, she says, will be her everlasting fame. 'This my children, this my wedding; and this my fame.'

As to why the sacrifice was to be to Artemis, the authorities are not quite clear. Perhaps it was in her capacity as goddess of virginity, since the unmarried state and eternal childlessness of the princess is heavily emphasized (as it is also in the case of Jephthah's daughter). Artemis was the sister of Apollo, with whom she shared some characteristics, such as that of hunting; they were born together, twins, on the island of Delos (as we shall see in a later chapter), the children of Zeus by Leto. Artemis, like Apollo, was connected with light—in her case, though, with the moon; and her main attribute was her chastity, which also, probably through that connection, was a quality which became associated with the moon. She spent her time with her hounds and maiden followers hunting in the hills of Arcadia, an outdoor existence which suited her hatred of the qualities of love and family life.

There is in fact something masculine and severe about her manner and behaviour, characteristics well displayed in the bronze statue, from the fourth century B.C., in the National Museum in Athens. It shows us a rather horsy-looking woman, with a healthy outdoor look, by great contrast with the softer, more feminine Athena in the next room. Artemis wears her hair swept back from her face and tied up in a practical, but not of course especially attractive, circlet; Athena's flows loose down her back —but that would get in the way while you are hunting. Athena wears a softly flowing gown. Artemis' gown is strapped round her, leaving her big arms free for action.

The cult of the virgin goddess has retained a strong hold down the centuries, culminating, no doubt, in the Mary-worship of the Middle Ages. In her capacity as the symbol of what might be called anti-sexuality Artemis is contrasted, in Greek myth, chiefly with Aphrodite. This straight dichotomy is represented best in the story of Hippolytus, the son of Theseus, who spent his time hunting and riding and refused to worship Aphrodite. The latter, out of jealousy of his loyalty to Artemis, caused his stepmother Phaedra (whom Theseus had recently married), to fall in love with him. This story has a curiously close parallel in the ancient Celtic tale of Tristram and Isoud, in which the hero, Tristram, spends his time hunting and has no inclination for the pursuit of love, but becomes eventually trapped into tragedy when he and his uncle's (in earlier versions, there is reason to think, perhaps his father's) new wife are caused to fall in love by the workings of magic.

It seems that you cannot worship them both. Artemis and Aphrodite are contradictory in character. It is hard, in fact, not to reveal a bias in the discussion of the matter, even at this distance. But each to his own taste. I would not wish to argue against hunting, except to point out that Hippolytus came to a nasty end.

While the Artemis of classical Greece is presented in this very definite style, a different aspect of her took root across the Aegean in the Ionian Greek colony, becoming the main cult of the great city of Ephesus. There the worship of Artemis (known to the Romans as Diana) grew into a world-famous feature, her temple in Ephesus becoming so well known that in the middle of the fourth century B.C. it was burnt down by a man called Herostratus (one of those names one can never remember) with the sole purpose of ensuring by doing so that his name would never be forgotten. (A subsequent decree that anyone who spoke his name would be put to death only made it more certain that his aim would succeed. This would also seem to contain a technical difficulty. *What* name is it we are not allowed to mention?) The successor to that, the post-Herostratian temple, was even greater, in fact the largest ever built, and became one of the Wonders of the World.

But this, the Ionian Artemis, was such a different goddess that some authorities consider them to be not one but two, using, as it were, the same name. The Artemis at Ephesus was a goddess of fertility and plenty, as may be seen by the statue of her with its many breasts, clearly a mother goddess. The attention which St Paul gave to Ephesus, where he stayed to preach the new religion with its male deity, seems to imply that he regarded this centre of the more ancient mother-goddess worship as a special threat. Legend claimed that the temple of Artemis at Ephesus was founded by Amazons, which certainly seems to indicate that it was regarded as a remnant of an earlier matriarchal system. The myth of Artemis contains much violence, and some of this perhaps provides the basis for a cult involving human sacrifice. There was the death of Actaeon, torn to pieces by his hounds for daring to watch the goddess swimming in the nude. More doubtfully perhaps Pausanias mentions rituals at Sparta, which he says derived from human sacrifice to Artemis. Certainly a tradition of human sacrifice is preserved in the version of the story in which Iphigenia is saved from the altar at Aulis and transported to the land of the Taurians, where, as priestess to Artemis, she officiates at the ritual slaughter of shipwrecked strangers.

This version, which was adopted by the later tradition and by Ovid, points to the eventual modification of that barbaric practice—if, as we guess, that is what lies at the base of the myth of Aulis. This adaptation has it that Artemis at the last moment substituted a stag for the maiden victim—reminding us again of the outcome of the Abraham and Isaac episode—so that Iphigenia lived on. But in spite of the inclusion of this theme in the ending (which he did not write) in this last play of his, Euripides seems to imply, with his ominous and unforgettable emphasis throughout on that blood-soaked altar and with the obvious intention of Iphigenia herself that the sacrifice should take place, that the modified one was not the only form of the story current in his time. The happy ending seems as imposed as it almost certainly is. It may well have been the case, at Aulis as at other sacrificial sites, that a custom of human sacrifice was adapted in later ages to become that of the sacrifice of an animal—here, evidently, as one would indeed expect from other instances, the animal emblematic of the deity in question. But if so then this change evidently took place at Aulis not so long ago that it had quite banished the remembrance of a previous tradition, the influence of which still affected the myth.

In any case the story seems to require Iphigenia's death, and the logic of the play too implies the inevitability of it, as she goes ceremonially towards the sacred grove around the altar of Artemis, in a scene tense with the inhumanity of ritual, to meet her savage end.

And so the Trojan War was launched. Heavy with all its consequences, it lumbered forward. From that long flat shore the Greeks felt the breath of a favourable breeze along the waters, and the thousand sails spread on their thousand masts as the sacred kings and demigods embarked, leaving Aulis behind them stained and changed.

SEVEN

AGAMEMNON AT MYCENAE

THERE ARE SOME in whom quiet insistence is more effective than a shout; but they turn out to be those in a position to imply a reservoir of authority, which perhaps is what makes it insistent, not just quiet. You get the same thing occasionally in music, in a slow passage of Bartok, say, when the quietness emphasizes the unsaid and induces more a shudder of awe than does (for instance) the thundering of Beethoven. And when you come up the valley it is not that the citadel rears or towers or does anything so obvious ahead of you, but simply that it is unavoidably, imperatively, the centre and focus of your view.

What there is left of Mycenae today—or, more accurately, what has been returned to view by the archaeologists—is in the form of a series of rising tiers encircling a small conical hill. This sits among a ring of larger hills at the top of the winding road by which you approach. Like the stage at Epidavros, like the volcano in the lagoon formed by Santorini's cliffs, it dominates the scene not by its size but by its significance and centrality.

It is impossible to come towards it up the narrow valley among the hills without a feeling as if of inferiority. 'Commanding' is the sort of word used for such hilltop positions as it occupies; but Mycenae is commanding in more than just the sense of looking down all around on its surroundings. Something perhaps about the hierarchical structure of its ramparts, tapering to a definite summit underlined and emphasized by the more substantial lower reaches, gives us the notion that the hill itself embodies authority. The idea of a High King, similarly, has this sort of innuendo, as if the use of terms like 'looking down on' and 'looking up to' were more than just metaphor. Mycenae plays with our traditional images in physical form.

From on top you look back in the direction of Argos. The wide fertile plain stretches away towards the sea, with no visible limit but just the haze of distance. The sudden break in land form, where the hills of Argolis sink to an unexpected end in the alluvial flatness, marks the contrast between the places. It is as much a pair of counterparts as peace and war.

Mycenae is in the form of a palace within a fortress, surrounded by royal tombs. For that reason, and because it occupies the crown of a hill, it appears as more or less concentric. The ramparts are stronger on the side of the view towards Argos, the inevitable direction of approach. On the other side the hill falls in crags and steep slopes to an encircling valley, and the palace looks out towards those bare, escarpmented hills. The main part of it is made of huge roughly dressed blocks, a style known as Cyclopean from the legend that these giant constructions were originally erected by the Cyclops. It is difficult to see how else it could have been done, and certainly the style is that of prehistoric giants rather than men. No other building feels so old. Everything about it overawes with an atmosphere of manifest antiquity.

The present village of Mikini, further down the valley towards the main road and the plain, is in bizarre contrast to the vast and eternal palace. Behind the breeze-block tourist restaurants along the road, it squats, understandably keeping out of sight: a cluster of farm huts and hovels, all made of mud bricks. Chickens and children scuttle among the stones. Clearly this, unlike the other, will not be with us in a few thousand years. Yet it too is in a way timeless, the accretion of poverty around the edges of wealth, in its tiny and inconspicuous way the same sort of reminder of reality as are those accumulations of shacks which embarrass great luxurious cities in Latin America. Though physically temporary it is, too, socially permanent, since probably very little about the life of its inhabitants has changed; whereas there are no High Kings here now, mighty with gold. An old woman huddled in a shawl turns a lamb on a spit in the open air, and another hurries down the track with a bucket. It reminds us aptly that it would be

E

a mistake to think of the Greek past as being all a world of palaces and pedigrees.

Perseus was the son of Danaë by Zeus, who visited her in the form of a shower of gold, in the prison where she had been confined by her father because it was foretold to him that his grandson would kill him. After many adventures (he killed, for instance, the gorgon Medusa) Perseus came to Argolis with a band of Cyclop builders, and built first Tiryns—apparently considered the older citadel of the two—and then Mycenae. Though no doubt it is intended that the house of Atreus should be found to be descended from Zeus through Perseus, so that their tenure of Mycenae was aboriginal, there seems to be a break somewhere in the lineage. The ownership of Mycenae changed lines, and we take it up again with Tantalus, whose son Pelops inherited his many kingdoms. Possibly Tantalus too was a son of Zeus. Of Pelops we shall hear more elsewhere, but it seems that he was a hero of Asian origin, probably from Lydia. He subjugated the whole of the area which then came to be called after him, the Peloponnese. As far as Mycenae is concerned, we know that Atreus was the son of Pelops, and that Atreus settled in Mycenae and there founded a dynasty.

Mycenae's history is on two levels, the one being its powerful central position in the imaginative story of the Greek world, the world-picture expressed through the myths. The other is the story of its real and factual effect on Greece's political geography. Two co-existing aspects of it operate, at one and the same time, like two ways of looking at the same thing: contrapuntal, co-extensive even, but not directly mutually translatable precisely because not operating in the same sphere, the same conceptual system. Like the mind and the brain. Like colours and light waves—the one being detectable by the eye, the other by the spectroscope. They are correlated, but not in the way that one is more fundamental than the other. It would be wrong too to try to describe the one in terms of the standards of the other. Sound is measured, noise perceived.

In physical terms it started in the Stone Age, since there are slight signs that the hill was occupied even then. Somewhere around 3000 B.C. the Bronze Age started; that is, men learnt to work with metal tools. From that point on Mycenae became more noticeably settled, until in about 2000 B.C., when a new population, a Greek-speaking tribe, arrived, a swift and definite advance in life-style and development took place. These were literate people, as is evidenced by their remarkable tablets in the script known as Linear B, which reveal that both these early Mycenaeans and their counterparts in Crete spoke the Greek language.

Archaeological Mycenae reached its climax in the later decades of the late Bronze Age—that is, some time about 1300 B.C. At the time of the probable fall of Troy, which may have been about 1250 B.C., it was already slightly past its peak, and from then on there seems to have been a steady decline. After the Dorian invasion, which signalled the rise of their new city of Sparta, Mycenae and the ancient world of the Achaeans was in effect over. This was perhaps during the eleventh or twelfth centuries, and Mycenae was certainly sacked in 1100 B.C. This did not imply the end of the fortress's occupied life, but probably simply the loss of its independent power. It was occupied and re-occupied for many centuries, and in fact entered the classical age as still a recognizable place. However, it had been from time to time subject to the control of its neighbour Argos, and was finally destroyed by Argos in the first half of the fifth century B.C. Thucydides certainly does not seem to have found the physical remains of it in his time, the late fifth century, particularly impressive. He said that Mycenae seemed, to his contemporaries, a small place; and other towns of that period did not seem very imposing. Yet that, he said, was not a reason for underestimating their power—not that there was ever really much danger of that. However, when Pausanias came this way some five hundred years later it was by then deserted.

We owe the partial reversal of this trend to Schliemann. A German businessman who made a fortune in Russia during the Crimean War, he devoted his life from the age of forty to archaeology in Greece. He seems not only to have been possessed of the knack of finding what he was looking for, but gifted with good luck too in there being something left to find. For instance, it is really amazing that the Mycenean graves remained to such an extent unplundered, so that Schliemann could unearth there, in the late 1870s, that great store of treasures. He had as his ideal the proof of Homer as literal truth; a mistaken concept, no doubt, since Homer dealt in the world of myth, which counterparts that of history but works, in doing so, in a different way. However, Schliemann did show that the Troy and Mycenae of the myths were shadowed by a Troy and a Mycenae in the physical world, and thus he added immensely to the depth and richness of our knowledge of both. Delving into the background and substrata of Homer's stories does for us something equivalent to the biographical investigation of a great writer or artist. Perhaps *A la recherche du temps perdu* is altered in no way at all by a knowledge of what Proust normally had for breakfast; but our understanding benefits by being enabled to spread out from the work itself into areas only marginally connected with it. So it is, I feel, with Agamemnon and archaeological Mycenae. But Schliemann did not feel that; he felt that he had shown Homer to be writing history.

He started to uncover Troy in 1872, but work was held up after 1874 by legal difficulties about possession of the treasure unearthed. This hiatus enabled him to work at Mycenae, which was anyway a logical continuation. In 1884 he progressed to Tiryns, and we would have had the benefit of his genius for discovery at both Ithaca and Knossos had he not died unexpectedly in Naples in 1890. As a result Knossos had to wait another ten years for Sir Arthur Evans, and Ithaca even longer, as we shall see in later chapters.

There is a great deal more to Mycenae, archaeologically, than just the cone-shaped ruins crowning the hill. It spreads out in the surrounding countryside for quite some distance, and the modern road up the valley runs more or less through the middle of the area over which it had expanded. Five of the major tombs, in fact, are out of view completely, over the top of the ridge on one's left as one comes up the road. Outskirts of the town which surrounded the palace lay as far away from it as the top of this ridge, and the remains of houses can also be seen in the valley on the right, far below the ramparts. The earliest grave circles, where the bulk of the treasure was found, lie in two areas, one inside the walls, the other near to the main approach. The former, down to the right as one comes into the citadel through the Lion Gate, was the scene of Schliemann's success, six deep shaft graves clearly of royal status. In them were the remains of nineteen people, the men wearing those remarkable gold masks, the women accompanied by gold ornaments. Other well-known objects, such as the swords and vases and the drinking cup, also came from here. The other graves, above the Tomb of Clytemnestra, below the path on the right near the entrance to the enclosure, were not discovered until 1951, and also contained golden treasure.

Although slightly later (the finest of them being of the period 1400 to 1300 B.C.), the great *tholos* tombs impress us more today than these primitive circles. *Tholos* simply means vault or dome, and describes their form. Until the Pantheon was built in Rome the largest and most advanced of these, known as the Treasury of Atreus, had the largest dome so far constructed, 48 feet wide and 45 feet high. This lies to the left, on the way up, just above the road; and from its position directly opposite the citadel it gives, particularly from the hill above its crest, a fine view across the valley to Mycenae. The others which are easily accessible (which the ones on the other side of the ridge are not) are known as the 'Tomb of Clytemnestra' and the 'Tomb of Aegisthus', and both are near the ramparts, sunk into the slope of the valley to the right below the entrance.

The *tholos* tombs are all dug into hillsides, and covered over; but, as one can see from the Tomb of Clytemnestra, the tops of their domes were visible above ground, so they were evidently not intended to be hidden. They are remarkable for a number of reasons, but chiefly for their echoing hollow darkness and their size. Clearly they sheltered a dynasty of considerable importance, and their emptiness now emphasizes their grand scale. They answer you with a *bou-oum* like the Marabar caves in Forster's *A Passage to India*. Feeling around in the huge empty darkness one is not just impressed but mystified. Why should it have been desirable to make them so big?

The comparison may seem unfair, but in the form of construction and the shape these 'beehive' tombs are reminiscent (though greatly superior in finish and very many times larger) of the 'beehive' cells in certain Irish tombs, the neatly domed chambers, for instance, at Dowth in the Boyne valley—a tomb of about the same period or before—which, along with the greater tomb at New Grange near by, has another feature in common with Mycenae. The stones of the Irish one and the funerary articles of the Greek both make use of the theme of the double spiral.

Without doubt the power and richness of historical Mycenae can be understood best not here, beside the Cyclopean walls or in front of the Lion Gate, but in the National Museum in Athens, where, as soon as you come in, that amazing hoard confronts you. Something about the soft colour and the hard surfaces of gold insists, with quiet superiority, on one's attention. The air of luxury combined with indestructibility which it has gives it an easy advantage over more common things. Presumably they knew what they were doing: that the lines of the eyebrows and the beards of the kings would be as precise and distinct now as when they beat them. That somebody, some day, would be impressed.

The masses of fine gold ornaments in those cases on the ground floor cannot but remind anyone who had seen them both, of that other great National Museum, the one in Dublin, where similarly fine beaten and patterned goldwork from about the same period fills similar cases. What is unavoidable too is the recognition that familiar patterns recur, particularly, as mentioned above, that series of double spirals on the vases and medallions, a pattern endlessly repeated in the room containing the Mycenaean grave ornaments, where, as at the burial mound of New Grange, one feels almost overwhelmed by it. Of course it proves nothing; proof is a more stringent matter altogether; all one can do is remark on the shape of the facts. No doubt the forms which patterns can take are limited; and the love of gold is permanent and universal.

Judging by their funerary masks the Achaean kings were

mostly small and fat. The great exception is that lean, sharp-featured face which Schliemann believed to be that of Agamemnon. An image of a man with cunning eyes and a cruel mouth shows through the formalized gold features. Its long sharp nose and deep-set eyes are made more prominent by hollow cheeks; a trimmed, winged moustache and a straight beard leave the long line of his lips and the prominent chin unhidden. By comparison with the other bulbous-featured faces, it seems a man of a different race. The effect is almost a bitter, certainly a weathered look. We cannot be surprised that Schliemann called it Agamemnon. None of the others bear a strength of character in their faces sufficient for them to have established themselves in myth as the High King and leader of the Greeks.

The conclusion from the cases in the National Museum must be that the civilization which flourished at Mycenae during the late Bronze Age was not only rich and powerful but advanced in artistic skill. To some extent one would have gained this view in any case from the site, from the magnificence of its well-dressed blocks around the entrance-way, from the Lion Gate itself, of course, an adequately royal and sophisticated entrance for the palace-fortress. Two lions stand, headless now, their fronts towards each other, a small pillar between them, their front feet raised on a step to give them a sort of rampant stance. The whole relief is framed by the corbelling of the wall stones which rise above the gate lintel, forming a triangular space. The lions themselves are finely formed, as if moulded in stone. In the massive stone at the side of the door can be seen the holes made for the beams which kept it shut, and the flagstone of the threshold shows the deep ruts of wheels, while the surface is hatched from side to side to give the draught animals foothold.

As you go up the stones get smaller, the atmosphere less that of a fortress, more of a dwelling. Without the guidebook it would as usual be impossible to guess at the function of the small rooms indicated now by only the bases of their walls. But at the very top the hill becomes a platform looking out towards the valley and the plain beyond, and it is no surprise to find these level spaces called the Great Court, the Anteroom, and the Throne Room.

We have to imagine these broken squares of wall as being a stately two-storey building, columned and paved and highly decorated. Such things as the bases of pillars in the Propylon, the formal entrance to the court rooms, are about all that is left now of the original architectural splendour. At present one enters the central palace area, by way of those modest stepped streets and terraces of the jumbled jigsaw of buildings below it, from what was probably a side entrance; the official approach is unfortunately not now usable, but can be seen by peering over the southern edge of this top plateau, leaning, as it were, out of the Great Court or the Anteroom. This, known as the Grand Staircase, is a broad and straight flight of stone steps with gentle rises, which must have had the effect of making the formal visitor fully aware, as he rose slowly against the soaring wall of the royal enclave towards the eventual achievement of the Anteroom, that he was indeed going somewhere special. One has to see the Staircase as being indoors, the wall on its outer side rising to curtain it off, rising within its own shell to double back on itself from a small landing before emerging directly into the Anteroom. It would make the journey to the royal presence both slow and secluded. The Throne Room, now looking very small and spare, was entered by a broad doorway, a few paces across the Anteroom floor.

At the back of the royal rooms lay a small temple, originally the sort of private chapel which all Mycenaean palaces probably contained; this, which was altered in later ages of occupation, now unfortunately reveals to us no more than its foundations. The rooms themselves ended (to one's right if one comes as if from the Grand Staircase) with a Megaron, a pillared hall in which the main occasions of the court presumably took place. This is entered out of the Great Court by way of two small rooms, themselves characteristic of the pillared and vaulted grandeur of Megarons. Here one can get an intimation of the splendour of the inner recesses of Mycenae, feeling the room rising from these sound footings to a roof held on four pillars, of which the bases are still in place, rising around the clearly identifiable large central hearth. There is plenty of evidence that the people of Bronze Age

Greece relished colour and decoration, and the hearth, the pillars, the floor, the walls and the ceiling would all have been painted and frescoed.

At the back of the Megaron were the private apartments, around the area of the temple. Not much more than an angle of one of these remains, in the far right-hand corner, as one passes inward from the Megaron, and because of its stepped floor this is assumed to be a bath. Traces of red stucco have given it the name 'the Red Bath', tempting speculation as to whether it was here that Agamemnon met his gory end. But that is not an authentic part of the tradition, and in classical times it was generally assumed that the murder of the king took place not here, in the ancient citadel, but at the lower palace at Argos.

What Mycenae infallibly impresses one with is its intimation of power. The king at the top of the citadel, where the Throne Room formed something reminiscent of the centre of a hive, would feel his dominion encircling him in the concentric tiers of the palace and fortress clasping the slopes below him. The position itself would induce greatness; it would demand it and produce it in one movement. The impression is akin to that which surrounds both political position and wealth, particularly when the two are (as is not unusual) combined. Charisma gets attached, unavoidably, to such a situation, to the fact of being surrounded by the physical proof of power, such as is this solidity and substance of Mycenae.

The power and dignity of the house of Atreus are, in the myth, the elements which give poignance to its misfortune. The quarrel arose between Atreus and his brother Thyestes through dispute as to the possession of the kingdom, complicated by the possession of a lamb. This was no ordinary lamb, but no doubt symbolic from the start, since both the kings, Thyestes and Atreus, seem to have been lords over sheep-owning people. Homer refers to Atreus as 'Shepherd of his people', and to Thyestes as 'rich in flocks'. Atreus had committed himself to the sacrifice of the finest animal in his possession, a sacrifice which, it seems, was not to any god of flocks, but rather to Artemis. Much as Poseidon did to Minos on another occasion, she tempted him by putting among his sheep a lamb with a golden fleece, which he could hardly resist keeping. In the end he sacrificed the beast, but kept the fleece. Glancing forwards we perhaps see the continuity of the theme in the circumstances which eventually forced his son, Agamemnon, to sacrifice his daughter to the same goddess, perhaps in expiation of Atreus' failure to fulfill the earlier obligation in full.

In any case Thyestes was in the meantime conspiring with Atreus' wife, with whom he was in love. But the wife, lamb and kingdom seem to be inextricably interrelated, since the myth implies that possession of any one of them brings possession of the other two. Whoever owns the lamb rules the kingdom, and since the brothers seem to have owned the flock jointly they both claimed the right to it. Evidently it was the symbol of kingship at Mycenae, in which case it would seem that we are dealing with kings who were also priests of a pastoral deity. The fraternal quarrel which arose was, with the aid of Zeus, settled in favour of Atreus, but only after he had discovered his wife's infidelity with his brother, who had, correspondingly, possessed the kingdom and the lamb for a period in the meantime.

Atreus pretended to seek reconciliation, and to wish to share the kingdom with his brother. He therefore invited Thyestes to a feast at Mycenae, but at it served the flesh of the guest's sons, whom he had killed in sacrificial fashion for the purpose. To add to the charm of the occasion he then revealed what Thyestes had, apparently with relish, been consuming. Only his youngest son Aegisthus escaped, being too young to feature on the menu.

It was from this deeply engraved internal family quarrel that the destruction of the rest of the descendants of Pelops sprang. Thyestes, when he understood what had just happened, pronounced a curse on all the seed of Atreus. It hangs morosely over Agamemnon in particular, shading his deeds wherever he moved. Something about that meal in the palace at Mycenae chills us still; but it is not the only time in the myths when people find that they have eaten human flesh. Could it be that this definitively revolting theme refers back to yet more barbarous or primal times, bearing a memory older than that implied at Aulis:

something more basic even than child-sacrifice? Does its recurrence imply a reference to a time when the flesh of the victim was eaten at a ritual feast? We find the gods doing it, or rather, with the exception of distracted Demeter, refusing to, when Tantalus served to them his son Pelops. The fact that these are the immediate ancestors of the kings who underwent the fatal feast at Mycenae reminds us that Heracles, a descendant of the other Mycenaean house, the line of Perseus, also killed and burnt (but apparently did not eat) his sons. Perhaps the ultimate precedent for child-eating is given by the archaic god Cronus, eventually to become the father of Zeus, who ate his children year by year for fear that they would dethrone him—another familiar, and more explicable, theme—until his wife Rhea tricked him by hiding the infant Zeus in a cave in Crete.

The myths do not condone these practices; rather, they show disapproval. This would accord with the supposition that the theme of the eating of the flesh of the child-victim recalled the custom of a previous religion, which had in fact involved a more literal form of communion with the deity, by way of the victim sacrificed as his representative. The sacrificial lamb which, perhaps, Thyestes would expect to eat at Mycenae on a sacred occasion, might have been the symbolized, allusive form taken by a nastier habit of his own predecessors there. Perhaps we should not find the concept of the eating of the god-victim's flesh too remote or irrelevant, since it is done in token form today; and in the minds of some the sacramental bread of the Christian communion does not just represent, but is, the flesh of Christ.

It would take us too far from Mycenae to discuss the whole complex of the sacrificial meal, the totemic feast, the god eaten in animal or effigy form. But we can at least note that what the myth concerns itself with here is both the sacrifice of a lamb by a king of sheep-herding people and the killing and eating of a king's sons. It is not too much to see the latter as being a form of apostasy, and the curse on the descendants of Pelops as arising from their reversion to, or refusal to relinquish, the habits of a more primitive age.

Be that as it may, Agamemnon and Menelaus come into being

with a curse hanging about them. But the ritualistic quarrels of their father and uncle peter out only slowly in the background of their entry into the myth. Atreus was finally killed at the instruction of Thyestes, who once again reigned, only to be, in his turn, driven out by Atreus' son Agamemnon. It is, in fact (as we shall see again at a later stage), as if the kingship of Mycenae alternates between two lines.

For the time being that was the end of the ding-dong battle between the two brothers, since up to and including the time of the Trojan War Agamemnon ruled as overlord of the Peloponnese. Homer presents him as an imposing figure, particularly at times of crisis. We see him tower above the assembled Achaeans, our attention fixed by some physical detail, such as his staff, the emblem of his kingship. This had been made by Hephaestus himself, the blacksmith of the gods. Hephaestus gave it to Zeus; Zeus gave it to Hermes; Hermes presented it to Pelops; Pelops bequeathed it to Atreus; Thyestes acquired it when Atreus died; Thyestes left it to Agamemnon, who stood with this symbol of the continuity of his right to the kingship beside Nestor's ship on the shore below Troy.

No doubt historically Troy was destroyed by enemies more than once. The date of the fall of the Homeric city—that is, the one of Mycenaean times—is given variously as being somewhere during the twelfth or thirteenth centuries B.C. A date which seems to command some consensus is *circa* 1250. We know from Schliemann's excavations that this was neither the first (which was as old as 3000 B.C.) nor the last (about 300 B.C.) of the foundations of that persistent city, which remained in occupation into the fifth century A.D. Certainly Thucydides, who is not usually credulous, takes Agamemnon's war as being historical. He says for instance that it only lasted as long as it did because the Greeks were short of money. Had they had more they would have raised a bigger force, and finished it sooner. As it was their troops were limited to the number which could live locally off the land (some of the force being permanently unavailable for attack because busy cultivating or plundering), since they could not afford to support the expedition with supplies from home.

When they set sail from Aulis Clytemnestra had threatened Agamemnon with the consequences of his sacrifice of Iphigenia, should he ever return. The threat was to be duly carried out, a further episode of the long family quarrel. As we have seen, Clytemnestra had small cause to love her husband. She too, like Helen, his brother's eloped wife, was a daughter of the king of Sparta and Leda (though Helen at least was conceived in secret adultery by Zeus). Agamemnon gained her by fighting against and killing her husband, the king of Pisa, a district around Olympia in the western Peloponnese. He carried her off, and she bore him several children, the only son among these being Orestes.

The long saga of bloodshed was not over, but was now in the process of running with logic and inevitability towards its end. The curse was only to be released by the suffering of Orestes, the consequence of his climactic commission of matricide, the last, and perhaps most terrible, of the family murders. But to follow it to its end we must go down on to the plain, to Argos.

The dynasty at Mycenae and Argos
(main characters)

```
                        Tantalus
                           |
                         Pelops
                           |
            _____
           |                                |
         Atreus                         Thyestes
           |                                |
      _____                    _____
     |            |                  |             |
 Agamemnon    Menelaus             sons        Aegisthus
     |                             killed
  _____
 |        |         |
Iphigenia Electra Orestes
```

EIGHT

AGAMEMNON AT ARGOS

PERHAPS THE MOST surprising thing about Argos and Mycenae is that they are so close together. In fact we might be tempted to wonder whether they should be regarded as one place rather than two, were it not for the implicit distinctions made between them in the tradition. They were grouped in separate forces in the catalogue of those attending the Trojan War. Euripides mentions both Mycenaeans and Argives, and as if they were different. And yet an ambiguity between the two places seems to hamper our understanding of the situation. It is Mycenae which provides the testimony in the form not just of those impressive ruins but of the golden artefacts and the hieroglyphic tablets, the indications of the civilization which has in fact come to be called Mycenaean. Yet it is to Argos that the classical authors allocate Agamemnon: in Aeschylus' focal play it is to Argos that he comes home after the Trojan War, and in Euripides' *Electra* it is there that his grave is and there that his widow and her new husband are living after his death.

Pausanias, much later, appears to point to a solution. Both Mycenae and Tiryns, he says, were destroyed by Argos after the war with Persia. Later he gives a very credible reason for this, in that the city of Argos was in constant danger from its southern neighbour Sparta, and became obliged to expand its strength by incorporating surrounding settlements. Certainly rivalry with Sparta for control of the Peloponnese must be regarded as a main factor in the activities of Argos from the very beginnings of those two places.

We are left with two possible interpretations: Either the kings of Mycenae had moved their power and influence down on to the plain by the time of the Persian war, sufficiently to dominate their former citadel. Or alternatively Argos, becoming increasingly powerful independently, decided, after incorporating Mycenae, to adopt its ancestral tradition as well, with the result that the story of Agamemnon became officially located not in Mycenae but in Argos. In either case we have a picture of Argos in ascent at the time when Mycenae was in decline. It was not until the seventh century B.C. that it reached its peak, some hundreds of years after the high period of Mycenae. Possibly (though such matters are disputed) both the rise of the one and the fall of the other were connected with the Dorian invasion of the Peloponnese.

Coming down now from the rock-built citadel on to the rural plain one cannot help feeling the essential difference between the places. The ancient city of Argos is represented now by a quiet Greek country town, its peace slightly disturbed by the passage of main-road traffic, its streets busy and occasionally raucous, the background of life muttering around them, the clink of backgammon discs and the rattle of arguments in echoing tavernas. Orange trees soften its main square, accurately giving a warm and southern feeling to this predominantly fruitful place.

It is from the hill above the town (topped now by a medieval castle, but the site of a fortified citadel from Mycenaean times onwards) that one can best apprehend the breadth and flatness of the plain around Argos, stretching in cultivated fruit-covered squares in one direction to the gulf, in the other towards the hills around Mycenae. A rich land with good soil bordered by a hard and stony one.

Argos is the sort of place best understood by such views, rather than by inspection of the little there is of ancient remains. Certainly these exist, in the form of the remnants of the old town walls of Cyclopean style, and a later theatre and stadium, together with an outlying temple. But after the stones of Mycenae it would be easy to be disappointed. The remains at Argos are rather scattered, ranging in an arc round the western and northern edges of the present town, which actually overlays a large part of the ancient one. The latter once spread in a broad circle between its two hills, the one with the castle on it now and the other to the left as you look townwards from there, which actually bore an even earlier citadel of the ancient city. In fact looking out from the castle and facing the town, one should imagine the great city of Argos as sprawling across the country immediately below one's feet, round the bases of the two hills, and occupying an area about the same as that of the modern town.

In the museum is much evidence—mainly in the form of pottery—of the continuous occupation of the area from Neolithic, through Bronze Age, into Iron Age times, giving us ample reason to suppose that some basis of fact underlies the tradition of the myth. Most of the ruins investigated are of a later period, but near the road leading out of town towards the castle a series of Mycenaean tombs were excavated in the 1950s. The occurrence of the Cyclopean style of building, too, certainly helps to justify the location here of the sequels to the Mycenaean stories; and why should not the High King of Mycenae have ventured down on to the plain to build a residence which would be more spacious and comfortable than that steeply terraced one, in times when his power had grown (as the Homeric Agamemnon's evidently had) to be beyond challenge?

One feels in fact that it is unlikely that whoever controlled Mycenae would not also have reaped the wealth of the plain. One feels also that if the Mycenaean palace at Argos had survived like its counterpart in the hills it would have given a rather different impression; a summer residence, perhaps, a stately and luxurious showpiece of the style of those golden treasures in the graves of Mycenae. Possibly that is why it is not there now, in the way that Tiryns and Mycenae are; they were built for more serious purposes, and, being intended to be durable, have endured. Mycenae above all means business; it is indomitable, the real and serious face of power; and perhaps that is why Agamemnon comes over to us so clearly as a king, so that even at this distance one may fear him. His purely Argive face might not have created that awe. But the durability of the story is of course not due to the stones themselves, so much as to the words of Aeschylus; and perhaps also to the fact that whether or not the events it claims to convey occurred, the situation behind them was clearly factual. Somebody, at an early period, controlled the Argive plain, and with it a large and important part of the Peloponnese. Whether or not the curse of Atreus' seed was real, some things are real about it: things such as power, wealth, political position.

The story as it comes to us is in the form of a continuation, by the classical authors, of the theme in Homer. In the *Odyssey* we are told of the heroes' return from Troy, and the plot of Clytemnestra's treachery is outlined. It occurs during the episode of Telemachus' visit to Nestor in search of his father Odysseus: in response to his questions Nestor tells him a simple version of the story. It is incidental to the theme of the *Odyssey*, and perhaps for that reason it is not developed. Aegisthus had seduced Clytemnestra while her husband Agamemnon was fighting below Troy. He succeeded in getting her to live with him, and between them they killed Agamemnon on his return. Seven years later the son Orestes returned and killed the usurper and, apparently, his mother as well.

That is the bones of the story, and because it occurs in Homer we know at least that it belongs to an ancient and authentic tradition. But the details omitted there and present in the later sources seem, in most cases, every bit as ancient, as much authentic mythic matter, and even of rather more psychological power and mystery than this simple tale of deceit and revenge.

Aeschylus told the story in full, producing his Oresteian trilogy during the 450s B.C. It was mainly Euripides who developed the later sections of this, the return of Orestes and his expiation of his matricide, in his plays *Electra* (415) and *Orestes*, written about ten years later. The later playwright in particular tends to see the inhuman events in largely human terms, portraying as a moral issue what we cannot help feeling was rather more a mystical one; it is in key both with his own concerns and methods and with the expectations of his audience, the preoccupations of the period, that this should be so. But for this reason, perhaps, the archaic feeling of the myth seems to show through the dramatic conventions in the Aeschylean plays more than it does in those of

Euripides. And if this is so then it perhaps in its turn marks a trend towards the humanization of the mysteries portrayed by the story, a move away from a primarily religious world in which the gods were powerful forces lurking behind our practical lives, into a more secular one in which they were outdated residues of a primitive and superstitious way of thought.

The story is best seen in its context—that is, as part of the family history in which it was set, which we have been concerned with in the last two chapters. In this saga the Trojan War was an interlude, though an important one. It features Agamemnon at the height of his power, commander-in-chief of the combined Greek forces, on the rare occasion of a united expedition against a foreign nation. We join them in the *Iliad* towards the end of their long siege of the city, and inevitably feel how, in those nine years, they must have come to miss their homes, their wives, and the children who were growing up without them. The events which bring the story towards the ending of the war are charged with this longing: the deaths of heroes on both sides, and the constant interference by the gods and goddesses.

To a large extent the *Iliad* is literally inconclusive. The episodes it tells of lead towards an end which they do not reach. It culminates with the death of Hector at the hands of Achilles, and Priam's humiliating supplication for the return of the body. Homer does not then complete the story: the episode of the wooden horse is recounted later, in the *Odyssey*, by the blind bard Demodocus, after Odysseus, on his homeward journey, has reached the court of Alcinous. It is a fine instance of Homer's artistic mastery, that he should have Odysseus hear about himself and the Achaeans at Troy, and that a bard should as it were act Homer, and fill out events not fully covered in the *Iliad*. It indicates too that others were at work in the same field, since the story of the wooden horse, for instance, is told as if already well known, being only roughly outlined and not explained, indicating that it had been added to the Trojan story by another story-teller in the meantime. This and other references back, forming a general revision and explanation, a tying up of loose ends of the *Iliad* in the *Odyssey*, seem to me to suggest both that they were basically the work of one man, and that the second chronologically was the second to be composed—both matters that have been doubted.

The other details of the outcome of the war likewise find a place, if somewhat artificially, in the *Odyssey*: it is the ghost of Agamemnon, at the end of the book, who tells of the death of Achilles—though we already know he is dead since Odysseus has met his ghost on his visit to Hades. And the death of Paris and the sacking and plunder of Troy are only fully recounted by later authors. The *Iliad* actually ends with the funeral rites of Hector. And the *Odyssey* for its part opens with the long-awaited dispersal having taken place. The background of suspense left over from the previous story gives the new narrative its impetus. We are only too well aware of how the Greeks were longing to get home.

It is with this as a backing that Aeschylus takes up the story. Homer had recounted bit by bit in the *Odyssey* the manner of the various warriors' return: how Nestor had come straight through to Pylos, whereas Menelaus had run into difficulty and been detained, driven off course, with the result that Agamemnon went home alone. Had Menelaus been at hand, it is implied, things would have been different. We take up the story in Aeschylus from the Argos end at the time of the fall of Troy, announced to the waiting citizens by a series of beacons relaying the message across the sea from mountain to mountain and island to island. When the light breaks out on a distant summit it brings the tension of ambivalence to those who see it in Argos, knowing as they do that things are not well. A messenger arrives not long after to confirm the news and, with a sort of telescoping of time —there is an assumed lapse of several days—Agamemnon himself follows. He comes bringing with him the Trojan princess Cassandra, a mournful figure who, on this occasion, adds yet further tension by her presence.

The scene with which Aeschylus portrays the first meeting, after ten years, of Agamemnon and his wife, is full of dramatic irony and innuendo. We and the Argive citizens know what has been going on. Their speech of welcome, in fact, contains a number of veiled hints. He, however, is occupied with the emotions of his victorious return, and with the anticipation of taking up his peacetime role as king of Argos. Clytemnestra greets him with much show and protestation of faithfulness, which everyone else present knows to be duplicity. Perhaps the playwright implies that she overdoes it, because Agamemnon hesitates to step down on to the cloth which she has spread as a welcoming carpet for him. She overcomes his diffidence and leads him in, all too plainly like a sacrificial victim. And then indeed follows that strongly hieratic scene, described with second sight by Cassandra from outside the palace, in which she drapes him in a net, and in the lustral bath where she has coaxed him to purify him, ritualistically, from the soil of battle, she fells him, helpless and unarmed, apparently with an axe.

Homer does not record the detail about the bath. In his version of the story, as told in the *Odyssey*, Agamemnon is invited to a feast by Aegisthus, and he and his men are killed while eating. That seems ritualistic enough, but the feature of the lustral bath unavoidably holds more power. It might have been one of those square pits of about eight-foot width, with steps going down to the bottom, some six feet deep and filled with water, such as one may see in good condition at several early sites in Crete. The dramatic tradition presents the murder scene, however, with a silver bath, of the tub kind, in which Clytemnestra has been cleansing her husband before enshrouding him. Either way it is a horrifying picture.

It is perhaps this detail, in any case, which fixes the event as being sacrificial. One could of course regard the bath murder as simply a circumstantial detail in the narrative; and it works on that level too, whether or not its primary function is symbolic. What makes it unlikely that it is mainly such a narrative device, included in the story simply because horrific, is the parallel it bears to episodes in other myths and rituals. The ritual cleansing of the victim is one aspect of this, in its turn comparable to the purifying immersion of believers in the rivers Ganges and Jordan. Washing and a change of clothes on ceremonial occasions have been a practice of several religions, including those of the Jews, Moslems and the classical Greeks. Water is also itself conveniently symbolic, not only for its cleansing but for its isolating, insulating effect. It marks a clear boundary between worlds; hence the Prayer Book's comparison of the rite of baptism with the crossings of the Jordan and the Red Sea, and with Noah's passage. Water is often viewed too as having healing properties, as in the case of Bethesda pool and of many springs, wells and fountains; and also has the function of bringing about some significant change of nature, as that caused by the crossing of rivers such as the Styx.

Moreover, it is through water that a symbolic form of rebirth takes place in the case of those heroes who should have died as infants, but instead return to take up a new existence in a new land. Perseus, for instance, was set adrift by his father, and washed ashore on the island of Seriphos, to be adopted by its king. The story of Moses, found in the river, is closely paralleled by the Welsh one of Taliesin, set afloat in the river Dyfi and discovered by a prince, caught in a weir. Similarly in the Arthurian group the child Mordred was put in a boat and sent to sea, but found and reared by a good man on a distant coast. In this way they escape their almost inevitable death, and pass into the next phase of their lives. We are reminded of the answer which Jesus gave to Nicodemus, who had asked how a man can be born again: can he enter the second time into his mother's womb, and be born? The answer is that he can be born 'of water, and of the Spirit'.

There is, however, even more to this event, in its relational position in myth, than this sort of common symbolism. The killing of the king in, or half in, the water of his bath, relates to a theme which can be conveniently categorized as the 'between-two-worlds' theme, where there is a state of complete ambiguity, things being neither this nor that. For instance, after it was prophesied of Lleu Llaw Gyffes, the hero of the Welsh tale already referred to in connection with the theme of the apparently impossible death, that he might be killed neither on horseback nor on foot, neither within a house nor out of doors, and apparently (from the outcome of the story) neither on water nor on dry land, he too was persuaded by his wife to take a bath, and killed (as we have seen) by her lover while half in it and half out, under a canopy but otherwise out of doors, and, for good measure, with one foot on the back of a she-goat. In some versions of the story of the death of Minos, he too was slaughtered in his bath.

We thus find Agamemnon to have placed himself in a position between two worlds: not on water nor on land. In changing his clothes from those of battle to those of home he would be between two worlds anyway. But Clytemnestra dresses him in a net, so that he is neither clothed nor naked. It is at such joining points of opposites that the seams of reality can be penetrated, at the point at which the neat categories into which we have ordered things no longer apply, where it is neither one thing nor the other. Chaos sneaks in, getting its blade between the joints of the structure, breaking through the otherwise impenetrable mesh of time and events. Perhaps even it is only there that contact can be made with the continuum of reality, as opposed to the framework through which we normally view it. So that at the joining points of the year (for instance on the eve of the first of November which was the start of the Celtic year), the dead walk and the witches rule and one can do things which are normally forbidden. That is because it is neither this year nor next year; and things like that do not take place this year or next year. Similarly the other joining points of seasons, the eve of May Day and in the modern calendar New Year's Eve, are times of pranks and unusual events. So midnight in general is the witching hour; and it is the moment of transition—for instance at initiation into adulthood when the initiate passes between statuses, or at marriage—which is felt to be exceptional and specially mystic. At the junction of territories, in the extensionless space of this type of no-man's-land. It is of course no coincidence that otherwise illicit kisses are traditionally permitted under the mistletoe, since the mistletoe is of sacred significance precisely because it too falls between realities, being neither a plant, with roots in the earth, nor not a plant; and hence, as we have seen, it came to be omitted when all things swore not to harm Balder, in the Norse myth; and consequently it was what finally killed him. The strong interest which Celtic myth shows in this idea of neither-this-nor-that is a clue that it may have been for some similar reason—its not conforming to categories and definitions—that the Druids included the mistletoe in their religious rituals.

If Agamemnon dies, like Lleu Llaw Gyffes, in the intersection between realities, he certainly does so in his capacity as sacred king. The sequence of killings in the house of Atreus might, perhaps, be regarded as indicating that it was a kingship subject to that sort of succession: that each successor must kill the previous holder, as Agamemnon had perhaps had Thyestes killed, who had killed the former's father Atreus, just as Orestes eventually killed Aegisthus, his father's murderer, who in his turn, the son of Thyestes, had killed his father's successor, Agamemnon.

This complicated, side-stepping inheritance, in which each of the kings seems to have been killed by the next one, seems to demand an explanation. Frazer has a chapter in *The Golden Bough* called 'The Killing of the Divine King'; and although it would be generally agreed that over-all he fails to make his case, which is anyway rather obscure, the evidence which he collected on the way (much of it peripheral to the issue) is of use for many other purposes. Frazer was concerned with providing an explanation for the complicated ritual surrounding the succession to the priest-hood of Nemi, in Italy, in which each holder of the office was killed by the next one, himself to be killed in the same way in due course. The theme of the killing of the king was therefore central to his argument, and he found much evidence of the widespread existence of the practice, a sort of universal current of ritual which closely parallels the instances of it in myth.

Frazer's thesis was that the king embodied the welfare of the nation. For that reason he must not be allowed to grow old, since in doing so he would bring decay and infertility to the land he governed. His strength and the land's were magically related. By killing him while still in his prime the people could ensure that the spirit of kingship, the sacred element of the king, would be transferred to a strong and healthy successor without the danger of decline. It is as it were a constant series of renewals, a periodic revitalization of the vehicle of the country's spiritual good. Having shown the extent to which primitive communities believed that the king embodied, in human form, the god, and the god in turn manifested his health and vigour in the conditions of nature, he first gives examples ranging from Cambodia to the Congo, and through various parts of Africa, of kings who were killed at the first sign of weakness or decay, then goes on to produce an equally impressive list of kings who were killed at the end of a fixed term. Whether or not we accept Frazer's interpretation of the purpose of these customs—that they were a way of catching the soul, the divinity, of the king, and transferring it to a more vigorous receptacle before it could suffer decline—there can be no doubt of the importance of the idea, the concept of the killing of the king. One might, for instance, regard it, perhaps more simply, as a precaution against anarchy on the one hand and despotism on the other: the king being maintained permanently capable of governing, but not allowed to govern indefinitely.

We cannot but recall that it was with the title 'King of the Jews' that Christ went to his execution. The death of kings has remained a popular theme in art, and the psychologists have, of course, come up with various explanations. Freud, for instance, regards it, in his generally exciting book *Totem and Taboo*, as being (along with the whole business of the ritual killing and eating of the god, whether in his animal form or some other) a re-enactment of the original primal killing of the father of the horde by his sons. Such a fantasy might strike us now, perhaps, as just another version of the myth.

Aegisthus succeeds to the throne of Argos by marrying Clytemnestra, as well as by killing Agamemnon—in the same way, in fact, as Oedipus succeeds to the throne of Thebes. He, as the son of Agamemnon's predecessor, might have had a claim to the succession in any case. She for her part was also, as we have seen, the daughter of a king, Tyndareus of Sparta, whose wife Leda was seduced by Zeus in the form of a swan. Although in some versions of the story she is apparently the twin of Helen, who was undoubtedly the progeny of that divine/avian liaison, Clytemnestra was evidently not regarded as having immortal parentage; apparently Tyndareus slept with his wife the same night, so that the twins had different fathers; and Clytemnestra is repeatedly referred to by the dramatists as 'daughter of

Tyndareus', whereas Helen is known as 'daughter of Zeus'. Those other twins, Castor and Polydeuces, were also offspring of the same union; and they too are sometimes regarded as having one a mortal and the other an immortal father.

The last part of the story too is told most fully by Aeschylus, though that as well is outlined briefly by Homer. In its essence it is the simple story of revenge, and is presented as such in the *Odyssey*. No mention is made there of what happened to Orestes after he had killed his father's murderer; nor is it made explicit that he killed his mother as well, though this is implied. Yet these are the central themes in the version which Aeschylus develops: the horror of matricide, and the subsequent need for expiation. The justice of revenge becomes secondary. By committing another crime Orestes too incurs nemesis.

The second play of the Aeschylean trilogy, the *Libation Bearers*, opens with Orestes having returned to Argos and found the grave of Agamemnon, to which, shortly afterwards, his sister Electra comes. When they eventually recognize each other they set about plotting the murders of their mother and the usurper. It is a crime to which Orestes has been directed by Apollo's oracle. He is confronted on the one hand by the fear of disobeying the oracle; and on the other by an underlying feeling that this is insufficient justification for the act. The events which follow are simply, even sparely, told, Orestes enacting the apparently inevitable with almost ritual directness. Characteristically Euripides, telling exactly the same story, shifts the emphasis a little further. Whereas to Aeschylus fate or destiny was incontrovertible, however unfortunate, to Euripides the blind following of such mindless principles as revenge, let alone the adherence to the commands of the oracle, was probably inhuman, certainly primitive. Only fifty years separate the productions, but they were fifty years of development and change in Greek thought. In the earlier play the gods could still impose their will on helpless men; in the later one it was only the participants who were to blame, if they insisted on going through with these automatic and unpleasant processes.

Both plays end with Orestes seeming unequivocally guilty. In the one by Aeschylus we are made aware of the horror which he suffers at the sight of the Furies approaching, the Eumenides, those old and ugly dog-faced women who haunt the shedders of kindred blood. In the *Electra* of Euripides the end of the series of crimes is foretold: Orestes must stand trial in Athens, on the hill of Ares where such trials are held. The matter is thus brought firmly to ground, to be decided not in some mythical country under the auspices of gods, but by the established social forces, and at home.

The idea of the pursuing Furies, like the idea of a relentless destiny, is a compelling one. It finds its expression in the third play of Aeschylus' trilogy, the *Eumenides*, in which Orestes is on his way, with his escort of Furies, to take sanctuary in Athena's temple in Athens. In this strange play the gods and the super-natural take an active part, as if abstractions are being reified in the way they are in medieval miracle plays, personalized just as though each was another human character. The Furies themselves form the Chorus, which was more normally a group of towns-people; Apollo too appears as a character in the action, rather than as an outside force. The case is tried before Athena herself by the citizens of Athens, who in the end are equally divided on the verdict; the goddess casts her vote in Orestes' favour, and the Furies become the Friendly Goddesses, who will henceforth act in league with Athena as guardians of Athens. They leave the stage, and in doing so pass out of the mainstream of literature, only to make a startling reappearance in 1939, in T. S. Eliot's verse play *The Family Reunion*.

By once again humanizing, de-mysticizing, this final episode of the story of the house of Atreus, Euripides makes us aware that the forces at work in human behaviour are human forces. In his play *Orestes* the insanity which has overcome Orestes is from within, from his own guilt. Crimes should be dealt with by the courts, and by taking the law into his own hands Orestes has merely made himself as much a criminal as his mother was. He has only himself to blame for the results. When Apollo intervenes at the end it is a curt, and rather awkward, gesture to tradition; but it has the effect of emphasizing the interminable mess which

the participants, left to themselves, have been getting themselves
into. In this way the playwright firmly winds up the long story,
with the over-all message that what was self-induced must be
self-cured. It is a direct reply to the supposition of destiny and
nemesis, and as such a part of the implied debate in art, particularly in drama, in later ages. Basically there are two sorts of
hero, the ones who, like Oedipus, are caught in a machine,
unwitting playthings of the designers of events; and those others
who bring about their difficulties through their own greed or
weakness. We feel the tension of the two viewpoints particularly
in the works of Shakespeare, as when, for instance, Gloucester's
complaint,

> As flies to wanton boys are we to the gods:
> They kill us for their sport.

might well be taken for a description of Lear's own misfortunes,
believing as he does that he is the helpless victim of circumstances;
whereas we, the audience, know that everything that happened
to him originated from his own mistake, from his folly and
weakness.

The concept which lies behind the debate is of course that a
thing can always be explained in more than one way, so that the
episodes at Argos could be due to the meddling of the gods in the
affairs of men or to the wilfulness and lack of foresight of
Orestes; it is simply a question of viewpoint. And this is generally
true—that events can be seen in the light of one type of explanation or of another. Two sorts of causes are at work, so that when
a train, for instance, leaves the station, it does so either as a result
of certain actions on the part of the driver or as an end effect of
policies and systems practised by the railway corporation. In
the second view, the apparent causes of the first view are not
causes, but rather a part of the process. It is not that Aeschylus is
right and Euripides wrong, about Orestes, but that both have valid
ways of describing the causal sequence. The difference is of
particular interest to us here, because it was the 'why' view of
causality (as opposed to the 'how' one), a view which seems to

beg the question by presupposing an intention, which characterized the habit of thought which gave rise to the human representation of the gods. Another type of causal view—the 'how' one,
which sees things only in terms of internal relations—might
never have led to this animistic and anthropomorphic result.

Certainly the matter being dealt with, in the myths collected
around the dynasty at Mycenae and Argos, is not simple. There
are residues of plain folk motifs, and there seem to be also
undercurrents of ritual and succession customs. There are perhaps
those more basically mythic elements, the psychological problems entangled in social and family life; and perhaps even larger
issues, which have their meanings on a different level and are not
translatable into other language. I have the feeling, personally,
that in instances of real myth things are being sorted out which
cannot be adequately dealt with in any other way.

Perhaps at the same time we are receiving records of a real
dynasty, distilled and mysticized by time. Certainly Homer spoke
realistically, and filled out his heroic episodes with naturalistic
detail. Much that he says—of the sort of life, the palaces and
surroundings—could refer to the memory of a real Mycenae and a
real Argos, which had occurred and declined some five hundred
years before the time, in about 750 B.C., at which he composed.
By then, by Homer's time, it had all gone. There was nothing
golden or palatial about the Greece in which he lived—although
the beginnings of renaissance must have been approaching, or
there would not have been an audience civilized enough to give
occasion for his great artistry. The practice of writing itself—
which the Linear B tablets tell us clearly had been common in a
fairly crude form in Mycenaean times—had been forgotten; it
was only then starting to spread back westwards into Greece, this
time in its full alphabetical form.

One of the great problems about the relation of Homer to
Agamemnon is how in such circumstances an apparently detailed
memory of a different, more golden, period had survived. One
feels, from internal evidence alone, that however dark had been
the intervening period, Homer composed during a time of re-
awakening values, of new national aspirations, of growing

sophistication in outlook and habit of mind. From such a position
he seems to have been looking back across the gulf which we
know to have existed, to something which the people of his time
could regard as an ideal past, in their terms. But how could the
view of it have been so clear?

Perhaps though this is not so puzzling. Perhaps it naturally
takes a period of roughly five hundred years for an important
national epoch to become fixed in literary form. Gold-tinted and
embellished, of course; but finding expression then as a sort of
heightened reflection of current ideals. Compare for instance
Geoffrey of Monmouth, writing in the early twelfth century
about the events leading to the loss of British independence in the
late sixth. Perhaps that is the sort of time scale needed for the
sequence: decline, dark ages, beginnings of renaissance.

What we do know is that the Mycenaean civilization collapsed
all over Greece during the period of the late thirteenth century
B.C. What brought this about is not clear, but we may presume
that it was a product both of internal forces—such as the natural
decay of an old, and perhaps over-expanded, system—and of
external forces in the form of the movement into the area of a new
people. It has been often assumed that this was the Dorian
invasion, which the Greeks of later ages supposed to have taken
place at about the same time. But not enough is known about this
to make it a historical, or archaeological, fact.

Argos, as we have seen, arose during the period of Mycenaean
decline, and entered the classical age as an important city. It
figures prominently, inevitably, in the Peloponnesian War, and
as the traditional enemy of its neighbour Sparta it led the coalition
of states against the Spartans. After that it declined in importance,
but survived as a city into Roman times, being inspected by the
indefatigable Pausanias on his travels; and it has in fact never
really gone out of existence. Today, by contrast with its blood-
spattered and anguished tradition, it goes about its business in a
mild-tempered, comfortable way, surrounded by the fruit-
bearing greenness of its plain.

NINE

HERACLES IN THE PELOPONNESE

AT HIS TRIAL, near to where the metro now enters Monastiraki station, his prosecutors accused Socrates of having said that the sun is not a god, but a piece of hot stone larger than the Peloponnese, looking so small because it is very far away. Strangely he denied it, attributing the view to someone else. I think out of modesty, but it might have been because the statement lacks the obvious, indestructible truth (the hallmark of real wisdom) which most of his pronouncements possess. Anybody familiar with the Peloponnese knows, firstly, that it is absolutely enormous, certainly too big to be stuck up in the sky; and, secondly, that the sun is a god.

Heracles is often regarded as a sun hero, in terms of the now outdated classification, which means roughly that his attributes are those, such as monster-slaying and journeying, which are associated with other sun heroes. His parentage also makes him solar, since his father was the sky god Zeus, who seduced his mother by taking on the form of her husband—a neat trick practised by several other supernatural beings, with the advantage of providing the lady with a water-tight excuse. Heracles' mother was the daughter of the High King of Mycenae, and thus granddaughter to the hero Perseus. He was thus born both into the house of Perseus and into demigodship, and came into being with the implacable hostility of Hera, Zeus's wife, against him.

In keeping with his great status in the mythology, Heracles is chiefly associated with the Peloponnese, an area, there is every reason to believe, which fostered more than any other the beginnings of Greek life, and which remained of major importance throughout antiquity. It takes a figure of his prominence

and superhuman qualities to match that formidable lump of
country; and in a very clear way the Peloponnese is his, his deeds
still coming to mind among those mountains or in the shadows
of those hanging valleys.

The Peloponnese was his territory not just by this compati-
bility of nature, but by inheritance. As a descendant of Perseus
he should have become High King of Mycenae—and thus have
ruled much of inhabited Greece—and would have done so had
not Zeus been unwary and boasted of his amorous indiscretion.
He swore that the child born that day into the house of Perseus
should become High King. Hera grew furious with jealousy, and
brought it about that another descendant of Perseus was born
first, the birth of Heracles being delayed. Thus his cousin Eurystheus became king of Mycenae, and for his part he ruled no
territory at all.

Although his life and deeds are centred on the Peloponnese and
his family territory there, his birth and upbringing are said by the
myth to have taken place at Thebes. Perhaps a movement of
people with their special cult is indicated. At any rate we hear of
his early adventures not in connection with Argolis, but in
Boeotia, where he killed serpents while in his cradle and a lion
in his youth, during the hunting of which he slept with the fifty
daughters of King Thespius. Everything about Heracles is on
this scale.

Whatever the reason for the movement of the story from
Thebes to Argos and Mycenae, it then becomes distinctly
localized. Several of his later adventures, indeed, are very widely
spread; but the first six labours, perhaps the ones most characteristic of the Heracles myth, are grouped within a relatively small
radius of Mycenae.

The story tells of his move to Argolis to start his adult adventures as being divided from his youth by a spell of madness. This
was imposed on him by Hera for reasons variously given, and
during it he killed, and threw into a fire, his children by Megara,
daughter of the king of Thebes. This crime entailed his exile, and
he sought the verdict of the oracle at Delphi as to how it must be
expiated.

It was thus that he came to undertake his labours. The oracle committed him to be subject for twelve years to the commands of his cousin Eurystheus, who was residing at Tiryns. Heracles came to Tiryns to receive Eurystheus' orders.

Perhaps Eurystheus is described as being at Tiryns rather than Mycenae because Tiryns, as we have seen, was regarded as being the older of the two fortresses, built by Perseus and his Cyclops builders before they went on to build Mycenae. Certainly it is appropriate that this impressive and evocative site should have a central role in this important myth.

Tiryns has a magnificence not found in many other sites, due both to the massiveness of its stones and to its compactness. It is built as a solid block, and still towers imperatively over the road to Navplion. Everything about it is very substantial, and very real. One of its entrance-ways, for instance, through an outer wall jutting from the west side, is in the form of a simple but vast piece of corbelling; there is a remarkable passageway in the same form running along the other side. It is due to such basic but monumental architectural forms, as effective now as they ever were, that we can immediately identify these ruins with the habitations of those distant, looming figures of the myth.

The relationship between Tiryns and Mycenae is firmly fixed in the myths, and historically too they must always have been connected. Perseus occupied them both, as did Eurystheus. The two provided troops at Troy and, interestingly, in this case Tiryns is grouped with Argos. Probably Tiryns was a dependency of Mycenae in the earlier period, coming under the domination of Argos when that city increased in power. It is reasonable to see it as being the port to the inland settlement, rather as, in Crete, Agia Triada can be guessed to be the port to Phaestos. It should be noted that the Argive plain has silted seawards; Tiryns, now three kilometres inland, would originally have been on the coast.

Perhaps the dependency of Tiryns on Mycenae is reflected in the servitude of Heracles (if this is to be regarded as being his rightful home) to Eurystheus. The historical site, which covered an area much larger than that represented by the citadel walls today, eventually suffered the same fate as Mycenae, being destroyed by the then powerful new city of Argos shortly after the Persian War. By then, however, it had been in occupation for more than a thousand years.

There is in fact archaeological justification for the tradition that

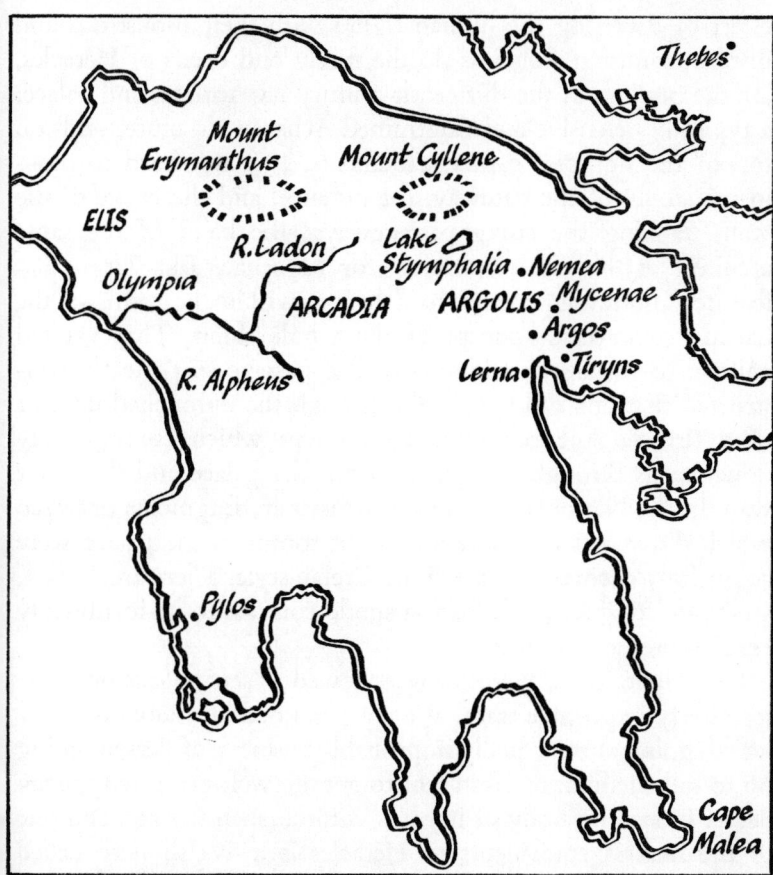

Tiryns was older than Mycenae, since whereas at Mycenae only slight traces have (so far) been found of occupation in the Stone Age, the settlement at Tiryns at that time was quite extensive. That is, before about 2000 B.C. The main rise in occupancy was contemporary with that at Mycenae, beginning with the Bronze Age and coming to a peak in about 1250 B.C. The citadel was

F

destroyed, like many other palaces of the Mycenaean age, in about 1200, when it was burnt and plundered. It was only sporadically resettled, and the later attack by Argos seems more a plundering expedition than a conquest.

The walls which we see now, which achieve the same sort of effect of dwarfing the human figure with their monstrous and uncompromising stones as do the might and deeds of Heracles, are the outlines of the thirteenth-century B.C. fortress and palace, a typically defensive and determined Achaean structure, built on top of the humbler earlier settlements. It is not hard to see— in the stones of the gateway, for instance, and the curve of the walls flanking the rising passageways—the hand of the same architect as the one responsible for Mycenae. But Tiryns has features amounting almost to delicacy, within the terms of the harshly militaristic concept of the whole thing. That vaulted gallery, for instance: a long corbelled passage so perfectly constructed that one can now walk through the untouched interior of a Bronze Age building. Those steps which curve steeply downwards through the gap between the palace and the outer wall. In the National Museum in Athens are fragments of fresco which show that the most important rooms of the palace were colourfully decorated in a delicate Cretan style. There are, in fact, aspects of Tiryns which form a subtle contrast to its formidably heroic outer appearance.

From here, then, Heracles was viewed as setting out on those seemingly impossible tasks. We are reminded inevitably of other heroes going about equally improbable business, of Perseus going off to kill Medusa, or Jason sent to get the well-protected golden fleece. Indeed no body of myth is without such themes, and one of the nearest equivalents to Heracles is a Welsh hero called Culhwch, who was sent monster-slaying by the father of the girl he loved. Culhwch was by no means alone in this predicament, since he had colleagues in Ireland such as Finn, who unsuccessfully wooed Grainne and was sent by her to collect two of every wild animal in Ireland and bringing them to Tara; and in the case of the wooing of Etain, daughter of the king of Ulster, in another Irish tale, the hero has to clear wooded plains and divert rivers.

In folklore and mythic tradition these apparently impossible tasks are normally associated with the winning of a bride, and the lack of this factor in Heracles' case sets him somewhat outside the convention. Perhaps there was once a wooing story involved in the relationship between him and his cousin, and it has somehow got lost or overshadowed by his heroic career. But the theme is not a very fixed one, and difficult tasks seem a natural part of a hero's make-up.

In Heracles' case they were twelve in number—Culhwch had nearly forty—which has been taken by some to be a further instance of his sun-hero status: twelve tasks corresponding to the twelve months of the year. Moreover, the sequence took him twelve years. But twelve is a common number in mythic circumstances, perhaps because of its property, like the points of the compass, of defining a centre or providing a convenient segmentation, in space or, as in the twelve hours of the day and the night, in time. For that reason, perhaps, Conchobar king of Ulster slept with the twelve warriors of Ulster grouped round him, and Charlemagne was likewise surrounded by the twelve peers of France, Arthur by his twelve knights, and Odysseus by his twelve companions. The number ensures a clearly defined centre, and it has that effect in the grouping of the twelve tribes of Israel round the holy tabernacle, as described in the second chapter of Numbers. Odin likewise, in Norse myth, was accompanied by twelve councillors, and indeed the same cycle says that not only were there twelve major gods but that Odin, the father of the gods, was called by twelve names.

No doubt this particular theme is so common that to cite all its instances would become tedious, but it must of course be mentioned that there is a symbolic relationship between Christ's twelve disciples and the twelve tribes of Israel. In Revelations we find the matter hammered home: the twelve gates of the holy city, with their twelve angels, bear the names of the twelve tribes; whereas the twelve walls of the holy city, with their twelve foundations, bear the names of the apostles. What, we cannot help wondering, is all this about? The signs of the zodiac reflect a possible structuring of the heavens in this form, but that in itself illustrates the fact that it is a conceptual rather than a discovered form. We are left with the one natural fact, that the moon goes through its phases twelve times during the course of the solar year. Indeed this would seem to be one of the very few facts which are given to us by nature rather than conceptually constructed.

The first six of Heracles' tasks are those based near to his starting point, the Peloponnesian tasks with which we shall be concerned. The second six are, by contrast, wide-ranging; in the course of one of them the hero travels all over Greece, in one he visits Hades, and in one he goes beyond the western borders of the Mediterranean, out into the ocean itself.

In the hill country inland from the route between Corinth and Argos dwelt an apparently invincible lion. Eurystheus demanded that Heracles should kill it and bring back the skin. Known to us now as the Nemean lion, it had by then depopulated the hinterland around Nemea, uncomfortably close to the king's court at Mycenae. Its skin was so tough that no blade could pierce it, so that when Heracles eventually found it, in a cave on the mountain, he had to strangle it with his two heroic hands. He then cut off the skin by using the lion's own sharp claws, since nothing else would work. It is this which he is always regarded as wearing, as his only garment, and the lion-skin cloak together with his club make him recognizable in representation on reliefs and jar paintings.

Nemea was in classical times the site of a temple of Zeus, and was well known for the ancient institution of the Nemean Games. These were of a status to equal those at Olympia and Delphi, and so have given us one set of the celebratory poems of Pindar, the Nemean Odes. Today we see there mostly the ruins of the fourth-century B.C. temple, lying in a soft valley which has the air of being set a little apart from the world, a pleasant, almost idyllic place surrounded by mild slopes. It lies some way east of the present town of Nemea, which sits on a hill overlooking its own valley and vineyards and a more abrasive terrain broken by strangely eroded escarpments. The area surrounding the sanctuary, which it seems formed part of the sacred precinct, is

still in the process, in the late 1970s, of being excavated. The
stadium where the Games were held has now been revealed,
some distance south-east of the temple, and the restoration of this,
together with the construction of a small museum to house the
finds unearthed in the process, now give the long neglected site
of Nemea the tourist lure which it has for so long lacked. Three
pillars stand of the temple itself, the rest lying in gigantic tumbled
blocks where they have fallen.

It is amazingly easy to get off the beaten track in the Peloponnese, and to travel at all in the region inland from Nemea is to do
so. You simply leave the main road, and you are at once immersed
in an atmosphere of utter remoteness. The land is so large, and
mountains close off a view out, a view of where one is. The
journeys between places are so long and complex, the roads so
vertically and horizontally bent. So few, and such small, settlements or habitations occur, that those that do appear to exist
simply to emphasize the breadth and emptiness of the landscape.
Should one try to get to anywhere specific, it will normally turn
out that travelling hopefully is not only better, but rather more
common, than arriving. Signposts are either non-existent or
point to places not mentioned on the map. Maps, in any case,
appear to be mainly constructed by guesswork. Often the track is
rather too obviously not beaten. Some of the roads they have not
yet finished building, others they have forgotten ever existed.
You find the road becoming more and more reminiscent of
hillside, and end up at a point where the distinction vanishes
completely, finding yourself facing a ravine.

Such is now the area of the hunt for the Nemean lion. One
cannot believe that it was ever otherwise, and it is through such
country that we must often imagine Heracles as striding. But the
second labour involved our hero in a descent to altogether gentler
country, to the bottom of the Argive plain itself, on the western
shore of the gulf which is now dominated by the port of
Navplion.

The hydra of Lerna was a many-headed water monster which at
the time disturbed the tranquillity of the low-lying, fertile area
where the plain meets the sea. The creature had nine heads and

breathed poisonous fumes, and one of its other characteristics was that if one of its heads was cut off two more immediately replaced it. It had been specially reared (according to Hesiod) by his enemy the goddess Hera to be Heracles' downfall—which, as we shall see, it eventually indirectly was. Heracles' normal method of attack was with his club, but battering the hydra's heads with this had no effect, and he had to resort to metal— though even then of course the heads proliferated. The solution was to cauterize the roots of the severed heads, which he did with brands from a fire his assistant started near by; the last head, said by some to be immortal, he buried. He then poisoned his arrows by dipping them in the monster's blood, for use on later occasions.

Lerna was the site of habitation from very early times—as early, in fact, as the fourth millennium B.C.—and the products of excavations there in the 1950s, including finds of imported pottery, can now be seen in the museum at Argos. Early remains are visible on the site itself. The area now is a flat fruit-growing plain at the head of the gulf, presumably in ancient times a much more mysterious swamp, lying where the edge of the plain below Argos meets the water, and under the foot of those hills which divide the valleys of Arcadia from the Argive plain. The snake-nature of the water monster may well be a reference to the worship here of the snake-goddess as part of the earth mother cult, such as appears to have existed before the coming of the Olympian religion in several important places in Greece. If that is so, then in this episode Heracles is performing a religious mission on behalf of the new Achaean gods. In later times it seems that the cult of Demeter—herself surely a descendant of the earth mother goddess—was practised there, involving mysteries of initiation in a sacred grove.

Such snake- or dragon-shaped monsters as the hydra are, in any case, common in myth, and may be susceptible to such an explanation (remnants of an old snake-worshipping religion which has to be destroyed) or to a psychological one, which would presumably see them as projected phallic products of the unconscious. They were encountered, as we have seen, by St George and other Christian pioneers, and, in the early English poem, by Sir Gawayne—and indeed by many Grail-hunting or adventure-seeking knights in medieval stories. They are not always water monsters, and Heracles' case is unusual for the detail of the multiplying heads; but generically serpent and dragon-like monsters which plague an area and must be killed may all be classed together.

The order in which the labours of Heracles occur is sometimes varied, but the next is usually said to have been the hunting of the huge boar of Erymanthus. This was a fearful beast which was causing devastation in the area of Psophis—a name now borne by an insignificant place lying on the bad road which passes from Kalavryta south of the Erymanthus range, once apparently the name of a territory. Heracles made his way there through the hills of the northern Peloponnese, and it was in the course of this journey that one of his subsidiary adventures occurred.

The centaur Pholus lived in the hill country called after him, Pholoe, through which the hero had to pass. Although the centaurs on the whole are depicted as rather wild and uncouth—they behaved extremely badly at the Lapith wedding feast—there were two of them, Cheiron and Pholus, who were unusually civilized. Cheiron we shall encounter again; Heracles had dealings with him too, and the horse-man emerges rather more creditably than the god-man. In this instance Pholus invited Heracles to stay for supper and, whether by the force of hospitality or under the persuasion of the guest, the centaur broached the cask of wine which Dionysus himself had given, many years before, to all the centaurs jointly. The other centaurs, who lived in other caves near by, smelt the strong bouquet which emerged when the jar was opened and came angrily around armed with stones and the branches of trees. Heracles fought them off with arrows, and so effective was his defence that they fled. They fled in fact all the way to Cape Malea, the wild and empty tip of the southern Peloponnese, where their leader Cheiron had already taken up residence. But in the process the gentle Pholus accidentally dropped one of Heracles' poisoned arrows on his foot, and died at once. After this sad little interlude the hunt for the Erymanthean boar continued.

Greece is a mountainous country. Everywhere vast bulks of mountain rise from the sea, rear in front of you and disappear into the clouds. The Peloponnese has its share of loftiness, and Erymanthus is a good example of that quality. It is a wild range of impressive bulkiness, fierce peaks jutting through the cumulus, rising above the gentle tree-covered land of Elis, in the north-west corner of the Peloponnese, inland of Patras. It forms the boundary of Elis, of Arcadia, and of Achaia in the north, its rivers flowing into those lands in their respective directions. We are told that the gods loved mountains, and certainly the size of these makes them unsuitable for men. It would simply take so long to get there.

The boar hunt, like so many of Heracles' adventures, is a familiar theme. King Arthur spends a large part of a Welsh tale hunting a monstrous boar through Ireland, Cornwall and South Wales. The Irish story of Diarmaid (mortally wounded while hunting a boar which had poisonous bristles) seems to be a close parallel to the Greek one of Adonis, fatally wounded by a wild boar sent by Ares. No doubt boar-hunting is simply a dangerous sport, but swine in general seem to have some special mystical significance in myth, judging by the frequency of their occurrence.

Heracles this time did not kill the monster, but caught it and brought it home. He captured it by driving it into a snowdrift, and carried it back on his shoulders to Tiryns. When the inde-fatigable Pausanias came through Psophis, following part of Heracles' course, he noted that there were still wild boars in the oak forests of Arcadia. Recording that the tusks of the one brought home by Heracles were said to be in the temple of Apollo in Cumae, in Italy, he added that this seemed highly improbable.

The next two tasks also involve much the same area, that is this still wild territory in the north of Arcadia. The capture of the Cerynian hind and the killing of the Stymphalian birds are both typical encounters with unnatural creatures. The hind had bronze hooves and golden horns, and as such sounds decidedly like a cult statue rather than a dangerous monster. Heracles had to bring it back, not kill it, and spent a whole year in the pursuit. Finally he cornered it on the banks of the Ladon—a river which runs through the mythology as it runs through the northern Peloponnese, making sudden unexpected appearances, its name now, as perhaps then, always seeming to carry overtones of importance. Its significance is perhaps due to its position, since it runs between Elis and Arcadia, broadening from its early form as a hill-country stream in those clefts and glens characteristic of the north-west of Arcadia, running with ever-increasing confidence southwards, until it becomes a respectable tributary of the Alpheus, the river in whose valley Olympia lies.

The hind was sacred to Artemis, as one would expect, and she at first objected to having it carried off, but was in the end persuaded to let Heracles take it to Eurystheus. He then proceeded at once to deal with the Stymphalian birds.

Around Lake Stymphalia is an area of marsh; at the time when Pausanias visited the area, in fact, this was rather an area of marsh which occasionally became a lake. During his own time it varied more than once, on one occasion becoming extensively flooded when its outflow became blocked by driftwood. In the course of history it has changed its form several times, sometimes being drained and at others dammed; and what evidently used to be a periodic patch of water is now a sizeable lake, the level of which has in fact risen to obliterate one of the archaeological sites in the area. Other sites, including an acropolis at the west end of the lake, have been identified. The lake—as it undoubtedly is now—and the marsh to which the myth refers, lie north-west of Nemea, but can really only practically be reached from the coast at Kiato, from where a good road rises inland and upwards towards the foothills around towering Mount Kyllini.

The Stymphalian birds were man-eaters, and sound particularly unpleasant. They had metal beaks and claws, and seem also to have been extremely numerous. Heracles frightened them out of their cover by the use of metal cymbals, and then shot them down with arrows. Pausanias identified the birds as being possibly a migrated flock of a species of aggressive ibis-like bird which he believed to exist in the Arabian desert. When he came to

Stymphalus there was a temple of Artemis there, on the ceiling oⱼ which birds answering the description were depicted. There is little to see now of what was, apparently, an important site in antiquity; only a lake in hill country, overlooked by that rising range which culminates in the fine peak of Mount Kyllini—the Cyllene of another story.

Heracles still has seven labours to go, but now approaches the last in this cycle, the last of the adventures in the territories neighbouring Mycenae which show him as a Peloponnesian hero. This one takes him a little further west, to the kingdom of Elis, which forms the north-west corner of the Peloponnese, between Patras and Olympia. This was a task of quite a different sort, and represents him rather as the clever, trick-playing sort of hero than, like the previous ones, as simply mighty.

It was, it seems, cattle country. King Augeas for some reason kept his cattle housed, and in an all too familiar way had long postponed the day of mucking-out. Perhaps, however, the story makes more sense the way Pausanias tells it: that there were simply so many cattle in the fields that the land had become useless under the dung which they left, and needed to be cleaned. But traditionally it is stables which have to be cleaned out, and so it is that image of the matter which seems to us correct. Heracles has to clean out King Augeas' stables, which are full of dung to an extraordinary extent; moreover he has to do it all in one day.

The task seems rather to have been interpolated into the list, since in this particular case Heracles negotiated with Augeas directly, agreeing to do the job for a percentage of the stock. He cleared away the accumulated dung not by any feat of strength, but by the trick of diverting two rivers. When these had done the work in the specified time Augeas refused to pay the fee, with the result that Heracles interrupted his labours at this point to go to war against him.

Heracles' further adventures in the undulating, wooded land of Elis really form another part of his story—and his adventures are so varied and numerous that we are only dealing here with a small selection of them—in which we find him instituting the Olympic games, measuring out the stadium at Olympia, and introducing there the worship of Zeus. But to this particular spot we shall return; and since he was not forgotten at Olympia we shall hear of him again.

Pylos was another kingdom which Heracles attacked during his career, apparently in reprisal for its having supported its neighbour, Elis. And he was not unknown either in the extreme south of the Peloponnese, since one version of the story outlined above has him pursuing the unfortunate centaurs who fled there to join their comrade Cheiron on wild Cape Malea. In this encounter in this remote and, even now, rather intimidating place, the wise centaur Cheiron (like Pholus in the earlier episode) was wounded by one of Heracles' venomous arrows. Something of the ambivalence of the whole idea of centaurs is distilled in these dealings with the semi-human hero. They for their part live in caves in mountains, away from men; but this apparent wildness was countered in the case of Cheiron by his great wisdom and compassion, his role as a teacher of moderation, truth and health. He it was who taught the healer Asclepius, and the heroes Achilles and Jason. He had taken to this retreat on Cape Malea, from his home on Mount Pelion, after the disgrace of the Lapith wedding. That Heracles should be responsible for Cheiron's death is particularly poignant, since they were both superhuman in such different ways.

The wise centaur met his end by accident, when Heracles was firing arrows generally at the other centaurs. One of the arrows struck him, and although he was only wounded, and was in any case, unlike the others, immortal, the pain of the wound grew so bad (presumably because of the viciousness of the poison) that he chose to die. Another sad episode ends, in the rocky country of the southern Peloponnese, over much of which even now one does not try to travel. Those long headlands of cliff, their coves approached by nothing better than a goat track, and often not even that, can best be reached by sea, by means of a small *pop-pop*ping boat swaying around their crags.

Heracles, like the centaurs, went largely to places where men tend not to go, to the extreme and uninviting heights, far above the valleys with their temple ruins and their institutions, to the places which are known most for being far distant, involving a long journey. Even now the Peloponnese throws up, without one's having to seek it, this sort of disconnecting effect: the isolation of a difficult and painful journey. Changes so powerful in urban places—a change of government, a change of economy —mean nothing there, nor has the passage of so much time had any great effect. Travelling around the Peloponnese (with such vast and arduous distances, such small and infrequent villages), one gradually becomes overwhelmed by a sense almost of hopelessness. At six o'clock in the morning the women are gathered patiently with their buckets round the village tap, and the men are already in the fields, picking beans. There is something formidably interminable about it, the same conditions, the same pattern of life persisting through millennia.

Of Heracles' many later adventures the most striking, perhaps, is his period at the court of Omphale, queen of Lydia, where he resided once again in subjection, having only recently freed himself from the domination of Eurystheus. When he had finished his twelve labours he set out to look for a new wife; it seems reasonable to assume that he could not go back to Megara, having killed her children, the start of the first set of difficulties. Once again, however, a king makes a bargain with him and then refuses to comply with it, and once again Heracles commits a murder while apparently in a state of unsound mind: having won the archery contest which should have given him the girl, he is driven away, vows revenge, and when accused of having stolen some horses kills the king's son. As Homer tells the story, towards the end of the *Odyssey*, it seems that Heracles acted inhumanly, killed an unsuspecting guest in his house, and that he really did steal the horses. Homer, alone among the sources of the story, shows him in a plainly unfavourable light. In any case he was now guilty again of murder, and again had to be purified.

Accordingly he went back to the Delphic oracle, and after some dispute there caused by the severity of his crime, he was sentenced to be sold into slavery, and consequently came to be owned by Queen Omphale, for whom he did a year's work in ridding her kingdom and other areas of various evils.

Heracles was immortal, whether by birth, as an inheritance from his father, or as a result of his achievements; and so he could in effect only die by choice. He had married again, and was living in Trachis, now the area of Lamia, inland of the westerly arm of the Gulf of Evvia. At the same time he continued to bring home mistresses, the last of which was the princess Iole, whose kingdom he had captured. It was apparently this habit which spurred his wife, Deianeira, to use what she believed to be a love potion which had been given to her by a dying centaur, killed by one of Heracles' fatal poisoned arrows. The potion was a mixture consisting of the centaur's blood and semen, which she now smeared on a new shirt which she sent to her husband to wear while sacrificing to Zeus. The poison, as of course it was, corroded his flesh, and drove him mad with pain. It was, ironically, the poisonous blood of the Lernean hydra, which had entered the blood of the centaur on Heracles' own arrowhead, and which, some time before, had driven the good centaur Cheiron to choose to die rather than suffer the continuing pain when he received it in the form of an accidental wound.

Heracles built himself a funeral pyre, on Mount Oeta in the land of Trachis, a mighty peak now known as Iti, inland of the Gulf of Lamia. And after some refusals somebody was persuaded to light it for him. In the cloud of smoke and flame he was transported to Olympus, to become a member of the family of the gods.

The myth goes on to tell how the descendants of Heracles attacked and eventually invaded the Peloponnese, and this is traditionally equated with the great Dorian invasion of the twelfth or thirteenth centuries B.C., in which peoples from northern Greece spread southwards and, perhaps, put an end to the long period of Mycenaean rule. The Spartans of the classical age, as Dorians, would thus be considered to be descendants of Heracles, but this does not seem to have unduly affected Athenian attitudes to the hero; Euripides treats him fairly in his play *Heracles*, though showing Athens to be the stable, humanitarian centre with which his guilt and madness are contrasted. In *Alcestis* he implies a note of something a little less than respect, by introducing Heracles' liking for wine which, perhaps originating from the episode with Pholus, became traditional for him; and of course Aristophanes gives us a typically deflating picture of the hero in the *Frogs*—but even this view of him retains some dignity. Perhaps these slight precedents led to the later tradition of presenting him rather as a buffoon, but they do not themselves constitute a departure from the straightforward hero-image which he clearly mainly represented.

TEN

ENCOUNTERS IN ARCADIA

ROUGHLY IT LIES between the further bank of the river Ladon and the east coastal hinterland of the Peloponnese, in a long diagonal stretch, an encircled central area between the ancient regions of Argolis, in the north-east, Achaia in the north, Elis along the west coast, Laconia (the southern territory around Sparta) and the south-western area of Messenia. The name, of course, carries a load of unwarranted overtones, through its misuse, from Roman times onward, in a way which has watered down its original fiery spirit with an insipid prettiness and romanticism.

Arcadia is rough and unequivocal, like Pan, its god, who can fairly be described as down-to-earth. Only in playtime travesties of its true nature do its shepherds dance and sing. Those leafy groves when you actually go into them offer no promise of besporting nymphs, but rather something more natural and less comprehensible, with a nervous threatening air, like a scent left by a wild animal to warn away others. Indeed the leafiness of them is itself not that of the stage scenery, but rather a reference to darkness at midday, the black shadow which is the obverse of the menacing sun.

Wooded quite thickly at its western edge, it opens into broader bare hillsides in its central region, where Tripolis sits at the bottom of a single valley flanked by round-shaped hills. Arcadia is essentially a country with many valleys, much going up and down. Most of all it is varied scenery, ranging from mountain to plain in quite short distances. Limestone alternates with sandstone in the uplands, giving a crumbling, gnawed look to its ridges. In the hills towns take the form of hillside places with precipitous streets stacked at the edge of ravines. In the valleys villages cower from the sun under heavy clumps of trees. Their well water splashes darkly in this deep shadow, under the black-leafed plane trees and the light-forbidding mulberries and the deep evergreen oaks. Out on the valley slopes the jingle of sheep bells comes from the depths of any patch of shade.

At their tops the valleys are full of crags and gorges; at their bottoms they are fertile and wide; and it is in between these extremes that the flocks graze. The goats spread out, like black insects in the distance, seen across the wide expanse of a smoothly eroded slope. The shaggy sheep group together helplessly under a rock or a tree.

People too live, and always did, among these nature-dominated slopes, in these small citadel settlements, permanently embattled against the weather or the sun. Indeed it is clear from Pausanias that the country, however wild it was then and is now, had long been inhabited. People travelled from early times through those mountain passes, where the villages still cling precariously together in a sort of self-reliant network, looking to each other, and to Tripolis, rather than towards the outside world.

That Arcadia always possessed an identity is clear too; it was separate and concise enough in spirit, in fact, to have its own gods. Pausanias implies that its people kept their sense of identity through such shared traditions and beliefs. The scattered and small settlements now give little immediate idea of how such places can, did and do, hang together. Now the only social lifeline in fact seems to be the country bus, an institution of almost mystical importance, the passage of which brings people to the doorways of their mountain hovels, the arrival of which is a major village event, in places where its driver-and-conductor team provide a constant social service. They throw out bundles, shouting, into shop doorways; leaving the road they drive bumping over fields to deliver a packet at a farmhouse; and in between they provide a travelling forum where to the background of wailing folksong music from their tapes the tasselled, beflagged, beaded, ikon-hung interior of the vehicle fills with the clatter of

Greek women gossiping, all the way on that long rough ride, from one remote hill hamlet to the next.

Once again of course the traveller, however well equipped, stands in constant risk of getting lost. It is, however, a lovely land to be lost in, so that in effect being lost becomes quite difficult to distinguish from its alternative. Another bonus is the the necessary contact then made with the mule driver in an olive grove or an old black-shawled woman carrying water, or a boy on a horse, or some young girls returning on the long foot journey from school, who will tell you where you are and where the track across the hills eventually leads to, and in doing so reveal, in their polite directness of manner, the spiritual nobility of Greek country people. One emerges every time with the feeling that it has been worthwhile.

They grow vegetables and keep chickens, supplying one another with subsistence produce and surviving through the mysterious cycles given us by the multiplier-effect; but primarily Arcadia is a land of pastoralists, a community engaged directly or otherwise in that family-oriented business in which care of the flocks seems to be shared by grandmothers and toddlers and little tattered boys. Goats and sheep both co-exist there and compete, and just as at Delphi there seemed to be a reference to the element of territorial rivalry in the story of the dispute and eventual settlement between the sheep-herding god Apollo and the goat-connected Dionysus, so here we have both gods with animal connections and stories of contests.

Pan is essentially a local god, in origin. He belongs to Arcadia; and in the later development of his legend he was said to be the son of the other god of this area, and of this chapter, Hermes. Originally, however, this distinctive and unusual deity must have been a local cult-god of a tribe and its area, since the hills of Arcadia are his home and the site of his shrines.

Since Pan is clearly a non-Olympian deity, he may indeed be part of the old order, part of a less humanized and more nature-oriented system of religion. We know about him chiefly (as indeed with Apollo and Hermes and several others) from a 'Homeric' hymn which tells his story. But this is either not as early as it appears or contains later additions, since it makes what seems to be an obvious mistake about his name. It seems likely that the connection with the word for 'all' was accidental, and that originally the name Pan came from the same root as the term for pasture, the root of eating and grazing terms. One might conjecture this simply from his specialized function, because he was not an all-nature god at all, but the guardian of flocks and shepherds, and connected with nature and wild places only through that role. The influence of the association with the adjectival form 'all', as in Panathenaic, pantheon and so on, led to a process by which the god took on the extra connotations of his name, developing into a universal nature god, almost an abstract principle. As a result of that his worship spread through Greece.

Plutarch tells a strangely haunting story, the effect of which is supposed to be that even gods or spirits can die. A shipful of Greeks with an Egyptian pilot on board was passing the island of Paxi on a voyage to Italy, when a voice from the land called to the pilot by his name, which was Thamus. The message across the water was that the great Pan was dead. The event took place in the reign of the emperor Tiberius, and hence it was supposed by later writers that it coincided directly with the birth of Christianity. In fact it has since been convincingly argued that the sailor Thamus actually heard the lament for the death of Tammuz (a Syrian-Babylonian deity adopted from as early as the seventh century B.C. by the Greeks, and later known by them as Adonis), whose priesthood annually bewailed his departure, prior to his magical rebirth. The mistake has the special charm of being entirely explicable, if instead of hearing 'The almighty Tammuz is dead' he heard 'Thamus, the great Pan is dead', since both would sound the same in Greek. Pan in any case was by no means considered to be dead, since Pausanias later reported that people still heard his pipes.

Pan's story tells that he wooed the nymphs of the area, usually unsuccessfully, and during one of these adventures cut himself some reeds, to temper his loneliness, and played a tune on them. We cannot really blame the nymphs for fleeing, since the creature was dark and hairy, having the lower quarters and the horns and beard of a goat. In the National Museum in Athens we can see what he was thought to look like from a small statue group, in which he, horned and hoofed and with his hairy legs, is shown making advances to Aphrodite herself, who is about to hit him in the face, in a rather unladylike but practical way, with her shoe, which she has taken off for the purpose. No one would really hold it against her.

When Pausanias, passing through Arcadia, mentions that people there still heard Pan's pipes in lonely places, he is perpetuating a tradition which had certainly by then been taken seriously for many centuries. The experience was connected with fear of the wilderness, fear of being lost and alone; and something similar seems to be at the root of the other main manifestation attributed to him, by which he springs out with a sudden shout on lonely travellers in wild places, a habit which has given us the word 'panic', from the Greek *panikos*, describing the reaction.

The pipes and the loneliness of his nature seem to go together, and to join with the fear of empty spaces which overcomes people who are too long alone on the mountain. If whistle-playing is indeed a habit of flock-watchers it would not be very surprising. Certainly in the African bush one often hears the sad, constant piping of a penny whistle, and knows from the sound that someone is attending cattle. They say there that it is necessary in order to keep the ghosts away, and there seems to be some sense in this. Anyone who stays still and on his own for long in such places might well get bothered by ghosts.

Instruments connect Pan with both Apollo and Hermes, who are also linked to him and to each other by a connection with flocks. Pan himself, in fact, is often regarded, along with Satyrs, Silenuses and Fauns (all to a greater or less extent goat-men), as being a member of the retinue of Dionysus, a part of the revelry which that god's cult involved. Apollo and Pan, in turn, competed as musicians, and Apollo, winning, became the acknowledged god of music. Much the same story is told of Apollo and Hermes, as we shall see; clearly what has happened is that shepherd gods have become music gods and have had to be realigned in the conceptual system, while tribes shift and time overlays old versions of a cult with new ones.

Hermes, for his part, was born (the son of Zeus by Maia, a land goddess) on Mount Cyllene, and Pausanias records that a shrine to him existed on the mountain's ridge. It is the highest of the great mountain blocks of the northern Peloponnese, and is mentioned by Homer as if specifically identifying Arcadia. Indeed as much as Pan Hermes was Arcadian in his roots, and like Pan he developed to have a universal function later. His cult must have spread out from Arcadia at an early date, since there is evidence that he was worshipped at Mycenaean Pylos. His main displacement, however, seems to have come at the time of the Dorian invasion, or whatever the historical equivalent of that traditional movement was; probably it was then that his equivalent flock-watcher and musician, Apollo, began to replace him in the Peloponnese. If so this impetus may well have led to the realization of Hermes' wider nature.

In the story he and Apollo got against each other from the start. As soon as Hermes was born he started to grow precociously, and set off immediately from the cave on the mountain. He travelled to Pieria, that rocky area in the north of Greece around the foothills of Mount Olympus, where Apollo was at the time grazing his cattle. Revealing at once his trickster nature, he stole a selection of the herd and evaded pursuit by disguising their footprints, either by making them shoes or, in other versions, by getting them to walk backwards. He then returned to his cave, still only a few days old.

Apollo, in his search for the lost cattle, reached Mount Cyllene (knowing as the god of divination what had happened) and accused the infant. The incipient quarrel between his sons was prevented by Zeus, who instructed Hermes to return the cattle. They were hidden in a cave near Pylos, far to the south, in a cave in fact traditionally identified as being in the cliffs flanking the little bay of Voidokilia, a small and sheltered inlet under the old castle, near which is indeed a cave with remarkable stalactitic formations which with an effort of imagination can be seen to look like an ox skin. Clearly, anyway, Hermes had come to have some close connection with the southern Peloponnese at an early stage.

The quarrel was significantly patched up by the gift of a musical instrument. Hermes had in the meantime invented the lyre, later to be viewed as the instrument characteristic of Apollo. He had fashioned it out of a tortoise shell and strings made of gut, and when he played it to Apollo on the occasion of the return of the cattle the effect was so powerful that he was at once forgiven for his mischief. Apollo even forgot about his desire for the cattle, which Hermes then took over; once he had been given the lyre Apollo became the god of music, delegating the care of flocks, herds and of their watchers to the new god Hermes.

Whatever disagreements, encroachments or territorial rivalry lay behind the act of theft by Hermes against Apollo, they evidently reached a satisfactory compromise. The two gods settled into a *modus vivendi*, viewed in fact as a traditional friendship between them. Apart from their Arcadian overlap they of course had their individual functions, and indeed Hermes is better known in the myths in general in his role as guide to travellers, and as the messenger who accompanies the various deities on their journeys to and from Olympus or Hades. As such he became the conductor of souls, the guide across the void between this world and the next. In the *Odyssey* and *Iliad* he acts as Zeus' personal messenger, and comes and goes between Olympus and the battleground.

Because of the need to travel speedily, he became traditionally a fast runner; and in most of the representations he is in fact shown as having wings on his heels. In this capacity he became a god of athletes, and as such had his statue in a prime position at Olympia. Through his less respectable connections, having been a thief since birth, he also became the patron of thieves and of trickery, and the arch-scoundrel Autolycus, a rustler and bandit who lived on Mount Parnassus, was said to be his son. This same Autolycus (whose name reappears in *A Winter's Tale*) was said in some versions of his pedigree to be the grandfather of the wily Odysseus; craft, it seems, continued to run in the family.

Hermes' major exploit, after his encounter with Apollo, was

the killing of the monster Argus, which Homer frequently mentions as an attribute of his, and which he undertook when sent to rescue Io, with whom Zeus was in love and who had been put by Hera into the custody of this hundred-eyed, ever-watchful giant. Hermes lulled him to sleep with music, and then cut off his head.

There is a connection too between Hermes and Dionysus, just as there is such a connection in the case of Apollo and Pan. He is often depicted as carrying the infant Dionysus on his arm, a reference to the episode in which he carried the newly born child, on Zeus' instructions, to foster parents, out of reach of the ever-jealous Hera. And it is in this form which he appears in the best-known statue of him, that called the 'Hermes of Praxiteles', which stood in the temple of Hera at Olympia. Pausanias saw it there, and there it was rediscovered in the excavations of 1877.

It is thought that it was Hermes' function as guardian of flocks which led him to be viewed as a sort of home-protector, with the result that the Greeks formed the habit of putting little statues of him, known now as 'herms', outside their front doors, and, perhaps now in his role as protector of travellers, at their boundaries and crossroads. From this habit the Romans, with typically suburban taste, developed that of using small statues of Hermes as garden ornaments, with the result that the messenger of Zeus is in a sense the direct ancestor of the garden gnome.

It is from his name, rather than from his character, that the alchemists derived the word 'Hermetic', equating him with an Egyptian god of arcane knowledge, the god Thoth. And from the alchemical practices, the so-called Hermetic philosophy, we in our turn get the word 'hermetic', which presumably derives from the way the vessels were sealed in that early form of chemistry. Hermes' Roman counterpart, Mercury, followed the chemical connection and gave his name to the substance quicksilver, which shared his qualities of speed and liveliness.

Hermes has, in fact, come a long way, and by an unexpected route, from those slopes of Arcadia, and in the process he lost his rural, pastoralist nature almost completely. But it was to the cults and legends connected with sheep-herding that he owed his origins, and in that backwoods country under Mount Cyllene, where they are still attending to their flocks, that he achieved the original impetus which launched him into the body of myth.

Even the sheep there have an ancientness about them which emphasizes the remarkably unchanging pattern of the life. Shaggy in the spring, tall and lean when shorn, they have long necks and drooping ears which give them a sad, downtrodden appearance. (The goats, by contrast, appear hard and fierce, black as shadows and as devilish.) Perhaps to us they carry overtones of past times largely through their resemblance to our image of biblical sheep (derived presumably from illustrated Bibles) and that blend of Middle Eastern lore which those in turn convey. Something about the activity itself too gives a direct line back to remote ages, to not just pre-industrial but even pre-agricultural, pre-settled and town-dwelling life—semi-nomadic, and therefore wandering. The fact that they are still moving across the slopes now, from an exhausted grazing ground to a fresh one, says a lot about the land-use pattern and the lack of change. It lies both behind the way of life there now and behind the myths. Those great herds in motion, driven by screaming old women. Or at rest, watched over by small children, Always, of course, watched and accompanied, as it is clear that they were in the times when the myths were formed, and as they are still in all Balkan countries and all over Africa. The paddock or the hefted flock seem to be unknown forms of land use in such places, so that Greeks travelling in western Europe are at first surprised to see sheep being allowed to wander about our hillsides on their own. This is one of those factors of economic form which separate our lives and world—in which everyone is busy doing other things, the farmer at market, the wife shopping, the children at school—from the lives of those who lived in the climate of the myths, making the important point that there really is this gap between the way most of us live, and a world which could encompass Hermes and Pan. In some places this gulf between the cultures and the times gapes widely; but not in Arcadia.

ELEVEN

BIRTHPLACES OF THE GODS

ALTHOUGH THEY OVERLAP and intermarry, interfere in each other's business and occasionally appear curiously ambiguous, the characters of Greek myths can definitely be divided into two classes: gods, and heroes. One main feature divides them; although again there are exceptions, since some of the heroes, such as Heracles, shared the privilege of being transported to the everlasting life of Olympus, the defining distinction is that of immortality. In such cases it always is. It was that for which Gilgamesh longed and lamented, in the Mesopotamian epic, being almost, but not quite, a god. Reading the often anguished words of Pindar one feels, in fact, that it was because of the human lack and need of immortality that the gods were necessary. To Pindar they are free of grief and secure in their citadel in the skies, for ever. We on the other hand are things of a day.

It seems a little remarkable to us that though the gods did not die they were not, as gods sometimes are, regarded as being completely out of time. They came into existence, in their stories, in a very human way: through the processes of procreation, pregnancy and birth. Though they had no end they had beginnings. This apparent contradiction is a striking instance of the realism which surrounds them, as if they were in a perfectly normal sense facts of the natural order. It is because they had such regular biographical details that it was possible to view them as part of the surrounding reality, walking about Arcadia or Attica and experiencing emotions and frustrations like anyone else. Or, to put it another way, it was because they were seen so vividly and naturalistically in Greek tradition that it was not inconsistent or conceptually awkward for them to have births.

The main shrines of some of the heroes were at the places of their supposed death or burial. Burial places in particular have always seemed appropriate cult centres, as they were in the cases of many of the early Christian saints. They bear the esteem of claiming the possession of treasured relics. No such claims were possible in the case of gods and goddesses, who must therefore become identified with their holy places in other ways. And in fact we find that their shrines were often located at the places where they were said to have been born.

Some of the places on the surface of Greece in fact became greatly famous for that reason, since the birth of a god, and particularly of one of the major deities, was obviously an important matter. Among them two stand out, as being universally known and revered: the place where the god Apollo was born, and the birthplace of the leader of the gods, Zeus himself.

Delos is by any standards small, and nothing about its physical form seems to mark it out as being significant. It was said that before Apollo's birth it was a barren island, and it is certainly rather barren now. Apparently it flowered and bloomed in between, both literally and in the figurative sense of having splendid buildings, dense population, supreme commercial success, and high status in Greek politics and religion. Now once again unpopulated, levelled and bare, it gives us not a little trouble in believing in its past. And yet at the same time there is nothing there to come between that past and the afternoon of searing heat on which, inevitably, one first sees it, come out on the tossing, crowded boat from Mykonos, wandering around the rough ground of the sacred precincts under the unavoidable sun. More than anywhere else in Greece Delos has been set aside, from the start, as a place of the past, dedicated and devoted to its own importance and the memory of its major event.

Certainly the effect of its reputation remains potent, so that in spite of its unimposing form one feels impressed by the sight of it, the first sight of something to which the charisma of sacredness is attached, as for instance if one walks in the evening to that far western headland of Mykonos from where it can be seen, out there across the water, a long low shape lying on the backcloth of the sunset.

Apollo and his sister Artemis were the progeny of one of Zeus' many extra-marital adventures. Their mother Leto was the daughter of Coeus and Phoebe, two members of the race of Titans, the previous generation, as it were, of the gods, a group consisting of the children of Uranus which had Cronus as its leader. Leto was therefore Zeus' cousin, but intermarriage is a common theme in that section of the myths. Indeed, given the circumstances of cosmic origin which are assumed, this would seem to be inevitable.

In many of these stories Hera plays a crucial part, and almost always a negative one. She prevents, obstructs or destroys. In this case she would not leave Leto in peace to give birth, but pursued her relentlessly through the world. With the assistance of Poseidon she came to Delos, having first given birth to Artemis on the neighbouring island. Then, according to the original source, she clasped a palm tree on the island of Delos, and Apollo was born. According to later embellishments Delos was, till then, a wandering island, drifting round the world in a sort of search for its eventual destiny. Poseidon fixed it firm for the purpose of providing a refuge for Leto.

The exact place was, as so often, clearly identified. It was on the north side of Mount Cynthus, that neatly peaked 350-foot hill which is the only physical feature of the small and low-lying island. On the upper slope of the hill is a natural grotto, which became, probably in very early times, a shrine and small temple, which may still be seen. It seems highly likely that this was one of the island's first sacred spots, regarded as being the actual birth-place of the god.

Certainly the cult was well established at an early date. The 'Homeric' hymn which is the most authentic source for the tradition is a work of the seventh century B.C., at the most as early as 700, but it undoubtedly conveys to us authentic material. Its theme implies that a need was felt, even then, for an explanation as to how and why such a humble island had been so honoured. During the classical period this poetic tale was taken to be the work of Homer, but in spite of this mistake (as we now know it to be) a point made by Thucydides still applies: the hymn is evidence that the festivals and ceremonies which it mentions were in existence and well known at least by the time it was written.

Actually Homer himself does mention Delos and its cult, on the occasion when Odysseus has landed on the island of the Phaeacians and, waking on the beach, finds himself looking at the princess Nausicaa. Wishing to impress her, he compares her grace and upright slenderness to the most prestigious example of such perfection he can think of: the palm-tree sapling sprung from the ground beside the altar of Apollo on the island of Delos. He went there, he recalls, on his way to Troy, with his troops accompanying him, not knowing about the future and its trials. He looks at her now, he says, with the same mesmerized wonder as he looked at that young tree.

What we can read into this little episode is at least that there were in Homer's time an altar and a sacred palm tree on Delos. The implication is that the tree was by then very old; it is described as a sapling in the days of the Trojan War, which Homer must have regarded as being at least a long time before his day. On the site itself there is certainly evidence of early habitation, and tombs of the Mycenaean period indicate that Homer may have been accurate in his dating of the beginnings of the cult. Delos is actually only archaeologically and historically detailed for later periods, but these early items of evidence are significant enough.

The author of the hymn mentions the festivities in connection with meetings held by the Ionians, and we may therefore imagine an Aegean-based Ionian league, which used Delos as its regular meeting place. This is the sort of role which the island thereafter maintained, even when its larger neighbour Naxos became the most prominent of the Cyclades; many of the monuments found on Delos were dedicated by Naxos, made in Naxian marble. The confederation of islands maintained a certain independence until the expansionist ambitions of Athens began to influence it. The

tyrant Peisistratus, successor to Solon during the mid-sixth
century, was chiefly responsible for promoting the idea of
Athenian domination of Greece, and he it was who brought
Delos into history, in about 540 B.C.

Peisistratus saw the importance of establishing Athens not just
politically but in the religious sphere, as the centre of every
kind of Greek activity. He turned his attention to Delos as the
most revered centre of worship. There had always been connections between the two; the development of the importance of
Athens now required an increase of interest in these links. The
Delphic oracle conveniently authorized the interference, which
took the form of clearing an area of the island of the burials
which had been made there. This was an act of purification, and is
more significant for its evidence of Peisistratus' power than for
any obvious effect. The same exercise was repeated at a later date,
during the Peloponnesian War, when all the graves on the island
were opened, an event which (as described by Thucydides)
accidentally became one of the first pieces of archaeology. From
the weapons and the form of burial, he says, it was apparent that
many of the burials were Carian—connected, that is, with the
people of the southern stretch of the Asiatic coast of the Aegean,
south of Lydia. These people, he records, like the Phoenicians,
occupied most of the islands until the rise of Cretan naval power,
when the Minoan colonists took their place.

It was after the second purification by Athens that the Athens-
dominated Delian games came into being. But already before that
the ties between the two places had become close, since Delos
had become the centre of the league organized by Athens immediately after the Persian wars, the aim of which was to prevent
any possibility of a repeat of that disaster.

When the league was formed, Athens was the political and
Delos the religious head of it. Part of the plan consisted of raising
funds, and every member of the league paid an annual contribution, partly at first consisting of troops or fighting ships, but
increasingly taking the form of cash. Delos was the treasury of the
league, but the security which its sanctity had traditionally
ensured seemed to be in jeopardy, as barbarian pirates began to

become a trouble throughout the Aegean. In the mid-fifth century the treasury, at the suggestion of the people of Samos, was transferred for its better protection to the Acropolis in Athens. We have seen in an earlier chapter how the integrity of this act was thrown into doubt by the fact that Pericles then spent the money beautifying the city. Plutarch records that Pericles replied to the accusation that as long as Athens remained powerful the cause for which the funds were raised would be fulfilled, and while that was the case the allies had no business asking what he did with the money. In what seems to us, even with all our subsequent experience of political double-talk, to be a highly agile piece of logical acrobatics, he argued that once Athens was fully equipped to carry on the defence it was only right that the surplus should be put to some general public use, such as encouraging artists and craftsmen and giving people employment. We have seen that one of the results was the Parthenon, so that perhaps one should not quibble. The effect for Delos was, however, critical: it came from then on in a very real way under the power of Athens.

During the Peloponnesian War the Delians achieved independence for a time, with Spartan help, at those periods when the fortunes of Athens were in decline; and when Athens was gaining power they lost it again. Their situation fluctuated similarly during the Macedonian rule of the next centuries; but it was during that time, the turn of the third to the second centuries, that the great commercial prominence of the island was achieved.

Pausanias points to the sort of symbiosis which exists between religion and commerce. Trade and sacredness have each something to offer the other. It was believed, he said, that the presence of the god made it safe to do business on Delos. On the other hand the sanctuary clearly flourished, those throngs of visitors which had always come to the festivals now including the richest of the Greek world, who no doubt were as anxious as anyone to keep in with the god. As the Roman power expanded eastward Delos had the good sense to remain neutral, and in the growing conflict between Rome and Macedonia it was thus able to trade with both sides. Indeed the sort of truce which always accompanied religious festivals must have provided many opportunities for people to do business who would otherwise have felt obliged to fight each other.

Delos had much to thank Apollo for. The god, it was said, loved the island more than any other place, and it seemed as if he showed it. For such a tiny and unauspicious spot to gain such prominence is indeed a phenomenon requiring explanation. During those years a dense population of varied nationality crowded its surface, and it flourished as few islands other than Manhattan have ever done. Only the painful intrigues and manœuvres of Roman politics could undermine it, and until these got the better of it it boomed.

We can see the results of this period most clearly, now, walking around that strangely bleak landscape. The statues which lined the sacred way, the colonnades and coloured pediments, have been broken and removed, and hardly any visible vestiges of magnificence remain. But the size and layout of the sanctuary, to which one can go directly from the sacred port, indicates a time of very considerable splendour. Elaborated over many centuries, it remained throughout the history of the island a focal point, the seat of the place's importance.

The remains on Delos fall easily into two parts: the area of the temples, and the commercial and residential city. The ruins of the latter, mostly Roman, run southwards along the shore. One can see how it has been forced by lack of space upward, out on to the steeper slopes of Mount Cynthus. Near to the sanctuary and the port are the markets, a smaller one of the period leading up to Delos' commercial climax, and a vast hall which must have been the main trading and business area of the city in its prime. Southwards from the sacred port, which connects with Apollo's sanctuary, a complex of docks and wharves, backed by warehouses, formed the trading section. Seeing the general extent of all this now, one can appreciate Pausanias' description of Delos as the common market-place of Greece. Perhaps it is a natural role for an island placed at the focal point of sea routes between Italy, Greece, Africa and the Near East. But considering how poor the island itself is in natural resources, it seems a really remarkable achievement.

It is not surprising if this area now looks chaotic and unplanned. To some extent it was. It underwent continual modification for centuries, and in any case was constructed under the pressure of population expansion and an equivalent increase in the bulk of commodities handled. By contrast the holy precincts seem more comprehensible, spacious even, and relaxing in mood. That could hardly be said of the cramped residential quarters, where people evidently lived shoulder to shoulder, with no proper streets, no squares or civic features, forced into proximity by the shortage of space. But here and there a larger, more comfortable dwelling occurs, and in some of these mosaic floors have survived which show a high level of artistic taste. We also find that there were, at the later period, proper sewers and plumbing, which is something that cannot always be said of the houses of the neighbouring Cycladic islands today.

The worship of the god, to which all this was due, was centred on the great sanctuary, as it had been evidently since the seventh century, the main plan of the extended version which we see now being laid out probably in the time of the expansion of the cult under the influence of Peisistratus. But the archaeology of the site is greatly confused by numerous additions and inexplicable divisions, so that the area of the temple is a network of structures, only some of which can properly be understood.

One of the greatest features of the sanctuary, and of the island, was the colossal statue of Apollo, dedicated by the people of Naxos in the early part of the sixth century B.C. We know that it stood more than twenty feet high, the whole thing, including the base, made of a single block of Naxian marble. Apparently it fell in an earthquake, and during an attempt to carry it away it became broken and dismembered. The base is now some distance from the other remaining parts, the torso and a section of the thigh, which may still be seen in the sanctuary. In the museum on the island is one of the hands.

Some distance from the sanctuary lies an open area of summer dust known as 'the Sacred Lake', supposed in later versions of the story to be the pool beside which Leto gave birth to the god Apollo. It is not generally impressive now, though it has some water in it in the winter. But what commands attention, and indeed would do so anywhere, is the row of marble lions on its western side. Although these must be among the most famous lions in the world they never fail to cause surprise, and sometimes disappointment. They are not grand; in fact they are relatively small for such a species, particularly when represented in monuments. Most of them have lost their bases, and the terrace on which they once grandly stood has disintegrated beneath them. Their faces are worn, so that the once-ferocious features have become tamed. In defiance of all these disadvantages they still look out over the lake heroically, undefeatable.

There is something about them that is recognizably primitive and ancient; not just the archaic style, which is perhaps an artistic manner rather than an expression of anything, but the idea of such an animal which they incorporate: an animal not monumental or formal, but wild, ravenous and powerful. Perhaps whoever made them knew simply that lions lived in the wilds and hunted for what food they could get. The Delos lions are thin sinewy beasts, and clearly all the more dangerous for that; their bellies have disappeared into their protruding ribs, and their haunches are all muscle and tendon. Their mouths are open in an endless roar of complaint, baying silently across the now bare and ruins-scattered ground, expressing the soundless agony of the arid land.

These guardians of Apollo's birthplace were presented by the island of Naxos in the seventh century B.C. There were originally nine of them, and five now remain on the site. The Venetians commandeered a sixth, which is still standing lonely guard outside the Arsenal in Venice.

Roman ruins now surround the sanctuary area and the edges of the Sacred Lake, but the more ancient and interesting relics are to be found a little way away, and on the mountain itself are not only the grotto which was probably the original shrine commemorating the birthplace, but temples to the other gods, including rather surprisingly Hera, who evidently became reconciled with Leto and her progeny. On top of the mountain there were temples to Zeus and Athena, not much of which can now be seen. What can indeed be seen from there is the all-round view of the other islands, filling the horizon very impressively, and demonstrating that central position of Delos which gave rise to the idea that the surrounding islands had gathered protectively round the holy spot.

The reason for the devastation which one sees all around, and also for Delos' remarkable temporal arrest, is that the whole of this prosperity and success came to a sudden end. It was in 88 B.C. that a general invading Greece on behalf of Mithridates, king of Pontus, violated the island's sacredness which had up to then been its protection. Delos, Pausanias points out, was completely helpless, unarmed and unfortified. Consequently everyone was massacred and the place was looted. Moreover, the invaders razed it to the ground; and although it was sporadically re-inhabited it was not much rebuilt, and never recovered from its desolation. As a result Pausanias is able to say that in his time it was uninhabited, if you took away the Athenian guards, just as it is now, if you take away the museum curator. That, he says, is how impermanent and uncertain human matters are.

Cicero tells us that tourists used to be shown the palm tree under which Apollo was born—which, however, he doubted could be the same one seen by Odysseus. Apollo was not the only deity thought to have been born under a tree, and when Pausanias was on the island of Samos he in turn was shown the willow tree, on the banks of the river Imbrasos, which marked the spot where the goddess Hera was born. Certainly there was a cult of Hera on the island of Samos from early times, to the extent that by the classical age the temple of Hera there had become the largest in Greece, and was one of the ancient wonders of the world.

The ruins of this lie on the coast near the river Imbrasos, and although only one column remains upright there can be no doubt about the site's importance and status. That it was an early shrine, a sanctuary round the supposed birthplace on the bank of

G

the river, is indicated from the discovery of a Mycenaean tomb and buildings there. The major extension of this shrine, which, together with rebuilding and alterations up to the third century, form the present ruins, took place during the sixth century B.C. Herodotus noted that it was the largest Greek temple of his time. This is now somewhat hard to grasp, since the place is remote and rural.

The great temple of Hera was built as a piece of political self-promotion by the ruler of Samos in the late sixth century— Polycrates, who had considerable influence on the surrounding Aegean through the ownership of a powerful navy. It is he of whom Herodotus tells that timeless story, so strong in its tone of folk-tale that it must, one feels, always have been a current legend. His success and good fortune were so strong that he began to fear the envy of the gods, and he therefore sacrificed the thing which was most precious to him, which happened to be the emerald ring he continually wore. He threw it ceremonially into the sea. A few days later a fisherman brought him a fish as a gift, and of course the ring was found inside it. Divine envy is apparently not so easily warded off, and he eventually died a savage death.

There is no doubt that Polycrates, in building the famous temple, was making use of the good fortune which his island possessed of being the supposed birthplace of the wife of Zeus. Hera was not just Zeus' wife but his sister as well, since she was the daughter of Cronus and Rhea, and although the details are rather scant we may imagine that Rhea was supposedly seeking a place safe from her husband's child-eating habit (as in the case of Zeus' birth in Crete) when she came to this distant and lovely island. Samos is not otherwise connected with Hera's story, which as we have seen consisted mostly of acts of jealousy brought about by her husband's total lack of fidelity. She and Zeus were not regarded as having much of a married life. It is remarkable in fact that Hera, as the goddess of matrimony, should embody to such an extent the unsuccessful side of that institution. Possibly we have to see this as a reaction against the matriarchal cults of the mother goddess, the imposition on Greek thought of the new male-dominated social form, in which there was no doubt about who wielded the thunderbolt.

At any rate the climate of the myths seems rather to have favoured Hera's counterpart, the goddess Aphrodite. In the scheme of the myths the functions of love and marriage are kept resolutely separate. Hera's assumption that Zeus should be sexually faithful to her seems not to have been generally shared; in any case it is shown as being constantly thwarted. He for his part was completely shameless. Most of his progeny were conceived and born out of wedlock, so that matrimony was not even accorded that function. Love, it seems, is thought of purely as extra-marital; and Aphrodite personifies this element with appropriate charm.

The name 'Aphrodite' has an apparent connection with the word for foam, *aphros*, and perhaps it was because of this association that she came to be regarded as foam-born, produced from the waters of the sea itself. The story of how this happened takes us back to a pre-Olympian episode in the origin of the gods. Uranus, the ancestor of all these deities, was the offspring of Gaea, the earth goddess, the representation of the mothering earth itself. Inevitably, under the circumstances, she and Uranus coupled, and produced the Titans. Cronus was one of these, and he it was who overcame the tyrannical father, Uranus, who had imprisoned his other children, the Cyclops, in the underworld. It was at the instigation of his mother Gaea that he carried out the first and one of the most startling assaults in this cosmogony, by castrating his father with a small sickle. This highly symbolic act had the effect of deposing the old god and ending his era; but the results of the mutilation carried over into the world of the new order. Some of the drops of blood fell on the earth, and gave birth to the Furies. By contrast the genitals themselves fell into the sea, and from the foam that resulted the goddess Aphrodite arose.

The sea they fell into was that off the coast of the southern Peloponnese. The wind took her gently southwards across the water, and she stepped ashore on the island of Cythera. Nothing in this scene can ever now be free of the paradigm depiction of it, that gentle, wistful tableau which Sandro Botticelli made of it in about 1478. I can never come before it in the Uffizi without amazement that something so well known and so often seen can strike one still as so beautiful; the immaculate finish and consistency of tone perhaps make the original more stunningly lovely than any reproduction. The thoughtful girl drifts shoreward in an atmosphere of dream, with a soft wind rippling that emerald water, the air suddenly full of flying flowers, a pale wash of chalky blue cooling the distances, herself a still, reposed centre to the motion which sweeps evenly across the picture, and the whole thing made as if in one thought, as if it were a single piece of imagining.

Kythira, as it now is, is a richly varied but in places rather rugged island which lies just off the coast of the southern finger of the Peloponnese, within sight in fact of Cape Malea, where Heracles finally confronted the Centaurs. The island's shore, where the goddess is supposed to have drifted to land, is in places quite idyllic, with soft clear water and the shelter of cove-making cliffs. There is evidence of Minoan colonization of the island (as indeed there is of several), so that perhaps once again an early goddess-cult developed there into the claim to this association with the birth of Aphrodite. Archaeologists have identified a substantial sanctuary near to the old town, which is assumed to be the sanctuary of Aphrodite traditionally located on the island. Pausanias speaks so highly of this that it is really surprising that it had in the meantime completely disappeared. Schliemann himself failed to find it. This sanctuary, Pausanias said, was the oldest and most sacred of all Aphrodite's sanctuaries, which gives us some reason to believe in the authenticity of the tradition, that it was in these parts that the goddess originated.

It must be said, however, that there are rivals for this honour. As early as Homer we have evidence for a strong and important Aphrodite cult in Cyprus, at Paphos. And not surprisingly that place also laid claim to being the spot at which the goddess came ashore, born from the waves off its coast. Certainly she was well established in Cyprus in antiquity, and it is perhaps with that centre of her worship, rather than with Kythira, that she is most commonly connected.

Aphrodite features in the body of myth mainly on account of her success in the beauty contest adjudicated by Paris, prince of Troy. The background and outcome of that adventure we have already investigated, in connection with the origins of the Trojan War. Aphrodite, however, had a generally romantic life, as indeed one would expect of a goddess so definitely representative of amorous inclination. Although she had affairs, in that gossip-columnists' world of Olympus, with several of the gods (including Hermes and the war god Ares), and anyway was ironically married to the unattractive craftsman god Hephaestus, it was Zeus who fell for her most desperately. The story implies that he received only frustration as a reward.

In the episode of the *Odyssey* in which the blind bard Demodocus entertains Odysseus and the court of the king of the Phaeacians, a long and full story is told of one of Aphrodite's major affairs, in which she was caught by her husband Hephaestus in bed with her lover Ares. Knowing of their liaison the god had made an ingenious net which imprisoned the guilty pair in the bed, and he then indignantly showed them in that plight to all the other gods. Homer, through the mouth of Demodocus, tells the story with a light touch, the narrative being full of convincing detail while at the same time moving swiftly to its climax.

Strangely Aphrodite is one of the few Homeric deities whose name or its equivalent has not yet been discovered in the Mycenaean tablets. Perhaps she came to Greece from a different direction at a later date, after the arrival of the Achaeans and the main Olympian gods. The name is thought to be Phoenician in origin, and the cult to have spread through the Aegean along the Phoenician trading routes. She is thus equated with the Middle Eastern goddesses Ishtar and Astarte, fertility goddesses who became, via their association with regeneration, goddesses of love. Such an Asian tradition might well have revitalized the related Minoan goddess cult in Greece to give us Aphrodite.

The remarkably explicit deposition of Uranus, which gave rise to the birth of Aphrodite, was the first of the overthrowals with which the established religion of Greece is depicted as coming into being in the early part of the mythology. We owe our view of this background mainly to Hesiod's *Theogony*, the story of the origins of the gods. In its turn this revolution led to the reign of Cronus, a darkly menacing figure lying in what feels like the prehistory of the Olympian dynasties, just before the dawn of the specially Greek understanding reveals the brilliant details of the more familiar and humanized pantheon.

Cronus, more accurately written as Kronos, was identified by the ancient Greeks with the principle of time itself, the eternity in which the world had already existed before men came to know about it. The Greek for 'time' is similar, but not identical, beginning as it does with the χ which we transliterate as *ch*. Chronos and Kronos sound similar enough for the association to be a natural one; Graves, however, points to a possible connection with the word for 'crow', raising the interesting suggestion that Cronus was one of the several ancient European crow gods, like the Celtic god Bran who became, in later developments, the guardian of the Holy Grail.

The theme of the overthrow of the established rule is a common one in all mythologies, and perhaps indicates an abiding fear possessed by each generation of the inevitable (but nevertheless resisted) rise to power of the next. Nothing, presumably, is more universal in the experience of mankind. At the same speed as the father ages, the son grows up. The end becomes all too obvious. In the Greek myths it is often foretold by an oracle that the son will kill the father. Whoever it was who told Cronus this, it is certainly shown to have been his main preoccupation. He was married, as his father was said to have been and as his son Zeus would be later, to his sister, in this case Rhea. Does this insistence on the habit of brother–sister incest among the early gods imply a belief that it was a custom at one time practised? It would be possible to explain it in dynastic terms as an offshoot of matriliny; and certainly while the practice of incest seems to have been comparatively rare in historical societies, and confined where it occurred to special cases such as the marriage of a sacred king, the theme of inbreeding is common in many traditions, not least in that of the Old Testament. While Lot, in the book of Genesis, had intercourse with his daughters, and both Isaac and Jacob married their first cousins, the prophet Abraham actually married his sister. Clearly it is possible to see a connection between these instances of brother–sister incest and the theme in which the mother's brother takes up the paternal position of hostility to the next generation.

Cronus' fear of being supplanted by his son led him to the rather extreme expedient of eating his offspring year by year as they were born. The detail is almost as startling as Uranus' castration and perhaps, like that, requires some sort of psychological explanation. He should no doubt be regarded as swallowing them, rather than as ripping them apart, as in the unforgettable Goya image of him among the 'black paintings' in the Prado. G. S. Kirk (in *Myth, Its Meaning and Function in Ancient and Other Cultures*) suggests a Hurrian comparison for the Cronus story and the theme of child-swallowing. Whether or not paedophagy can be definitely identified as a general theme—we have seen it done by accident in the story of Atreus and Thyestes—the theme of child-killing is a very widespread one, in Greek myth and elsewhere.

The structure of events is usually the same, and closely parallels those of the case of Cronus. It is in fact rather unusual for a hero to be born without this attempt by the ruling power to kill him shortly after birth; and this is usually in response to a prophecy that he, when he grows up, will depose or kill his father, or the ruling king, or (as they are often the same person) both, and take over the kingdom. He is then subjected to almost certain death— but not quite certain, since the frail chance of his escaping still remains. It happened to Oedipus, Paris and Perseus; in Roman myth it happened to Romulus and Remus; we know that the Hebrews told the same tale of Moses, and that the element came to be incorporated in the story of Jesus Christ; in Celtic myth both Tristram and Arthur were the subjects of such attempted destruction, as was also Arthur's eventual rival Mordred. All, of course, miraculously escaped. And so did Zeus.

On the advice of Gaea, the earth, their joint mother, Rhea put an end to the yearly occurrence of her child's death by hiding during her pregnancy in Crete. She gave Cronus a stone to swallow instead, which apparently fooled him. Zeus was saved, and was reared secretly in the Cretan mountains.

Rival traditions associate the event of the birth of Zeus with two separate places, a cave on Mount Ida and one on Mount Dikte. Presumably as a compromise it is said by the developed versions of the story that he was born in the Dikte cave and reared near the Ida one; but undoubtedly a genuine and strong tradition of his birth existed at one time or another at each.

On the face of it the Diktean cave, the more exciting and impressive of the two, would seem to be a most unsuitable place for the birth of a god associated with light, air and heights. On the other hand as a hiding place it is ideal. These chthonic, slippery depths are the last place one would seek a new-born sky god. Dark, dank, deep in the earth, it is nothing if not of the under-world, the internal and normally unseen depths inside the earth itself. As such, of course, it seems the natural place for a mother-earth cult, and since there is archaeological evidence of Minoan use it is probably fair to assume that it was the site of a pre-Olympian, pre-Achaean cult connected with the earth goddess.

One comes up the treed hillsides among those tangled, ancient oaks, to turn and find at one's feet a sheer view across the Lassiti plain, its absolute levelness completely enclosed by protective hills, making a sort of flat-bottomed bowl. By contrast with this clear and breezy upland outlook, the cold and uncomfortable depths of the supposed birthplace itself come as an inevitable shock. It is so deep and so sheer, and at the same time so dark and mysterious. There is something about the complete receptive silence of these underground depths that makes one feel the insulating, enclosing presence of the rock. By the tiny light of hand-held candles you look towards the unrevealing darkness; in this deep colourlessness and cold the shadows of the unearthly forms of fat and wrinkled stalactites break and obstruct the dim glow of the light. With the mystery of sheer unknowableness a black underground lake curves away out of sight into the darkness beyond candle-reach. The huge conjoining stalactites form passages and chambers, and in the far deep corner of one such is the supposed birth spot, an uncomfortable, cold and unpropitious corner, where archaeology long ago revealed the figurines associated with early Cretan worship.

It is perhaps on the way back up that one grasps the association with childbirth which, if this was originally a shrine to the earth mother, might have caused the event of the birth of the new god to be located here. Looking up that slippery slope to the slit of daylight, with the huge dripping depths around you, you get an apprehension of what it would be like to be born seeing.

Zeus was a god of air and sky and high mountain, and although the Diktean cave lies in hilly country densely foliaged with his sacred tree, the oak, it lacks the clarity and space which one would more readily associate with him. As you come up to the plain through tiny mountain villages and out on to the rocky hillsides, the oaks themselves—a dark Mediterranean variety with an oak's rough bark but the small, spiky leaves of a holly—seem rather to absorb light than to take colour from it, giving back in return only a deep green darkness. In the bright heat their rich black-green is a luxury, a relief to the eye. But it is not really Zeus country.

Going up to Ida is a different matter altogether. The upper part of the mountain is quite bare, and the whole of that flank in which the cave of Zeus lies is unclothed except for a smattering of the small dry scrub which occurs even on the most barren hillsides. From all directions Ida is a serenely lofty mountain, the folds of its slopes falling like drapery, cascading in a stiff gown around it. A barrier of crags and gullies marks it off at most points from normal life. It is, and feels, remote, and difficult to get to. One can see at once how it came to be thought of as a birthplace of the sky god; such bulk and inaccessibility is only too easy to associate with the lives of gods. But Ida has a beauty and femininity too which made it a natural place to locate the seclusion of Zeus' mother.

You get there from the mountain village of Anogia, a prototypical Cretan upland place, where tall and dangerous-looking men stand in the shadows dressed in knee boots, headbands and black riding clothes, and in every doorway there is a cackle of crones. The cave of Zeus is by any standards remote—Anogia itself is remote, and the cave is far up the mountain from Anogia, through upland valleys where sheep graze, past the hovels used by the semi-nomadic shepherds, along the edges of rock-bedded gorges. The swoop and soar of eagles, the sky god's sacred and symbolic bird, sets the mood of the area. Ida throws a broad shadow ahead.

Perhaps one should remember that in ancient times all places must have been more or less remote. The Minoan villas which the road up to Anogia passes were obviously far-flung pioneering outposts. But so were many others, to a greater or lesser extent. If one expected to have to take a trip of several days by goat paths and mule tracks to get anywhere at all, then perhaps the cave of Zeus under the flank of Ida would not seem as far from every normal place as it does now. It does seem strange to us that cults originated in such very distant places. But perhaps it was their distance, their security from normality, which made them sacred. Until the road was built during the late 1970s Mount Ida was not really within most people's reach; and even now the long winding drive is impressive, and intimidating in bad weather or the threat of it. The combination there of eagles and thunder can be more than one can comfortably experience.

Zeus was (as indeed the myth implies) not an indigenous Cretan god. He is an ancient Indo-European god, but probably came into Greece with the proto-Greeks, and to Crete with the Achaean invasion during the early part of the second millennium B.C. The archaeology of the two caves indicates that the cult in the Idean one was later than that on Dikte (which reached its climax at about 800 B.C.), and if this is correct then Ida is more likely to represent an original place of Zeus-worship, which was then perhaps transferred to the more ancient sacred cave as the new religion gradually took over from the old.

The Idean cave is spectacular mainly because of its position, high among the limestone crags of Ida, with the shadows of eagles veering by and vast clouds rolling past the slopes. By contrast with the one on Dikte it is comparatively tame inside: a large gaping grotto, more of an open mouth than that other uterine orifice.

From a distance it appears as a black gash on the huge bare flank which soars with astonishing eminence and magnificence above it. The size and height of the peak, most of the year streaked with clean snow, makes it in any but the gentlest weather a sort of looming emblem of natural power, inducing in a very real way the primitive emotion of fear.

TWELVE

HOMES OF THE GODS

AT SOME TIME during the coming into being of the particular style of thought which characterized the classical age, it seems that a literal, physical belief in the existence of the gods must have become impossible. By the time of Euripides this was clearly the state of affairs, and when he portrays the gods as appearing in person and entering into human affairs, he is, we feel, using an established artistic convention. Socrates was accused of not believing in the officially accepted deities, and significantly did not properly reply. From his works we may guess (though of course we see the matter mainly through the eyes of Plato) that he believed in some more abstract principle, which he could refer to as God.

It is equally certain, however, that at some less precisely identified time the Greeks in general did believe in the real physical existence, in idealized human form, of the personages of their pantheon. We know that when they did so they included the assumption that one does not nowadays see these figures; they no longer come among men and walk about Attica, although there was a time when they did. It is of that time that the tales tell, when gods fought amongst the troops before Troy, and appeared in aid of their mortal relatives in those episodes later to be presented by the dramatists and poets. It was of that time that we speak, they clearly felt, when we say that Apollo loved Delos, his birthplace, more than any spot on earth; or that Zeus holds court on Mount Olympus.

That last belief, however, may well have survived the abandoning of the sort of credulity which could lead one to expect actually to see, to meet, one of the deities. So few, if any, of the people of early times can ever have achieved that inhospitable summit. There was no real reason for doing so, it would be a great deal easier not to, and moreover the force of lingering superstition would have deterred even the sceptical. The tops of high, unapproachable mountains could well have sheltered the remnants of a belief in the visible identity of the gods. Similarly people at a quite late date believed that Pan lurked in wild and lonely places. There was simply no good evidence that he did not.

A different sort of belief must have accompanied the reverence of those many sanctuaries and sacred sites where, within the awe-inspiring inner cells of their ancient temples, the various deities graced with their presence their special shrines. No doubt it was possible, and necessary, to regard the presiding gods as being both real and never seen, in some way maintaining themselves invisible, and appearing by proxy in the form of their cult statues, which we know were greatly revered.

Although as mystic presences they may have been regarded as inhabiting the splendid houses built for them in their sanctuaries, as anthropomorphized characters the gods were viewed, in the mythology, as being gathered together in a highly regulated community on Mount Olympus itself. The tradition stems strongly from Homer, particularly from the *Odyssey*, where he implies at one point that although the physical mountain is meant it is at the same time changed: not that eternally snow-streaked, cloud-shrouded rocky height, but a version of it on which no snow or rain ever falls, where in a windless air a bright light shines over everything. It is nevertheless located where our physical equivalent of it is, so that one crosses Pieria when one comes down from it, as Hermes does on one occasion, and one descends to the inhabited zones from its high flanks, as Athena does when she sets off for Ithaca.

Homer too gives us the clearest picture of the sort of life the gods are imagined to have lived there. We find them as the *Odyssey* opens all gathered (except Poseidon, who is occupied elsewhere) at a sort of country-house weekend house party in Zeus' palace. It is something of a family gathering, of course, and the natural activity into which they fall is a sort of argumentative gossipy conversation.

Zeus is firmly presented as a father-figure, the father both of the gods and of mortal men; in its Latin form, in fact, his name, Jupiter, is equivalent to the combination Zeus-*pater*, meaning Father Zeus. He ruled over the small community on top of Olympus with a distinctly autocratic paternalism, and in fact his strictly wilful rule at times led to Olympus becoming a place to be avoided. We have seen how Demeter shunned Zeus' court there in protest at his behaviour, and other gods such as Pan preferred a more relaxed life in humbler places. In any case the strictly Olympian pantheon never included certain deities, such as the Furies, who were consigned to a cave under the Acropolis, or the gods of the underworld, Hades (though he was Zeus' brother) and his wife Persephone. Of the gods who lived at court there Zeus and Poseidon were the most important, and in the second rank came Apollo, Hephaestus, Hermes, Ares and Dionysus. To these seven male divinities tradition adds five goddesses, making a satisfactorily mystical dozen: Hera, Athena, Demeter, Artemis and Aphrodite.

It was appropriate, perhaps inevitable, that Zeus as sky and thunder god should site his palace on the highest point of land available to him, the summit, as it were, of Greece, the 9,571-foot limestone peak of Mount Olympus. It towers in a huge mound above Thessaly, in largely empty, rocky and wild-looking country near the coast, just inland of the road which crosses the alluvial plain between Thessalonika and Larissa. Olympus is so large that it is rather difficult to see, since one finds oneself always under its shoulders and obstructed by its foothills. From the sea, from far out in the gulf of Therme, it rears at dawn to a shimmering climax, supported from the shore upwards by rising buttresses of lesser mountains. But even from there it is much of the time an inferred presence behind the obscurity of clouds, the last stretches of it retreating tantalizingly out of reach of the experience of vision.

In order actually to get there, you start from the little mountain village of Litochoron, a few miles inland from the main road.

There the necessary guides and mules can be acquired for the long, but normally quite feasible, trip. It is a three-day outing, the last stages of which are partly reliant on the weather, involving overnight stays in two well-equipped mountain huts. The first phase is a deceptively gentle and wooded ride through rising country; the second takes you out on to an enormous plateau, increasingly exposed and weather-dominated, from which views of the distinctly intimidating chain of rocky summits ahead, with their soar of sheer cliff and their habit of looming briefly, disquietingly, from the rolling cloud, provide an impressive experience for some hours. The upper refuge hut is relatively close to the summit, and only on the last stretch along the main ridge to the throne of Zeus itself is there anything like serious mountaineering to be undertaken. There the weathered rocks, in the cold clear air, form the vast seats on which it was supposed that the gods gathered in council, around the bowl formed by the curve of the summit peaks.

No doubt this unpropitious place, with its trailing wisps of cloud and its immense proportions, perfectly suits the superhuman concepts surrounding the deities. It is always easier to believe in the supernatural on the top of a high mountain than elsewhere, the obstruction of human associations being necessarily withdrawn to a distance and, particularly, put into perspective. Pindar tells us that Apollo loved Parnassus, and it seems to us natural and appropriate that on those occasions when the elders of Israel actually heard and saw the God of the Old Testament it was on the heights of Mount Sinai, and when Moses was summoned into the divine presence he climbed out of sight into the summit cloud.

But although this soaring rockscape suits the idea of divinity in general, it suits the nature of Zeus best of all, the patriarchal, iron-willed, irascible character of that supreme god of the sky, of thunder and all high places. His special functions seems to have been with him from his origins, the name in Greek being traceable to the Sanskrit *Dyaus*, which appears in the Vedas as '*Dyaus pitar*', 'Father Dyaus', and which at the same time connotes a bright sky, giving to the Latin languages their word for daytime, *dies.* In its Olympian form Zeus' character was developed to express supreme power, the overlordship, the idea of a presiding ruler, which we cannot but associate with the palaces of the Achaeans, with their kings and territories. He is the High King of the gods, a sort of universal Agamemnon.

There is something massive and ominous about the very idea of Zeus; and this huge and heavy air of power hangs too over the tumbled ruins of his other principal home, the dark-stoned, sombre Doric temple of Olympia.

Olympia lies in the valley of the river Alpheus, in the softly rolling, wooded country of the north-west Peloponnese. It is a low-lying site, rather viewless and with a feeling of enclosure. The country round about is noticeably pretty, pleasant with cypress trees and little churches, like parts of Italy. The temple site itself, however, lies in a slightly mournful hollow, lacking both outlook and eminence. As a result it has the air of being a strangely docile, unemphatic place, with its pine trees and still air, a place which does not immediately suggest the worship of Zeus. The ruins themselves, of course, are quite another matter; their huge and splendid disarray now presents a battlefield of fallen columns, lying with all the immenseness of the work of giants, where old earthquakes have toppled them. The ominous mood of the grey stones, the lack of view and of brilliance in the light, give as complete a contrast as one could get to Apollo's shrine at Delphi.

The myth traces the origin of the site to the arrival in the area of Pelops, the son of Tantalus—both of them dynastic names which appear to have come from Asia Minor. Tantalus, it was said, lived in a time when the gods consorted freely with men, and the two races even feasted together. On one such occasion, when Zeus and other gods were dining at the table of Tantalus, the host proceeded to test the omniscience of the deities. The form this trick took is so strange that it cannot but be seen to reflect a memory of some primordial sacrifice: he cut up and cooked his son, Pelops. All the gods at once knew what had happened, and refused to eat. All, that is, except Demeter, who was at the time still distracted by the loss of her daughter; she ate from one of the shoulders, with the result that when Pelops was restored by Zeus to his original shape it was necessary to add a piece of ivory. Tantalus was punished for the crime by being eternally hungry and thirsty, fixed in the abyss of the underworld, with water which recedes from him when he stoops to it, and fruit which lifts away from him when he reaches up to it. In the process he has given us a verb, just as his son, expanding his rule over various kingdoms, gave us a place-name.

Pelops came to the territories of Elis and Pisa in search of a bride, and chose the daughter of the king of Elis, a lady called Hippodaemia, whose hand, however, could only be won by the suitor who could win a chariot race against her father. It seems that a part of the arrangement was that those who failed were killed, and needless to say the king, Oenomaus, was in the habit of winning. Pelops resorted to the rather unsporting gambit of tampering with Oenomaus' chariot, with the result that the wheels fell off; the king died, Pelops married the girl and gained with her her father's kingdom. With the experience of other such stories in mind, we cannot but see a dynastic expansion being achieved by marriage into a kingdom practising matrilinear succession.

The cult of Pelops, of which this story is the doctrine, seems to have been established at Olympia since the very beginning of the use for worship of that ancient and sacred place. He had his own temple within the sanctuary, which may even have preceded there the introduction of the worship of Zeus. It was, the tradition says, in memory of that first chariot race that the four-yearly games took place, from mythic times onwards. A horse-cult seems to lie at the root of this, since even the name of the legend-ary bride, Hippodaemia, suggests a definite connection with horses. It is clear, however, from the episode at the end of the *Iliad* in which the funeral of Patroclus is celebrated by means of games, including a chariot race, that the tradition may well have stemmed too from a funeral custom, an elaborate ceremony surrounding the burial of a hero. Why the games should have come to be held regularly every four years, if that is the case, is not quite clear, unless it was the custom also for the reigning king to be replaced at four-yearly intervals, the outgoing king suffering a symbolic death.

That is one way of viewing the arrival of Pelops. In any case it almost certainly reflects a change of hands due to invasion, since it is clear that the sacred site at Olympia did change hands at least once, giving us the superimposition of cults which the site clearly shows. Pausanias states that the shrine was originally sacred to Cronus, who, we have seen, was ousted in Greek religion by Zeus, so that the site must by then have been regarded as having been in sacred use even before the arrival of Pelops.

A further invader in the mythic sequence was the hero Heracles, who conquered Elis and took Olympia during his battle with Augeas, arising out of the latter's failure to keep his bargain after the labour involving the cleaning out of his cowsheds. Heracles, we are told, took part in the games (which in this version apparently already existed), and won the wrestling match, as one would expect. Pindar confuses the chronology slightly further by implying that Heracles founded the worship of Cronus there, which clashes with the otherwise convenient view of the coming of Pelops as being equivalent to the invasion of the Achaeans, and the arrival of Heracles as counterparting that of the Dorians. It can be said, though, that both historical and mythic tradition see more than one set of invasions of an anciently important site. Archaeologically we have evidence of occupation since the early part of the second millennium B.C.

Traditionally the first Olympics are put in the year 776 B.C. This gives us a sort of starting point for Greek history, since records of the winners were kept from then on. It was the games that made Olympia famous and of national importance to the Greeks of the ancient world. It gave them a sort of ethnic rallying point, a reinforcement of their sense of joint identity, in exactly the way the National Eisteddfod does for the Welsh today. The festival was preceded by a truce throughout Greek lands, so that all Greeks could travel to Olympia. Although by the classical period their colonies had spread over much of Europe and Asia Minor they possessed that crucial symptom of identity, a common language. There must therefore have been a strong feeling of belonging, and of the colonials' experience of homecoming, about these gatherings. We can read into Plutarch's later account of the games of 476 B.C. a sense, too, of being at the heart of great events. After the battle of Salamis, he tells us, Themistocles attended the games, and the presence of the saviour of Greece in the Olympic stadium distracted the crowd's attention, all day, from the competitive events.

It is clear, however, that the games, whatever their social and political importance, were never entirely secular. It was because Olympia was the home of Zeus that they possessed their special charisma. The grove and the area around it came to be thought of, in fact, as inhabited exclusively by gods. It is interesting that Olympia was not a town. No mortals lived there.

The site lay, and indeed lies, between two rivers. The Alpheus is much the more impressive of the two, the other being little more than a stream. Pausanias describes the Alpheus as having the greatest volume of water of any river, and in terms of Greek rivers at least he is probably not exaggerating. It is not surprising that it is a powerful and capacious torrent, since it forms the sum of many individually significant tributaries which between them drain the central mountain block of the Peloponnese. It carries to the coast the melting snow and upland rains of Arcadia. The grove in which the worship of Zeus became established (known as the Altis, from the Greek word for grove, *altos*) lies under a prominent hill, and formed a walled enclosure of fairly modest size, some 600 by 500 feet, in which lay the altar of Zeus, the shrine of Pelops and very little else. The stadium and hippodrome were outside the sacred precinct.

It is the hill under which the Altis lies, rather than the grove itself, which is primevally sacrosanct. Worshipping Zeus in a grove is thought to be a Dorian characteristic, and it was only during the later occupations that first his altar, then, a good deal later, his temple, arose there. The hill, however, is the hill of Cronus, and forms the place of worship of that ancient and rather savage god. Moreover it was around this rocky hill that various goddesses, perhaps more ancient still, were worshipped. And among them was the earth mother herself, Gaea, mother of Cronus and indeed, in Hesiod's tracing of their ancestry, of his father Uranus too. Gaea, the personified earth, who had existed almost from the beginning of all things.

She was worshipped, we know, on the side of this hill, her shrine being on a rock which juts out towards the Altis, on the hill's south-west side. There her oracle offered prophecies, taking the interesting form (in view of all the associations of earth-worship with the depths of the unconscious) of the interpretation of dreams.

It was the conquest by Elis of the territory of Pisa, in which Olympia lies, which marked the first great expansion of the constructed site. Before that Zeus had an altar in the sacred grove; after that he was to have a temple. This magnificent monument was one of the largest of its time, and seems to have taken some nine years to build. It was the work of a local architect, Libon of Elis, and was completed in the year 457 B.C., at the height, in fact, of the classical period. The great sculptor Pheidias arrived from Athens when he had finished his work on the Acropolis, to add to it a statue of Zeus worthy of the place's importance.

This, sadly, we can no longer see. Much of the other statuary survives, though in broken fragments, but the gold and ivory Zeus was perishable, and it perished in a fire in Constantinople in the fifth century A.D. Fortunately we have at least a complete description, since Pausanias meticulously catalogued everything he saw at Olympia towards the end of the second century. It stood more than thirty feet high, and showed Zeus with his emblems of staff and eagle, sitting on a jewelled throne. The god was pleased, and indicated this to Pheidias by a flash of lightning. For many centuries the statue continued to inspire in those who came to see it a feeling of religious awe, recorded for us by various witnesses of the later period. It seems to have symptomized, or perhaps even to have helped to bring about, a movement in religious feeling towards monotheism. It showed a Zeus who would allow power to no other gods. At the same time, however, religious belief began to ebb, so that some who viewed it in later periods were concerned only to criticize it for its great size. Strabo, for instance, memorably pointed out that it could not stand up without going through the roof.

Pheidias set up a workshop for the long task of this major work, just outside the Altis and evidently as close as possible to the temple where he was constructing the statue; excavation of the site of it revealed not only some of the moulds used for the metal parts of Zeus, but a drinking cup which, from the inscription on it, must have belonged to Pheidias himself.

The temple of Zeus which housed the statue was a late addition to the enclosed sanctuary, and there was at least one early building there before it. The temple of Hera was built below the Gaeon (the earth mother's ancient shrine on the rock) sometime probably late in the seventh century. It seems to perpetuate the idea of goddess-worship, and so to mark Olympia's most anciently holy spot. The ruins of it, showing its outline clearly and the bases of many pillars, lie to the left as one enters the Altis, under the protruding buttress of the hill. This Doric temple of the early classical period was in fact the third to be built on this site. Two complete pillars, and some with new additions, have been reconstructed, of the forty-four which surrounded it originally. In Pausanias' time it housed many works of art, and it was here that the 'Hermes of Praxiteles' was, both when he saw it and when it was found in 1877—a fortunate, and rare, case of a statue not being removed to the home of later conquerors. The resurrected pillars seem to us, by comparison with later works, rather ungainly, implying a certain squatness in the building. They apparently replaced, when necessary, earlier wooden ones, and so were put up one by one without over-all consistency. But their design seems to indicate that a lot was learnt from then on in the realm of architectural technique.

The temple of Zeus itself was evidently a masterpiece of that later style, though still in the rather plain Doric form. Going from the Hera temple further into the Altis, towards it, one passes, midway between them, the site of the shrine to Pelops. The unmistakable grandeur of the sad ruins of Zeus' temple rise ahead, over the flat and tree-dotted ground of his sacred grove.

We have to try to imagine a solid sturdy building, its stone

stuccoed to give a smooth finish, its main features picked out in
blue and red, with gilded details. Nothing could really seem
further from the tumbled segments hugely scattered now around
these bare foundations, the coarse-grained local conglomerate
stone absorbing the light, the whole area having more the look of
defeated might than the memory of its living glory. Even on
returning after seeing the pediment statuary in the museum one
can only with difficulty envisage the splendour which this view
must once have had.

What still impresses us is its undoubted size. Walking round the
floors of it one can grasp, too, its ingenious complexity; rooms
within rooms within arcades protected the god's sacredness. The
great statue stood to one end of the inner cell, facing east. An
upper gallery allowed a closer look at the heights of this highly
ornamented work. It evidently became a considerable tourist
attraction, Olympia's centrepiece.

Outside the Altis undoubtedly the most conspicuous feature is
the reconstructed stadium, the longest such track in Greece, said
in one version to have been paced out by Heracles himself when
he instituted the games. It lies below the hill of Cronus, which
must have provided a grandstand view. One looks down now
from this direction from the modern road, which flanks the hill
and thus separates its upper slopes from the ruins below. The
stadium which has been restored is that of the late classical period,
only one of the long succession of stadiums which occupied more
or less the same area. The result, with replicas of the embankments
of that time, gives a fair impression of the site of the important
contests, looking a little empty now, as stadiums always do when
not in use. Entering it by the arched passageway from the Altis
one inevitably gets a trace of the feeling of excitement always
given by entry to a wide public area, the feeling of coming on
stage.

It was an earthquake of the sixth century A.D. which finally
toppled the great temples of Olympia. The site was then completely obliterated by the alteration, during the Middle Ages, of
the course of the river Alpheus, which covered the whole area
with a thick layer of silt, presenting a level surface on which the

first excavators could only guess at the whereabouts of the ruins. Some evidence was washed away by the river, such as the Hippodrome, which is no longer traceable; other important finds, however, had been preserved by the covering of sand and clay. As a result the museum is now full of remarkable treasures, covering a wide range of styles and periods, making it one of the richest and most important collections of Greek art.

Foremost among the museum items are the statues from the pediments on the two ends, the front and the back, of the temple of Zeus. Those from the east pediment, which was the entrance and the most important aspect of the building, depict the occasion of the great chariot race between Pelops and Oenomaus, over which, an upright figure on a larger scale, Zeus himself presides. Reclining figures in the two corners represent the gods of the two rivers between which Olympia lies. The contesting heroes stand either side of Zeus, their horses ready near by. The tableau has the stillness of tension and expectancy about it, even in its present crumbled form. By contrast that on the back of the building was all movement, a scene of great violence, depicting the occasion mentioned above: the wedding of Perithous, king of the Lapiths, to which he invited both the Athenian leader Theseus and the centaurs, who were related to his family. The centaurs became drunk and abducted the bride and other Lapith women, and we see here (and in a similar scene from the Parthenon, now in the British Museum) the battle between the humans and the hybrid horses which resulted. The proper ordering of this group has long been disputed, but it seems most probably correct that the two heroes, Perithous and Theseus, should be fighting back to back on either side of the central god. This latter figure was said by Pausanias to be the king, Perithous himself, but its central position and greater size, together with that characteristically godlike stance of cool command, make it seem certain that Pausanias was inexplicably mistaken. If it is a god, it is agreed, it is Apollo. It is a remarkably impressive figure and, like several of the better-preserved specimens of the pediment, represents a masterly co-ordination of style and subject.

We are particularly lucky also to be able to see as much as we can of the scenes carved in marble relief on the metopes, the panels punctuating the temple's Doric frieze. Some of these are whole enough to be graphically clear, and still convey the excitement of their narrative form. They represent the twelve labours of Heracles, the best of them perhaps being that in which (helped by Athena) he holds up the burden of the sky for Atlas, while the latter is fetching for him the golden apples of the Hesperides. There is another moment of excitement preserved for us, in which the hero is shown by Athena the spot at which to breach the walls of Augeas' cowsheds with his crowbar. Through all these tense little encounters he is shown as sturdily, likeably, human and she as unchangingly serene.

Though both the pediments and the metopes are by unknown artists, it seems clear that they were done by two different people, and also that each was the work of one of the great innovatory geniuses of any period of sculpture. They have a vigour and immediacy about them which owes nothing to convention or fashionable style. They communicate directly to us from some quite exceptional imagination. That two such men should have been available at Olympia during the fifth century is remarkable, and indicative of the sort of surge of inspiration which lay behind the building of the temple.

There are numerous other works of interest in that remarkable collection, many of them early and strangely primitive, like the early-sixth-century head of Hera; and some, such as the famous 'Hermes of Praxiteles', masterly in quite a different way. This justly famous work of art succeeds in combining a balance of physical form which Michelangelo would have envied with a virtuoso finish of almost audacious perfection. The thoughtful face with its classically perfect features sets a tone for the later realization of the calmness, the restfulness inherent in marble. The pose, between stillness and motion, counterpoints the athleticism of the form with the indolence of the moment in which it is fixed. Of course the statue is late-classical in concept, and lacks the austerity or simplicity of earlier works. In its naturalism it borders on being showy, and no doubt by contrast with the strength and purity of the archaic and early-classical sculptures with which it shares the Olympia museum it could easily seem unpleasantly sentimental. But none of these qualifications detracts from the sculptor's mastery of a certain form.

Praxiteles was an Athenian of the fourth century B.C., whose work we know only through copies. This was for some time thought to be his only surviving original, but doubt must now be cast even on that. It is indeed hard to believe that such a skilful piece of art is the work of a copyist, rather than the result of the original conception of the creating artist; and the matter is still not agreed. Peter Levi, in his characteristically erudite and civilized notes to his translation of Pausanias, accepts the 'sad but important truth' that it is a later copy. To argue that this should not matter would be to overlook the importance of the personal element in artistic communication. It would be sad as well as important if we are not in fact receiving directly the effect created in the marble by the man who was inspired with the idea, in the first quarter of the fourth century B.C.

Olympia's decline is really the decline of paganism, which coincided with the weakening of Roman rule to the extent of allowing such forces as Alaric and his Visigoths to overrun Greece. The great statue of Zeus had been removed to Constantinople towards the end of the fourth century A.D., and hence escaped for a few years the wave of destruction which flowed across Greek lands. The temple itself was burnt during the Christian eradication of pagan worship, under the fifth-century emperor Theodosius II, and the statue suffered a similar fate in its new home in an accidental fire which devastated the eastern capital in 462. Earthquakes in the next century completed the process of wiping Olympia from the world, crashing the pillars to their present fallen state, and changing the courses of both the rivers.

Considering that Greece is a country still subject to earthquakes it is perhaps remarkable that any of the buildings of antiquity have remained upright for so long. Several temples have, however, been more fortunate than that of Zeus. Perhaps it is not surprising that his brother and rival Poseidon, lord of the earth-quake, spared so much of his own home shrine, on the promontory of Sounion.

Sounion owes to the good fortune of having many columns standing much of its great, and justified, fame. But probably its special place in the affection of so many people arises from the qualities peculiar to itself, many of which it owes in turn to its connection with its owner, the god of the sea.

Poseidon held, in Greek religion, a position parallel and of comparable status to that of Zeus. In the myth he had the same parents as Zeus—Cronus and Rhea—and it seems from one account at least that he was regarded as the older brother. Rhea hid him, as she was later to hide Zeus, from her child-devouring husband, whom she told that she had given birth to a horse, giving him a foal to swallow instead. Perhaps the implication of his seniority reflects the fact that Poseidon was a very ancient deity indeed, existing before Zeus in Greece and indeed elsewhere, He may have been, in fact, a lord of the earth in his own right, later moved by Zeus into second place.

The story tells that on the deposition of Cronus his three sons, Zeus, Poseidon and Hades, divided between them the material universe. The lots they drew awarded Zeus the sky, Poseidon the sea and Hades the world under the earth's surface; the land they continued to share in common. Along with the sea Poseidon ruled over watercourses in general, springs, streams, rivers and lakes.

In that capacity he was regarded as being responsible for droughts and floods. But irrigation has never been the pressing problem in Greece that it is in the Middle East, whereas to this country with the longest coastline in Europe, where communities are settled on remote promontories and scattered disorderedly through widespread archipelagos, where land communications are obstructed by distance and terrain, and a living is often hard to get from the earth's rocky terraces, the sea always has been, is, and must always be, of supreme importance.

It is a theme we find in writers from Homer to Thucydides, and a fact of which one cannot help being made aware in any effort to move around in that demanding country. The sea is a constant background to the way of life, making itself felt and occurring in one's movements and one's incidental experiences, the background to many evenings being the chug-chugging of small boats thumping their way bravely through the heavy seas round the headlands, in the turbulence of the land-encumbered water outside the coves and harbours, water hardly ever still. They are, as much as the mules on the hillsides, the land's lifelines, holding together precarious social units. Greece is, in a very practical sense, its sea. Without mastery of the sea, without making it collaborate, it could not hold together as a country. There is good reason to think of Poseidon, then, as being in many ways more important than Zeus.

Poseidon is shown as being from time to time in competition with the other deities, as for instance when he debated the rule of Attica with Athena, a contest which also bears the male–female domination theme. On that occasion he lost, being able only to produce on the Acropolis a salt-water spring, which the judging gods rightly considered to be of less use than the olive tree provided by Athena. Attica and Athens settled for a land-based economy. But Poseidon was a dangerous power to thwart, and in revenge he flooded the Thriasian plain, the flat land around Elevsis. In another competition story (of which there are several) he tried to claim the rule of the Corinth isthmus from the sun god Helios, the dispute in that case being settled by their sharing it between them. No doubt these themes reflect the long experience which coast-dwellers have of the perpetual hunger which the sea shows for the land.

Poseidon was regarded as living in a deep-sea palace out in the Aegean. He appeared in the midst of storms, riding a smooth path across the waves in a gold chariot drawn by brass-hoofed, golden-maned horses. Homer depicts such a scene in the *Iliad*, when the lord of the sea makes his way to join the Greeks battling below Troy. The sea monsters rose from the depths, to play around his chariot, and the sea itself made way for his passage. Sea storms were the symptoms of his anger, and he was an easily angered god. Odysseus found him, as we shall see, a hard enemy.

Like his brother Zeus, Poseidon was notably maritally unfaithful. His wife Amphitrite seems to have suffered more placidly than Hera these many illicit affairs. On one of these occasions he courted his sister Demeter, who, however, was pining for her lost daughter (as usual) and so unwilling to accept his attentions. She changed herself into a mare to avoid him, and grazed among a herd; but this did nothing to deter Poseidon, to whom the horse was in any case sacred. He changed himself into a stallion, and they mated. If Demeter is to be regarded as a variant of the ancient European horse goddess, then Poseidon must be her male equivalent. In some versions of his story he is said to have created the horse, a reference perhaps to the fact that horses were at one time unknown in Greece, being introduced from the Middle East sometime after the beginning of the Bronze Age, in about 2000 B.C. We know that the Mycenaeans learnt then to use a small breed of horse for drawing chariots, but the common use of horses in their period, and therefore presumably the ultimate source of any horse-cult, belonged to the more northerly areas of Europe.

It is interesting in this connection that Nestor, king of Pylos, is always represented by Homer as a great charioteer. During the funeral games with which the *Iliad* draws to a close he gives such detailed and authentic instructions to his son on how to drive in the chariot race that one cannot believe that Homer too was not an experienced chariot-driver. Curiously the tradition is closely paralleled by archaeological discovery, since the Mycenaean tablets record large numbers of chariots kept at the palaces, and although the records of the chariots at Pylos itself have not yet been found, their existence can be inferred from the cataloguing of a large number of wheels. In this connection Poseidon recurs, as horse god and charioteer, since Homer shows Nestor of Pylos sacrificing to Poseidon, seemingly as his patron, at the palace shrine.

'Lord Poseidon, Girdler of the Earth . . .' There is, in connection with him, always a note of mastery, of the command of force. A bronze statue of the mid-fifth century B.C. in the National Museum in Athens is thought by some to be not Poseidon but his brother Zeus; but it shows a noble and commanding figure, and it is symptomatic of the conviction and belief which the Greek gods inspire that one wants to say (as I have heard people say in front of it) that it looks like Poseidon. By now, one feels, one knows quite well what Poseidon looks like. The clear gaze, the wilful gesture; he is not somebody to argue with—and although the brothers had that attribute in common, this figure does not possess the aloof majesty we associate with Zeus, but rather a sort of impetuosity. The statue, with its masterful combination of poise and momentum, is one of the most powerful in the museum.

Sounion often does justice to its god. The sea below the cliff sucks and heaves, in any but the gentlest weather, with the threatening mutter of unstable forces. The gleaming white temple stands a little arrogantly on its headland. It fits the place so well that one feels that it must always have been there, and this Doric rebuilding of the Periclean period indeed replaced an earlier version which was burnt by the Persians in 480 B.C. Of its original thirty-four columns, nine on one side, six on the other, and one, along with two pillars, in the middle now stand; several of these, however, have been re-erected in modern times. The specially bright appearance of the stones owes something to the strength of the light, as well as the cleanness of the air; in fact the columns are of a local greyish marble. Their special elegance, which makes them seem more than usually tall and stately, may be due to the fact that they are shaped into only sixteen, rather than the usual twenty, flutes. There is also an unusual simplicity and lack of decorated detail about the frieze, though the pediments, which no longer exist, bore sculptures. An inscription was discovered which confirms the dedication to Poseidon.

One comes to the temple through the rather tame countryside of Attica, the peninsula as a whole now much affected by the long string of concrete resorts which trail southwards from Athens. But the temple of Poseidon at Sounion stands on a promontory of its own, in a sort of extension of the land beyond its normal limits, at the end of a headland itself at the end of the peninsula. It looks out over the sea in almost all directions, dominating the bare, rather featureless landscape, with cliffs round its base giving an unbroken view down to the clear water. As the boats come past it, turning the corner from one section of the sea to another, it has the air, distinctly, of overseeing their domain.

Inevitably one comes and goes past it oneself from time to time, down there, the journey to and from many islands involving the turning of that corner into the open sea, or back to the last leg home. From the sea the clear white of these eighteen standing pillars shows up as a landmark, a sign that you have reached a critical point of the journey. It gleams very brightly in the sun, against the burnt land, tall and succinct. There is never any doubt as to what it is, or what it means. It is as much concerned with seagoing as a lighthouse.

There is nothing mortal or human about either Poseidon or Sounion. As a pair they embody a potent and permanent abstraction, an enduring recognition of the transcendent power in elemental forces. Matters as basic but rather more particular are dealt with too, one feels, across the water on the eastern coast of the Peloponnese, where a cult concerned with human welfare and survival flourished for many centuries in a gladed, rounded landscape which forms a notable contrast to Sounion's uncompromising exposure.

The grove of Epidavros, far out at the edge of Argolis, was a place associated with healing and cure for nearly a thousand years. Of course it is best known now (and more often in its latinized form, Epidaurus) for its theatre and its festivals of drama. In Greek the second syllable is stressed, a long *ee* sound, the *d* is soft, almost a *th*, and of course the *u* has no place, being properly a *v*, as in Elevsis.

The original settlement there was some distance from the sanctuary, at what is now called Old Epidavros, a small town on the coast. To its harbour the boats come, taking trips to the festival or sightseers to the famous theatre. The walls which formed, at this point, a fortified promontory, can still be seen south of the present town.

That Asclepius' shrine came into being some way away from the settlement must mean that its site had some ancient reason for being sacred. It is thought that his cult in fact came from Thessaly, and became located in Epidavros from the late sixth century onwards. Clearly a cult was there before that, and this is identified as being connected with a version of Apollo, himself a healer god, and in the myth the father of Asclepius. There is evidence for the early Bronze Age use of the site.

The buildings which may be looked at now belong largely to the late fifth century B.C. Expansion of the cult was promoted by the increased interest of Athens from about 420. Since this occurs in the period after the arrival in Athens of the plague which had ravaged Greece during the Peloponnesian War, that disaster may well explain this new attention to the cult of a healer god. Expansion continued during the fourth and third centuries, when the large guest houses built for pilgrims indicate a spreading fame and an increase in the movement of people which no doubt itself arose from improved communications.

It was during the main period of building of the third century B.C. that the great theatre was constructed, still today one of the most effective and attractive theatres in Greece, and presumably the best open-air theatre in Europe. It has been famous from early times for its particularly beautiful acoustics, and if one adds to that remarkable technical quality the fact that it seats 14,000 people, then its fame is not the least surprising. The approach to it through the pine trees gives one infallibly a sense of occasion, of expectancy.

Set in a natural bowl of hillside, facing on to a secluded valley, enclosed by soft slopes, pine trees gently circling it as if in protection: everything about it is both relaxing and mentally clarifying. The whole effect is one of concentration of attention, of complete dedication to a focal point. The sight of it around one is unfailingly amazing, as one sits in those carved seats, not only for the size of the thing but for the almost perfect state of preservation, after some two thousand years; but most of all one cannot help being impressed by those exceptional acoustics, which never fail to live up to their great fame. The casual conversation of people

on the far side of the auditorium, so far distant across this great
bowl as to be apparently not present—their physical person
across so many ranks of seats diminished by distance to insigni-
ficance—is clearly audible. It is as if all the possible elements—
sound, form, surroundings—were combined to advance the
purposes of theatre.

No doubt the theatre came into being as a result of the success
of earlier, simpler performances, themselves a developed form of
the rituals originally accompanying the worship of the god. In
open-air Greek theatres one always has a sense of their probable
ancestry, the dances on the threshing floor on the hillside after
a harvest ceremony, the depiction there (as a convenient public
place) of the story linking the god to the occasion. The intensi-
fying effect of the structure—audience on the slopes round a
circular stage—would magnify the issues being dealt with. One
feels, for instance, how this effect must have developed on that
more primitive threshing floor, the theatre of Dionysus under the
Acropolis, where many of the great plays came into being. At
Epidavros it is clear that only the largest ideas and concerns
could remain undaunted by the size of the surroundings. Its size
too, as anyone who has attended the festivals must know, gives
to these matters the added reinforcement of the attention of so
many people. Significance is underlined by the response of so
large a crowd, as when for instance 14,000 people react together
with a gasp at the monstrous lie with which Clytemnestra greets
her returning husband, or with a laugh at Agamemnon's sarcastic
reply. In the perfect auditory conditions such massive spontaneous
sounds come like the reactions of a single creature.

The festival which takes place there every year now is the
remote descendant of a four-yearly festival, the Asclepia, which
became, although not in the first rank like Olympia and Corinth,
one of the great festivals of classical Greece. It involved, like the
others, games and artistic contests, and it was the latter which led
to the development of its wonderful theatre. But primarily
Asclepius at Epidavros was always concerned with the cure of
sickness, and it was the ill and disabled who flocked to the
sanctuary.

Sounion: Temple of Poseidon

Fishing boats

Buying fish

Gournia

Agia Triada

Originally the cure of illnesses was mystically effected, with rites and sacrifices, purifying immersions, and rituals involving Asclepius' sacred animal, the snake. Later cures came to be undertaken by more physical means, by the use of medicines and diet, so that in effect the god of Epidavros is the ancestor of the medical profession. The element of faith healing, however, continued, and belief in the powers of the shrine lasted well into Christian times. The site had been plundered, like all others, by Alaric in 395, but it did not go out of use until the edict of Theodosius II banned all pagan cults in A.D. 426. Later earthquakes then, as elsewhere, obscured the ruins, which were not discovered again until the 1880s.

Only the foundations of the buildings now remain, on the site. Many of the carved capitals and friezes, pillars, ceilings and paved floors, are in the small museum (which is, as a result, a miniature treasure house of finely worked stone) and other statuary is in the National Museum in Athens, including the fine relief of the demigod himself, movingly portrayed as a benevolent sage. To understand the ruins of the site one should in this case visit the museum first. They cannot be appreciated on their own.

The modern entrance to the site involves, unfortunately, arriving in it from the back, passing the guest house and gymnasium on the way towards the sanctuary itself. The original main gate, the Propylaea, is at the far north of the site, the side furthest away from the museum. The ruins are all low and uninspiring, but with an effort of imagination one can replace the highly elaborate decoration of the capitals and friezes on the bare base of the most important building, the temple of Asclepius. This was a small but ornate construction of the early fourth century B.C., which housed in its inner cell the cult statue of the god. He was shown accompanied by his sacred snake and, also an animal sacred to him, a dog. The altar, as is normal, was outside the temple, a little to its north-east. An older building, evidently replaced by this one, can be seen near by, and probably was the temple of Apollo, whose cult preceded that of Asclepius and at a later stage fostered it as an offshoot. Many Roman ruins fill the area of the sanctuary and its surrounds.

H

Undoubtedly the feature of most interest, because so unusual and puzzling, is the building known as the Tholos, a name deriving purely from its circular shape. Built slightly later than the temple, it seems to have been equally prominent and important, and is also, like the temple, remarkably small. From the museum exhibits we can see that this too was highly decorated. An outer circle of twenty-six Doric columns enclosed an inner one of fourteen very beautiful Corinthian ones. An inscription was found which records that this remarkable building was designed by the architect who built the theatre itself, Polycleitos, perhaps a man of Argos.

Its use (like the use of the rotunda at Delphi) has for many ages been a mystery. The most convincing explanation is that it was a symbolic tomb, in this case the place of the worship of Asclepius as a mortal hero, his supposed burial spot. The only part of it we can see now is its foundations, and this suggestion draws some confirmation from the fact that these are revealed to be in the form of an underground labyrinth, a curious circling and redoubling maze which may well, like the more common form of the double spiral, be a representation of the idea of death and rebirth. Small

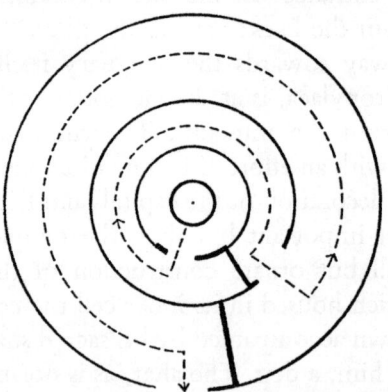

walls block the passageways which curve round it, forcing a roundabout route through the doorways in its curves. If this is rebirth, it is not easy. Such a thought, however, is very relevant to the myth of Asclepius.

Asclepius was the son of Apollo by a princess called Coronis, whose name would suggest a word for crow even it if were not for the fact that the myth shows her as being accompanied by that bird. In the story the crow reports to Apollo her infidelity with a mortal, whereupon he has her and her new husband put to death, but at the last moment snatches from her funeral pyre her unborn child. After this startlingly violent beginning the demigod Asclepius entered a life of gentleness and peace, which he began under the tutelage of the centaur Cheiron in his cave on Mount Pelion. It was Cheiron who taught him there the art of healing.

Asclepius' life was not, however, destined to be entirely without trouble. And in fact his story seems to reflect an ineradicable Greek belief in the inevitability of a tragic outcome. The healer had in the course of his career restored a number of dead men to life. This denial of the rules of nature began to anger Hades, who was being robbed of citizens due for his underworld kingdom. He complained to Zeus, and the accusation was not just that Asclepius had healed the dead but, tellingly, that he had done so for money. Perhaps a reference is made by the myth to the fact that patients at the sanctuary were always made to pay, sometimes large amounts. Zeus heard his brother's complaint, and struck Asclepius himself dead with his omnipotent thunderbolt. Pindar tells the story in his third Pythian Ode, one of the most consistent examples of sustained control of powerful feeling he achieved. Its theme is the need to come to terms with our condition.

Death preoccupied the ancient Greeks, and indeed fascinates the people of Greece still. With their open coffins and their lavish funerals they parade their obsession, in raw hilltop villages and down the streets of great cities. A sudden fatality never fails to draw a crowd; and anyone who has heard the wail of island women confronted with its occurrence will never forget either the sound or its implicit message. The feeling which it expresses so formidably is like that of the howl of a dog: a shriek both of pain and of protest, the wail of a bewildered animal.

That, I suppose, is the theme of the myth of Asclepius. The one prerogative most jealously guarded by the gods, most envied by men, is that of immortality. Consciousness itself we have poached from them, as in those myths which depict (like the one in which Prometheus steals fire from heaven and is eternally punished) a fall from grace, grace being equivalent to innocence, a fall from the Adam-and-Eve state in which one had no worries, which we have all, in effect, known, up to the age of six. After the first sin which occurs with the knowledge of what sin means, the human being is saddled for ever with moral responsibility. But that theft and its punishment are recognized as being now irrevocable. What they will not permit is that we should take the fruit of the tree of life, in the words of Genesis, 'and eat, and live for ever.'

THIRTEEN

ODYSSEUS AT SEA

WHEN HE CLIMBED ashore at last on his own island, forewarned, foredoomed, now heavily loaded with the wisdom of experience, he found himself confronted by the goddess Athena. She stood before him now in human form, and in reply to his telling her an entirely fictitious story delivered herself of what sounds like a heartfelt opinion. In it we can perhaps hear the note of that special sort of affection which does not rely on respect. 'Still lying,' she said, 'still playing tricks, arch-deceiver. Clever enough to take precautions, even now, instead of rushing home. How like you it is to be so cautious, lover of deceit and intrigue.' But she could not desert him now, she said, after all they had been through.

This speech by the goddess seems to summarize a curious aspect of the fascination which surrounds the character of Odysseus. One loves him in spite of his faults, with the sort of ambivalence which is always a trouble to the conscience. One knows that one should not admire him, yet an attitude very similar to admiration creeps in. Homer has used the subtlety of a double standard of values to keep us continually interested in the doings of this early anti-hero, and from time to time, as we forget to disapprove, we seem to catch the story-teller smiling at our predicament.

The figure of the trickster is a common one in myth and folk-tale, in cultures as wide apart as those of Africa and America, to be found both in the tales of Sioux Indians and South African bushmen, as well as being exemplified in Teutonic myth in the figure of the god Loki. The theme of the voyage of search too occurs in many mythologies, and for instance in Irish myth we find a hero visiting a long series of islands which have various supernatural qualities. The *Odyssey* starts with the advantage of combining these two promising subjects, and is able in the process of reworking them to include many other favourite folk themes and popular stories.

There is of course no record of Greek myth before Homer, but we cannot believe that Odysseus has not in some way or other always existed. It was Homer's achievement to give him such a fully rounded, credible form that he has remained thereafter an identified figure. Although there is a seemingly imposed attempt to give him a genealogy and to link him to the main body of Greek myth, he still stands very much on his own, with his own independent career which, in tone and subject matter, is quite unlike those of the other heroes. Before and during the Trojan War he is shown as being slightly apart, slightly different; it is only then, when on his return journey he gets blown off course and out of the normal world of heroes and quasi-history, that he takes on him all the accumulated adventures of the timeless wandering hero.

What Homer attributed to Odysseus was in fact a sort of anthology of folk-tale episodes, drawn from the wide range of sources influencing the eastern Mediterranean of his time. At the risk of entering a disputed area it might be said that he made of these basic folk elements something which is no longer folk-tale but myth. That is to say, in the *Odyssey* we are not just being entertained. We are at the same time undergoing a form of treatment for various diseases of the imagination.

Odysseus as first described in the *Iliad* shows only the potential for becoming the vehicle for such work. He is sketched in some detail, much of which is of retrospective interest. We find, for instance, that Homer viewed him as a short man: Menelaus towered above him when they were both standing, but he looked the more impressive of the two when they were seated. Perhaps this touch of characterization is a forewarning of the sort of thing Homer has in store for him. Not the life of a hero, but the energetic, complicated, wilful, uphill life of a man small in stature. We see him, early in the *Iliad*, showing a liking for the intricacies of politics. He is not easily daunted or impressed; he tells Agamemnon at one point that he is talking nonsense, and receives an immediate apology, instead of a rebuke, from the commander-in-chief and High King of the Achaeans, a response which has about it both a note of affection and a note of fear. His reputation among the troops is made clear from the start, as is the story-teller's own ambivalent attitude towards him. Both parties call him by names which straddle the boundary of praise and censure: resourceful, wily, arch-deceiver, Odysseus of the nimble wits. Achilles, contrastingly portrayed as straightforward and conventionally heroic, perhaps expresses one of the views we are expected to take when he says in reply to Odysseus that he hates like the gates of hell the sort of man who says one thing and means another.

To underline his status as a rascal (which, we shall see, evolves in the course of his misfortunes into the more sympathetic quality of survival by cunning) Homer gives Odysseus a murkily sinister background. His mother was the daughter of the bandit and cattle-rustler Autolycus, who in his turn was the son of Hermes, one of whose attributes (due to the theft with which he started his life) was the patronage of thieves. Later sources added even less respectable details to his story, such as the feigning of madness as an attempt to evade the recruiting for the Trojan War. The classical playwrights treated him unfavourably, Sophocles using him as an emblem of duplicity and Euripides, in *Hecuba*, showing through him the cruelty and hypocrisy of war. Perhaps it is no coincidence that the round pointed hat which he is always shown as wearing, which became in fact the mark by which he can be recognized, has come, via the pranks of the harlequinade, to be the clown's hat of today.

It was this sort of disrespect which became dominant, in the end, in times when more respectable qualities commanded a premium. But Homer achieves a remarkable tension, almost throughout, between sympathy and disapproval. This lovable rogue too has his remote descendants, in the picaresque heroes of the early novels and their multitudinous anti-heroic progeny.

The *Odyssey* is a curious book, being at the same time highly sophisticated and subtle in form and yet very accessible and apparently straightforward. One peers at the dovetail joints and the smooth inlaying in puzzlement, trying to see how Homer has done it. It sits there almost smugly, in its undisputed and unchallengeable central niche in literature, secure in the certainty that it will never be demoted from its high status in the literature of the whole world and of all time. It is as eternal as the seasons, and always as new; however well one knows it it retains the power to thrill and surprise, rather in the way that it is impossible, in a seasonal climate, not to be impressed by the feeling of the world rolling slowly into a different relationship with the sun.

When we begin, with the scene of the council of the gods on Olympus, the hero (who does not appear in person until a quarter of the way through the work) is languishing in the hospitable arms of the goddess Calypso. The gods are concerned about his delayed homecoming and the trouble it is causing on his island, and Athena sets off to stir his son Telemachus to take action to find his father. Telemachus at once does this, visiting those who have successfully returned, first Nestor at Pylos, then Menelaus at Sparta.

This prolonged introductory section has the effect of setting the later adventures in a credible world, referring as it does to historically real places. The comparatively recent discovery of the Mycenaean palace at Pylos, for instance, might well make us think that Homer possessed a fairly detailed tradition of what life there was like, in spite of the fact that by his time the site had already disappeared. We now know too that it was far from fanciful to view the small and otherwise inconspicuous island of Ithaca as the seat of an early kingdom, no doubt controlling territory on the near-by coastline of the western Peloponnese.

It seems that the situation Homer is depicting, the trouble arising from Odysseus' prolonged absence, is connected with the question of the inheritance of that kingdom, which it is assumed will pass to whoever marries the supposedly widowed queen. That is clearly why Telemachus finds himself in competition with a large number of suitors, who were, as he tells Menelaus, treating his family's possessions as if they were their own. The discovery of many signs of Bronze Age habitation in the area of Stavros, in the north of the island of Ithaca, gives the archaeologists at least sufficient reason to go on looking for the more important buildings of this traditional kingdom. It is possible too to identify, admittedly speculatively, several other features of the island as described by Homer. And a number of finds in a cave on the coast not far from Stavros show it to have been in use as a shrine from Bronze Age days until the end of the classical period, and remarkably included a fragment with an inscribed dedication to Odysseus himself, evidence at least that the Homeric Ithaca was identified with this Ithaca, this steep-sloped, mounded little island lying among broader neighbours in the mid-Ionian sea.

It is not hard to get to Ithaca—the boats leave Patras three times a week—and can never have been so, coming out of the Gulf of Corinth or up along the headlands of the Peloponnese. But the Ithaca of the *Odyssey* lies, like Grail Castle, in a place not easily found. Grail Castle does not move, as one of the medieval tales puts it, but rather it is bewitched in such a way that it can only be found by chance. One may know quite well where such things are, know the way to them even, yet not be able to get there when one wants to. It is characteristic of Homer that he should have chosen such a definite spot on the Greek map, a factual and identifiable place, as a goal for his hero's roundabout quest.

When at last we join Odysseus we find him homesick, pining on Calypso's shore. We meet him in fact towards the chronological end of his adventures, and have yet to retrace his progress to reach that point. Calypso accepts that he will not be happy until he reaches his home, and his mortal but much-loved wife, and with some nobility she sadly lets him go. Another shipwreck during another storm throws him naked on the shores of Phaeacia. There he is befriended by the princess and the king, and in the course of banqueting at that hospitable court he reveals his identity and then tells his story. The coil of the tale unfolds, to reach again that point, and then starts to tighten again towards Ithaca.

Leaving Troy Odysseus set off into the Aegean, on the voyage across to Greece which should have taken several days. He paused in Thrace, where he sacked a city, and a little later reached Cape Malea and the island of Kythira, at the very tip of the southern Peloponnese. This was a point at which he might have felt considerable relief, rounding the corner on the last leg home, back into his home water, the Ionian Sea. Just at that difficult turning, where the swell and the current combine with the wind to make one's course uncertain, a storm closed in on his small fleet and swept him off the map. He drifted uncontrollably for nine days, and drifted into a different world.

It is clear that at this point Homer moves (though imperceptibly) into another convention. Keeping his habitual painstaking naturalism, he now however deals with a type of space not found in the geographical Aegean but in the imagination. Though this seems clear, it has not prevented people from trying to trace the continuing course of Odysseus' ships—locating the lotus-eaters on the north African coast, and so on. The voyage now proceeds, however, with no directions given, and little idea of time. At one point Ithaca comes within sight again, as if tantalizingly looming out of the mist. But surely that mist which we feel obstructs their view of the familiar world is the mist of nightmare, through which one struggles to break clear of an engulfing dream world.

Certainly a complicated voyage is a very Greek thing, and this long succession of islands may on one level refer, from its standpoint of fantasy, to epitomized, typified places around that strange archipelago. In that one archetypal journey Odysseus encountered the paradigms of the experiences which, island-hopping, we cannot completely avoid; the storms and dangers, homesickness, guilt, seduction, and occasionally pleasure such that its completeness itself seemed like a threat which drove him on. There is something anyway troublesome about that unsettled sea, whose land-bound waters always threaten sudden violent storms, whose old boats and diverse routes make the going hard and unpredictable, and across which one goes with some side-tracked and thwarted purpose, blundering inevitably everywhere into unforeseen adventures.

The first theme is one of the most fruitful: the country of those blissfully indolent people whose diet of lotus has freed them from

ever thinking of their responsibilities, made them forget that there
was anywhere else where they perhaps ought to have been. No
doubt they are still there, growing a little lonely but by now
quite lacking the moral strength to take any sort of action, a
slightly lost look in their eyes, sitting with yet another drink
under the canopies on the quay. Hungry for fresh company they
tempt you with the addictive fruit of the climate and the soft sea,
under the vine and the jasmine, under the retsina barrel, wrapped
in the thick air of unreality. Struggling back to the surface of life
one leaves them in their bitter idyll, locked in a small island world
of gossip and nostalgia.

And while they sit and plan their unfulfillable future projects
the battered boats carry us on, in the spray and discomfort of an
often unfriendly sea. At sea, with the storms, the bright nights,
the passing islands, 'we sailed on', Odysseus told the king of the
Phaeacians, 'sick at heart'. You come out to stand on deck at dawn
and see in the distance some calm brown place, some quiet rural
spot with its two or three olive trees sheltering a mud-brick hut,
a goat, a mule, an old woman come to the door in the early light
to watch you pass. Coves and olive trees which will remain, one
feels longingly aware, out of reach for ever. Returning islanders
go ashore to their normal lives with all their bundles around them,
in tiny, bobbing boats. It was to such a tempting place that they
came next, only knowing in retrospect of the dangers which lay
near by.

Homer contrasts the beauty of the natural surroundings with
the elemental forces of destruction represented by the Cyclops.
These, though they were partly seen as men, were also partly
uncivilized monsters. In fact they are thoroughly ambiguous,
since though they seem to represent the disorder of untamed
nature, their leader, Polyphemus, is nevertheless the son of the god
Poseidon.

The Cyclops have their origin in some deep recess of the human
mind which has spawned almost universal tales of giants and
ogres. Like Odin, and like the giants encountered also by more
than one Irish hero, they have one eye. Like many other figures
in widespread stories they are of enormous size; and like some of

these figures too they turn out to be man-eating. In common as well with many such monsters Polyphemus gets outwitted, after a near escape, by the small and wily human whom he is blunderingly attacking.

It was, as the story tells it, largely his greed which led Odysseus to wait in the Cyclop's cave for the monster's return, hoping that somebody as evidently prosperous as Polyphemus would make him generous gifts. His men, with a more straightforward approach to the same end, had wanted to grab what they could and escape; but he thought that they would do better by waiting for their host. It seems he had a habit of entering people's homes in this spirit, saying, as it were, 'Here I am; what are you going to give me?' Himself he brought in this case a sample of some strong wine which he had been given on a previous occasion, evidently a concentrated wine intended to be mixed with water later, like that of the drought-governed island of Santorini. Once in the cave they helped themselves to food, and waited.

Polyphemus, as one would expect with Homer's approach, gets quite fair treatment. The Cyclops are fortunate in not having to till and plant—the land yields food of its own accord—but we find their leader to be a most conscientious shepherd. Indeed he seems to be largely pastoral and cheese-eating; but he has this one fault, the habit of eating people. And it is in his case too excessive greed which brings about his downfall. When invited to drink he takes two bowls too many of that strong wine.

The well-known story should perhaps be taken at its face value: as an extreme form of the sort of adventure in which the hero is trapped but against all likelihood escapes by means of his great ingenuity. Many a comic strip and detective thriller since has used the same techniques, though perhaps none have improved on this archetype. It hardly needs to be said that the hero escapes; he has to, in order for the story to go on. This piece of information which we possess from the start perhaps adds to the fun: we know that he must get out of the cave, because here he is telling the story; but because it seems impossible we are intrigued to know how it is done.

The episode is a long and obviously central one, with its sequel of escape from the island, the other Cyclops being evaded by the clever use of a pun, one more risk taken as Odysseus calls to Polyphemus from the departing ships, and the final curse which the giant calls down on them from his father Poseidon, 'girdler of the earth'. This, coming as it does about midway through the book, forms a pivot on which the various themes turn, the setbacks and storms, the long-delayed return. If (calls Polyphemus to the god) the vicious Odysseus is ever to reach his home in Ithaca, let it be late and in a sorry state, alone, in someone else's ship, and with trouble awaiting him.

It is the fulfilment of this curse—which Poseidon granted—that occupies the rest of the story. But before the complications begin the travelling Greeks are given a small and single respite, a brief pause for breath on an island on which no terrors greet them and nothing goes wrong. The floating island of Aeolia, home of Aeolus, guardian of the winds, where they were feasted for a month, was a haven which was not to recur on their thenceforth troubled journey. When they were blown back to it some time later it faced them with hostility, its attitude towards them having changed.

Aeolus agreed to help Odysseus. He sewed up the winds in a leather bag, and gave it to them to carry with them. A single quiet westerly remained at large, and this blew them steadily towards Ithaca. On the tenth day they could actually see their island, and had even come within view of the habitations there. Odysseus, relaxing in relief, fell asleep through accumulated exhaustion. Unfortunately he had not revealed to his crew what it was that was in the leather bag, and they, suspecting him of hiding some treasure from them, took the opportunity to find out.

Once the bag was undone it was too late to regret their mistake. The winds rushed out in a violent storm, and he woke to see Ithaca disappearing in the distance. For a moment he contemplated jumping overboard, but instead, with rare dejection, covered his head with his cloak. The winds drove them back to the isle of Aeolus, where, when the king heard what had happened, they were rejected as cursed by the gods. They left this time sadly, obliged to row across an endless calm.

Some days of this brought them to another island. Only in a Greek story could there be so many islands in so small a sea that a few days' rowing would inevitably bring you to one. One cannot but think of that perpetual network of ferries and caiques which meshes the Aegean, the island boats on which so many Greeks seem to spend empty days and nights out of their lives. Exhausted sailors asleep with their heads on the tables. Hawkers moving, rasping, through the dawn squalor of the saloon. Peasant women encamped among their bundles and whimpering children. All around, on those early mornings, the tired, sad eyes of the Greeks.

The one they came to next turned out to be the least pleasant of all. The description of the land as one where dusk and dawn draw so close together that the shepherds bringing in their flocks can call to those taking them out again, seems to imply a rumour of some far-northern place. The harbour was good, the land uncultivated, smoke in the distance indicated habitation. It was, however, another race of giants, man-eaters again, and they pelted with rocks the fleet enclosed in the cliff-bound harbour, destroying all but Odysseus' own ship, which hurriedly put to sea.

This episode, the island of the Laestrygonians, is briefly and violently told. All the companions except his own crew are now lost, and Odysseus travels on lonely and dispirited. In this way he comes to the island of the goddess Circe, where the remaining mariners fall exhausted on the beach. They are lost, with no plan, and blunder a few days later towards Circe's house as much for want of anything else to do as in the hopes of help.

One of the *Odyssey*'s most recognizable folk-motifs is the transformation of men into animals which then follows. It occurs elsewhere in Greek myth, in an episode connected with Mount Lykaeon in the Peloponnese, where it was said that every year a man was turned into a wolf, and, if he refrained from eating human flesh, back into a man ten years later. We cannot but be reminded of the central-European cycles of werewolves and

vampires which have given us such red-fanged films. The theme
has a poignant occurrence in one of the Welsh *Mabinogion* tales,
in which two men are punished for the crime of rape by being
turned into male and female deer, then, a year later, into a wild
boar and sow, the one previously male becoming female, and
similarly a year later into a he-wolf and she-wolf, so that each
has in the end suffered the humiliation of having borne offspring
by the other.

The horrors of Circe's farm, in fact, are rather of the order of
those of lands of man-eating giants. Clearly Circe is the close
relative of many evil witches elsewhere. This fairy-tale quality,
however, is transformed by Homer in the course of the episode
into something rather more serious. When she is overcome by
Odysseus with the aid of a drug of which the god Hermes
tells him, she develops into the noticeably more adult figure
of the arch-seductress. In no time at all she has got Odysseus
into bed.

The men whom she had turned into swine became human again,
and they all feasted (and in his case slept with the goddess) for
a year, in the sort of timeless freedom from age and want which
also occurs to such companies in enchanted castles elsewhere. But
reality began to impose itself, and his men grew homesick and
reminded him of his task. Surprisingly the goddess let them go;
but it could not be a direct journey, or a quick one. First, she said,
he must make a journey of a different kind: he must go into the
realm of Hades to consult the prophet Teiresias.

The 'Book of the Dead', in the *Odyssey*, is one of the best and
fullest of such heroic other-world visits, a form typified for later
Europeans by the very similar journey described by Dante. The
theme has been an influential one in later times too. Ezra Pound,
for instance, whose work is in general deeply influenced by Greek
myth, opened that fascinating and uneven work, *The Cantos*, by
re-translating Homer's description—using, for good measure, an
Anglo-Saxon verse style.

The fruitfulness of the idea is so persistent as to seem to need
explanation. But again we are dealing with something which was
neither original to Homer nor peculiar to Greece. The theme

of the mystic voyage combines with that of the journey to the underworld to produce a synthesis which evidently had deep roots in the subconscious. We find it referred to when Gilgamesh seeks to reach Utnapishtim across the waters of death, in the Mesopotamian epic which is probably as early as 2000 B.C. We find a similar idea in the crossing of those grim rivers such as the Styx, which the dead in several mythologies are said to have to negotiate.

Homer uses the occasion (just as Dante later did) to make some telling points about the people who are there, and to fill in stories which we have not had the opportunity to hear in full in the course of the narrative. His picture of the dead as envious shadows is a strangely convincing one. The ghost of Achilles, for instance, gives the pitiful opinion that it would be preferable to be a serf on earth than a king of the dead.

After interviewing several of the ancient heroes and hearing their version of their stories—never, says Agamemnon, be too nice to your wife—Odysseus sets off again, equipped now with the instructions given him by Teiresias. Poseidon is still vindictive, the prophet tells him, and his way home will not be easy. During the course of his message Teiresias delivers that intriguing prophecy of the way Odysseus is eventually to expiate his quarrel with Poseidon. He is to carry inland one of his oars, walking until he comes to a people who have never seen the sea or heard of ships, and who do not know what the oar is. When somebody refers to it as his winnowing fan he has reached his goal, and must there sacrifice to Poseidon—thus, presumably, carrying the cult into a new area.

In particular Teiresias warned him about the sun god's cattle. The sun sees everything, and only if they leave his stock untouched when they reach his island will they stand any chance of getting home safely. We glance forward to almost inevitable disaster; but first there are other horrifying dangers to be negotiated.

These now come thick and fast. After a brief return to Circe, who warns them of some of the perils to come, they set off to face the first of these, the Sirens. No one, Circe said, had heard their song and escaped. They sit among the rotting bones of people who have fallen for their spell. The thought of something so compelling that it would lure the passing traveller to such a terrible end has proved endlessly fascinating. As Sir Thomas Browne memorably put it, in the fifth chapter of *Urn Burial*: 'What song the Syrens sang, or what name Achilles assumed when he hid himself among women, though puzzling Questions, are not beyond all conjecture.' Great classical scholar that he was, he knew that the questions had already been asked of Roman scholars by Tiberius. As to the conjectured answers, some mythologists have treated the challenge as not merely fanciful— Robert Graves, for instance, gives some possible names which Achilles might have used; but Homer indicates that the Sirens sang different songs to different people, when he says that what they offered Odysseus was information. Evidently banking on his insatiable curiosity, they promised to tell him everything that was going to happen. At Circe's suggestion his crew had bound him to the mast, themselves being made immune to the Sirens' messages by means of wax ear-plugs. He struggled unsuccessfully to free himself from the bonds, and so became the only man to hear the song and survive; his ear-plugged crew rowed on obliviously.

If there is some idea of seduction in the Sirens' ploys to trap Odysseus it is, it seems, the intellectual seduction of the Faustian search for forbidden knowledge. Others perhaps might founder on more sensual rocks. His next adventure has a similar but more physical theme, the steering of a course between dangers, each of which threatens to frighten his ship into range of the other.

In many ways the symbolism latent in Scylla and Charybdis (more than that in several of the episodes) is too obvious to be productive of development. That perhaps is both because it is a simple and direct instance of a dilemma (other Odyssean dilemmas being more devious), and because it lacks the personal and psychological qualities which inform most of the doings of that complicated hero. The display which he now gives of his powers of leadership and decision-making simply makes the point that he seems more himself when involved, in his adventures, not in simple heroics but in personal entanglement, in emotional dilemma and the steering of a cunning course through moral danger.

Since Charybdis is represented as a purely nautical pheno-menon, a sucking in of the waters, she is clearly more a whirl-pool than a monster. Scylla on the other hand is more personified, depicted as a creature living in a cave among the rocks, a twelve-footed, six-necked, sharp-toothed fiend with a dog's bark. Avoiding the whirl-pool one risks the perils of the rocks. And it was not without loss that they passed through, his crew sadly depleted by Scylla's ravenous claws.

They beached then on the island where Hyperion, the sun god, kept his cattle. Circe as well as Teiresias had warned them that laying a finger on these beautiful beasts would be fatal for them, and Odysseus wanted to travel on, in evasion of this prophesied threat. But the exhausted men overruled him; of course they promised not to eat the cattle, and all seemed likely to be well. As long as their provisions lasted they were safe enough, and he warned them repeatedly of the danger. But a south wind held them on that shore for more than a month, until they were reduced to catching fish and birds and were gnawed by the pains of hunger and the fear of dying. It seemed foredoomed, since in the end the thought of drowning later was preferable to that of suffering the aching death of starvation now. With due ceremonial precautions they slaughtered one of Hyperion's fat cows, spitted the meat, chopped in small pieces, on skewers, and the smell of grilling woke Odysseus up from the deep sleep he had fallen into.

Of all the preordained catastrophes which signal our common helplessness in this tale (as in so many), nothing seems quite so unavoidable and yet so obviously fatal as that feast. At once satisfying their hunger and bringing about their deaths, Odysseus' men tasted both together the flavours of mortality and life, the day they made *souvlaki* out of the sun god's cattle.

It was not long now before the consequences loomed over them. The sun threatened that if Zeus did not avenge him he would go down to Hades and shine on the dead; and the sun, after all, is a god who must eventually be appeased. Even Zeus could not abide the thought of a sunless world, and he at once tempted the ship back to sea. There he blasted it briefly with fury, one of those storms, it seems, in which the sea turns black and the clouds touch the waves. There was nothing left of it or them except Odysseus clinging to some wreckage.

Even in this pitiful state he is still not wafted home, but once more, this time alone, narrowly escapes the grasps of Scylla and Charybdis. Now in his solitude he no doubt regretted the loss of the companions who had several times been a trouble to him, who had in the end brought about his downfall. Freed of the responsibility of controlling them, he nevertheless lacks with it some aspects of his character, since he is not a loner by nature but rather a manipulator.

The *Odyssey* has already dealt with the episode which follows, since Odysseus had opened his account to King Alcinous of the Phaeacians by telling of his long and sad sojourn with the goddess Calypso. When he now breaks off with the phrase 'but I told you that only yesterday' we realize we have been tricked by the story-teller's double use of time. It seemed that the time scale of the *Odyssey* had been the long and exhausting period of Odysseus' wanderings, whereas it turns out now to have been only the time taken in the telling of the tale. What is more Calypso forms the key by which the spring of the story is rewound, since once again we are taken back to the beginning, at which the council of the gods decides to free Odysseus from Calypso's possessive spell. Four books later we returned to that same moment, when Hermes, the gods' messenger, arrived in Ogygia to ask Calypso to send Odysseus home.

She, like Circe, had kept him with her out of sexual attraction. She offered him immortality, which he had so far declined, apparently preferring his mortal state. The price he would have had to pay for it was giving her his affection, which he told Alcinous he was unable to do. Whereas he stayed with Circe by choice until his men persuaded him to leave, in this case the desire was all on Calypso's side, and he pined on her island, staying against his will. The promise of immortality seems like a bribe, designed to get him to love her. She clothed him meanwhile in the imperishable garments of the gods. But he wept, in his beautiful clothes, and sat morosely on the shore. Perhaps the contrast between the two goddesses contains the idea that there are two kinds of sexual gratification: the one you have to pay for, and the one for which you get paid.

The periodic back-tracking which gives to the *Odyssey* its remarkable narrative tension comes to a sudden end when the tale reaches (for the fourth time) the period spent on Calypso's island. It unwinds now into a long end-sequence telling of the long-awaited return itself. Amazingly we have still more than a third of the total work to go. But King Alcinous' ships now actually convey Odysseus back to Ithaca and, significantly, on the journey he falls into a deep sleep, and still asleep they put him ashore on the island's minutely described coast. So that when he wakes again into the real world it is (as with the heroes of so many fairy-tales) as if from a long and terrible dream.

One cannot but feel that the homecoming sequence, for all its adventures, represents a winding down. It is the islands which typify the *Odyssey*, much as the islands of the Aegean typify Greece. Travelling amongst the islands must always have been a part of the background of Greek lore. There is the probability that the voyages of Odysseus contain at least a subconscious reference to the ancient Mycenaean trade routes. Thucydides records the importance attributed to the opening up of sea communications when piracy became controlled by Cretan naval power. In his terms we may perhaps see in Odysseus the figure of the pirate chief, an occupation which he points out was in ancient times regarded as respectable. Until very recently the more remote islands retained the vestiges of fear of piracy, locating their village on the top of an inland mountain, from where they could look down on the sea all around. Only during the middle of this century have they come to the conclusion, after staring for hundreds of years at the horizon, that the pirates are not coming back; indeed in the process of building new settlements on the coast they seem to have grown to realize that any boat appearing in the distance is likely to be bearing people who are coming not to rob but to be robbed.

Islands still form the main lure and seduction of the Aegean, such places as those where the stillness emphasizes the characteristic sounds, which then become elements of the general island feeling. The fishermen thumping octopuses against the rocks, all the afternoon; the pop-pop-pop of a boat below the cliffs; the flowing jangle of goat bells across a distant mountainside. They and their ports too necessarily embody the emotions of departure and arrival, even the worst of them bearing this tension of being a place in a temporal succession. And what is so compelling, in this context, about the *Odyssey*, is its recognition of this basic appeal as well: the intrinsic emotional thrill of any journey.

Many who have studied the *Odyssey* have seen in it too an overlay which arises from this idea, the journey seen as symbol of the individual's progress through life, Odysseus as Everyman, 'the pilgrim', with the various adventures each allotted their abstract nouns. This is of course too simple to do Homer justice, since a real myth such as that of Odysseus operates (like a good poem, and like any potent symbol) on several levels at once, its effect being due to the alchemical combination of elements in an instantaneous image. Not as if we were to feel, or think, now one thing, now the next. The whole has a nature other than that possessed by its components in isolation, just as water, for instance, refuses to float off into the air or to promote combustion, but instead does things like flowing downhill which are all its own.

No doubt it is because of the fascination and depth of the original achievement that we owe so much subsequent literature to Homer. The *Odyssey*, as already mentioned, provided Pound with a partial framework for his longest (if perhaps not his greatest) work, *The Cantos*. It did the same more definitely and firmly for the much more successful and influential work written at about the same time by Pound's contemporary and friend James Joyce. Joyce's *Ulysses* in fact used the background of Odysseus' journey on one level and a highly lit depiction of early twentieth-century Dublin on another to provide the basis for a display of literary forms and techniques which is still quite dazzling. The underlying impetus of the journey and the quest provides such later embellishments with the narrative force which is needed to sustain them.

Ultimately it is the idea of going home. Odysseus several times speaks directly, and with pride, of his rugged island. The theme has been with us from the beginning, and in our wait for its resolution the *Odyssey* keeps us in prolonged suspense.

Homer does not in fact follow Odysseus through to his death in old age, which Teiresias had foretold for him after the penitential journey with the oar. Later sources provide the ending, giving him some further adventures, and the legends of the Peloponnese, as recorded by Pausanias, indicate perhaps that it was in that direction that he was thought to have gone on his oar-carrying walk. Homer leaves us with Odysseus still at home, in fact at home in the sense of being securely so for the first time, the suitors conquered, peace made with their kin, his family around him. Ithaca has never been represented as being anything but a small and rather barren place. Its importance to Odysseus throughout lay in something quite different.

It is, in the real world, very much as he says it is. In some places the slopes fall steeply to the sea; a central mountain dominates it, bulking over the narrow neck of land which divides the island into two halves. It is not high, and in fact is dwarfed by the neighbouring island's peak across the strait. The land is stony and clothed largely with rough scrub. Perhaps the description given by Telemachus to Menelaus best sums it up: it is one of those islands that slope down to the sea, and not the kind of place where you can drive a horse. Odysseus tells Alcinous the same thing with a rather more defiant tone. It is, he says, a rough land; but it rears men well.

It is true, he goes on, that his homeland and parents are what is dearest to a man, however well off he may be living in exile. Ithaca may not be much to come back to, but that is irrelevant. There may be a contrast involved between the idea and the reality; but in any case it is the homecoming itself which is what is sought. The Alexandrian Greek poet C. P. Cavafy has perhaps best expressed this final message of the *Odyssey*, in his poem 'Ithaca'. Pray, he says, that the road will be long, the summer mornings many, entering ports seen for the first time. Do not hurry the voyage at all, because it is the gaining of wisdom and experience on the way that is what Ithaca has to offer, even if, on arrival, you find her poor.

> It is better to let it last for long years;
> and even to anchor at the isle when you are old,
> rich with all that you have gained on the way,
> not expecting that Ithaca will offer you riches.

> Ithaca has given you the beautiful voyage.
> Without her you would never have taken the road.
> But she has nothing more to give you.

FOURTEEN

MINOS IN CRETE

THERE IS NOTHING ordinary about Crete, nothing that is not dramatic and powerful in its impact. Its general effect is in a way unsettling, disturbing; and one feels that the Greeks have always been unsure about it, unsure as to whether they have quite got the measure of that unusual island and its people. Greek but not Greek, it lies on the margin of the ordered Aegean world. It bears the disorienting qualities of ambiguity and overlap. Not entirely European, it is not quite African or Asian either. Rather it is a continent in itself, an alchemical blending of elements into a new compound, something definite but unclassified, the sort of thing that customary taxonomy somehow fails to take account of.

For several thousands of years it has played this role, lying just on, yet just off, the Greek horizon, representing another sort of outlook and another historical causal sequence. Sir Arthur Evans dated the start of his archaeological categories as early as 3000 B.C., and even if the actual dating of his epochs can be questioned there is no doubt that the palace-city of Knossos at the time of its great destruction was the product of more than a thousand years of peace and independent rule. When this came to an end, in about 1450 B.C., Greece had still a thousand years to go before the classical age of Athens; and that seems so long ago to us now.

No wonder then if Minos appears as a dark and distant figure. He seemed to them too the embodiment of all that was outside their realm of systematic clarification: the forces at the interface —almost, but not quite, somebody else's problem. Minos was at one and the same time the name of a real power, the ancient sea rule of the colonizing Cretans (which no doubt possessed for the Greeks the overtones of culturally inherited fear), and on the other hand, in his god-form, the infernal judge of the dead, the bogy-man awaiting us, who will know of our misdeeds.

It is no wonder either that this dark, inhuman atmosphere hangs round the Cretan myth. It is the note of fear which we receive, something which the largely lucid and explicable body of mainland myth, for all its startling violence and often brutal realism, does not seem to have: the themes of human sacrifice to an animal god, the note of bestiality, the whole sinister business of the monster in the labyrinth.

We find the first expression of the idea of Minos firmly set out in Homer, where, towards the end of the *Odyssey*, Odysseus in disguise gives to his wife an entirely fictional account of who he is and where he has been. He is a Cretan prince, he explains, and at once (though it is hardly called for) he gives a potted geographical description of that island. Densely populated, with ninety cities, several different races of people speaking their own languages, including an indigenous residue, the 'genuine Cretans'. The incident is fortunate for us, since it provides a direct link between the otherwise numinous figure of Minos and the greatest city of Crete, which Homer names 'Knosos', over which Minos ruled. There is thus no doubt of the authenticity of the tradition that Minos was king of Knossos, and when several hundred years later Thucydides gave a rationalized version of the same situation he was probably very close to the truth. Minos, he says, was traditionally the first ruler to have an organized navy; he thus both prevented piracy, allowing sea communications to improve, and put his own people in control of colonized islands such as the Cyclades. It is implied, and we do not in fact really need to be told, that the name Minos was dynastic: that traditionally all the ancient kings of Crete were called Minos, so that it became synonymous with the kingship. Thus the name has a clear application. When it is used historically it may be taken to mean 'the ruler of Crete', and when it is used mythically, to mean 'the original Minos, after whom the kings of Crete are named'.

The theme of sea power, introduced by Thucydides, is all-important to the understanding of the whole relation of Crete to the rest of Greece. We have seen several times how control of the sea was crucial to the Greeks of various periods, as it was in the story of the vast fleet which combined under the leadership of Agamemnon at Aulis. If before the Mycenaean domination of Greece another power, namely that of 'Minos', ruled the sea, it too must (like 'Agamemnon' later) have had effective rule over the form taken by every aspect of Greek life: trade, settlements, artefacts and even thought. Moreover if this power was as great as we have reason to suppose, it would in itself explain the otherwise incredible flourishing of civilization which took place during those thousand-odd years at Knossos. It was the luxuriant blossoming which comes with perfect security.

The geographical location of their island of course strengthened the Cretans' success. We have to remember that the great Egyptian dynasties were flourishing at the same time as Knossos, and Crete consequently lay in the position of a natural go-between, a pivot round which any interchange between Africa and Europe must take place. To that one may add the extraordinary variety and abundance latent in the land itself, which not only made it self-sufficient in such things as timber for ship-building, but, with its hot climate tempered by upland rains, allowed the development of organized agriculture which in turn gives opportunity for the non-essential activities of art.

Homer refers at one point to the wizard Minos, as if he were the practitioner of an alien cult; but possibly this is simply another expression of the feeling that there is something deeply un-Greek about this representative of the pre-Achaean power. Nevertheless the mythical first Minos was given a conventional Olympian pedigree, being, like so many other figures, regarded by later mythographers as one of the offspring of Zeus. Zeus fell in love with a Phoenician princess, Europa, sister to Cadmus, the founder of Thebes. The theme of cattle has already been introduced into the history of that family, since it was through the signs given by an apparently sacred heifer that Cadmus knew the spot at which to found his city. Now this connection is reinforced, since Zeus attracts the attention of his love by assuming the form of a beautiful white bull.

The girl found the bull placid and gentle, and began to stroke it affectionately. Ovid gives us an attractive picture of her feeding it with flowers. Eventually she climbed on its back, and it bore her away, rather to her surprise, into the sea. They journeyed through the water to the coast of Crete, and there on the shore Zeus mated with her. She bore him three sons, Minos, Rhadamantys and Sarpedon, who were adopted by the reigning king of Crete, whom she in the meantime married. It was thus that Minos, the son of a bull-god, came to be king of Crete.

No doubt this episode of the story contains references to the European colonization of Crete, and probably also to the introduction at some point both of a bull worshipping religion and of the cult of Zeus. We know from the figurines found in the shrines in the sacred caves (which were the only equivalents to temples the Minoans had) that the original Cretan religion was a mother and son cult, which was later described in the story of Rhea and Zeus associated with the caves on Mount Ida and Mount Dikte. Zeus, in fact, was introduced into the structure of Cretan religion in several different ways.

Of the other offspring Sarpedon disappears from the mainstream of myth, and Rhadamantys reappears briefly as king of the Homeric paradise, the Elysian fields. Minos in the meantime married an apparently native princess, Pasiphaë, who bore him several children, including the daughters Ariadne and Phaedra. These, by recurring in the mainland story of Theseus, perhaps provide a parallel to the flowing back of Cretan influence to Attica and elsewhere, after the re-establishment of stability following the Achaean invasion. That, however, is the sequel; it is at this point that the main myth of Minos starts.

The bull theme and the sea theme return: Minos, preparing to sacrifice to Poseidon, asked the god to send him a bull for that purpose. The demand seems to have been intended to prove his special relationship with the god of the sea; and the point was duly proved, when an exceptionally fine bull at once emerged from the waves and swam ashore. So beautiful was the bull, however, that the cattle-loving king, doubtless with an eye to improving his stock, refrained from killing it, sending it instead to join his herd. He killed a normal bull in its place; but that, in

Poseidon's view, was a breach of the bargain. It is as if Minos had overreached himself, misusing his borrowed power. Did he think perhaps that he had mastered the unmasterable? In any case Poseidon reacted sharply to the act of deceit. In revenge he made the queen fall in love with the animal he had sent.

The very literal conditions of the myth force us to take this seriously. It was not a whim on Pasiphaë's part, but a consuming passion. I see her mesmerized in that uncompromising landscape, the hollow bowl of hard land below Knossos, creeping to gaze on the divine form of the animal on which she doted. I picture her hiding her guilty obsession from Minos, sure that if she looked at him he would read it in her eyes. Governed, herself, not by disgust at her lust but with a sort of amazement, revelling and rebelling at once at the beauty and the awfulness of it. More and more unable to do anything other than, with increasingly unconvincing excuses, hang about the cattle meadows in a state of hopeless longing.

Finally she had to tell the truth to somebody, to ask for help. Daedalus was the Cretan royal craftsman, an Athenian who had gone into exile following a crime he had committed in Athens. He is credited in the myths with the invention of tools such as the saw, with the implication, perhaps, that Cretan workmanship was more advanced at an earlier age than that of the mainland. His Attic origin, however, might also be taken to show a belief in an ancient exchange of craftsmen.

Daedalus constructed for Pasiphaë a hollow cow made of copper, which, with the queen enclosed, was placed among the herd. Sure enough the god's bull mounted it, and by means of the purpose-built construction devised by Daedalus' skill succeeded in penetrating to the queen inside; and she, poor thing, achieved that requital and consummation of her passion which she had longed for, and, presumably, a unique experience, though not without a certain loss of dignity.

The myth is a horror story, not a romance. The union was to be blessed with offspring, in the form of a monstrous hybrid, a bull-man named Asterion, and better known to us as the Minotaur. It is the first of a long line of horror-film family secrets which have to be hidden away in the cellar. It was for this purpose, the myth says, that Daedalus designed the labyrinth for Minos.

Several themes converge to make up this idea. We know now that the term labyrinth describes Knossos by way of a sort of semantic confusion, Knossos being correctly the home of the *labrys*, a sacred and traditional emblem of the place, the double-headed axe. These symbols (as one may see in the museum in Heraclion) were carried in procession, perhaps used at sacrifices, and are carved in various places on the palace walls. According to Sir Arthur Evans they indicate an Asiatic connection, being also found in Anatolia. Perhaps it was from the word *labrys* that *labyrinthos* came, and perhaps that word in turn came to signify a maze because of the extraordinarily complex ground-plan of some of the lower storeys of Knossos. It has been suggested that strangers normally lost their way there, and they might well think that they had done so even when on the right track, among those dog-leg, almost key-pattern passageways. But possibly also (and I think more credibly) the prototype labyrinth was actually a maze, in the form of a pattern marked out in mosaic tiling on a dance floor, where ritual dances took place, perhaps originally ceremonial or religious, later no doubt becoming mere festivities. This is certainly indicated by the reference in the *Iliad* to the dancing floor which Daedalus made for Ariadne at Knossos, which Homer mentions as being among the scenes depicted by Hephaestus on the shield he made for Achilles.

No doubt a combination of ideas went to make up that of the labyrinth, which has been a fruitful and a fascinating one to later writers, such as the great Argentine story-teller Jorge Luis Borges. In this particular case, the original labyrinth of Knossos, there is the additional strand of the theme of the monstrous beast, the product of the queen and the bull.

The story goes on to say that the Minotaur in the labyrinth periodically devoured the victims sent to him for the purpose, a fairly explicit reference, it would seem, to a habit of human sacrifice to a bull-god. This is in turn no doubt closely connected with the Cretan habit of acrobatic games involving bulls, a sort of bull dance, of which we know from the famous fresco showing vaulting youths participating in what must have been a highly dangerous corrida, and from a little ivory statuette of the same feat, both of these works now in the Heraclion museum. Bull-running and bullfighting no doubt developed into popular entertainments, like gladiatorial shows, coming out into the light from some much deeper and more serious root in a past full of dark religions.

The figure of the Minotaur has a special symbolic poignancy, nicely brought out in Watts's painting in the Tate Gallery, the semi-human beast gazing with longing from its prison. It inevitably bears a sort of theme about our nature, since (whatever philosophical problems this gives rise to) we do habitually feel ourselves to be existent on two levels, to be two different kinds of thing uncomfortably trapped within the same space-time co-ordinates—though to set out to distinguish them would be like trying to disentangle sex and love.

A connection between the powers of Crete and Athens now returns to the story, since the sacrificial victims given to the bull-monster were said to be taken from a tribute of young Athenians sent at fixed intervals to Minos. The reference, it seems, must be to some period at which the Minoan sea power held Attica in subjection; and the story tells of the breaking of this bond, by the advent of the Attic hero Theseus.

Theseus became the traditional hero of the Athenians, who attributed to him the unification of the various cities of Attica under Athens. Plutarch, writing in Greece in Roman times, looked back across many centuries to what he evidently regarded as being at least partly historical fact, and included the life of Theseus among those of his other more concrete figures. The hero's father, in the legend, was a king of Athens, his mother a princess of the rather insignificant town of Troezen, on the coast of Argolis. From there he came to Athens, and comparatively early in his heroic career he became involved in the Cretan story. Later he was to figure prominently in the myths of Attica, married by then to King Minos' daughter Phaedra, who fell in love (through Aphrodite's spite) with her stepson Hippolytus, Theseus' son by the Amazon Antiope. Hippolytus died in an

accident with his chariot on the seashore, dashed by the anger of
Poseidon roused against him by his jealous father.

When Theseus came to Crete he did so as a member of the
tribute of youths, taking his place among them as a means of
bringing to an end the dreadful payment. He arranged with his
father when he left that the usual black sails of the sad ship would
be changed to white on its return if he was successful in his
mission.

It was his good fortune that on his arrival he caught the eye of
Minos' daughter Ariadne, who promised her help against the
Minotaur, in exchange for which, it was arranged, she would
become Theseus' wife. In this part of the tale the labyrinth is
certainly taken to be the series of underground passageways which
the basements of Knossos may well have seemed like to strangers,
as indeed the streets of many an Arab medina seem to Europeans
today. The problem for the victims was to find their way out; and
for this purpose Ariadne provided Theseus with a ball of string.
It seems a simple enough device, and indeed one wonders why
no one had thought of it, but perhaps the simplicity is the
retrospective deceptive obviousness of a stroke of genius. By
attaching one end to the entrance and unrolling it as he went,
the Athenian was able to reach the lair of the monster in the
centre with the knowledge of being able to rewind his way
back.

Needless to say he killed the Minotaur, and prudently left the
island at once, taking Ariadne with him. For some reason (rather
surprisingly, not clearly stated) Theseus abandoned her, in contravention of his bargain, on the island of Naxos. One would have
thought a credible motive should be supplied for such an
unchivalrous act, and indeed some versions attempt this, with
apparently added features such as his forgetting her under the
influence of a spell. She was heartbroken, and was only comforted
by the arrival of the god Dionysus, who married her. Part of her
regalia was later set among the stars, where we find it now called
the Corona Borealis, that half-circle of seven stars which hangs
below the constellation of Hercules.

At any rate, at a later stage we find Theseus married to the other daughter, Phaedra, with all the complications which that then entailed. Theseus had a stormy reign in Athens, and in fact ended his days, the tale says, in exile on the fierce little island of Skyros, after unrest and insurrection had broken out in his absence. There he was treacherously pushed to his death by the king of the island, from the top of that rearing crag which towers over the small white town, and his bones were only (supposedly) brought back to Athens towards the beginning of the rise of that city to political domination, by the influential leader Cimon, in 474 B.C., at which point his story was resurrected for the purpose of Athenian propaganda.

Tragedy struck Theseus before that, however, on his return from Crete, perhaps in punishment for his abandoning of Ariadne. In his enthusiasm at his successful return to Athens he forgot to change the black sails of the ship. His father the king, Aegeus, kept watch for him from the Acropolis, and when he saw the black-sailed vessel approaching across the water he jumped from there to his death—from, it is specified, that high platform of rock on which the pretty little Nike temple now stands.

The Cretan matter flows on forcefully towards a succession of bitter endings. Minos and his technician Daedalus had fallen out, either because the king suspected him of being more involved than he should have been in Pasiphaë's affairs, or because of his indirect assistance to Theseus in providing Ariadne with the ball of thread. For one reason or another Daedalus and his son Icarus were imprisoned in Knossos, perhaps in that very labyrinth which he had constructed.

Not for long, however. The craftsman, never at a loss for an appropriate invention, made them both sets of wings. It is for the failure of his pair that Icarus is so rightly famous, the image which he preserves being that of the impetuous enthusiasm, the exuberance and unwitting arrogance of flying too near the sun. The wings were made of feathers held by wax, and before they set off the designer of these had warned his son against the danger which he in the end encountered. He was to follow his father, and fly a middle course. But when you are airborne it is easy to forget, with the power of the wind under your arms and the feeling of gaining height. The sheer sense of soaring is almost impossible to resist.

Somewhere out beyond Lipsos and Patmos the wax of Icarus' wings melted, and his father buried him on the nearest island, an explanation of the name of the closest neighbour to Samos, Ikaria. Daedalus continued to Sicily, pursued now by Minos and his fleet, and was there given the protection of the king. The latter refused to give up his guest—a sign, surely, that Minos' power was now failing—and instead it was the Cretan monarch who met his end there, drowned, perhaps by a trick of Daedalus, in his bath. Herodotus tells the story, in explanation of an oracle which dissuaded the Cretans from joining the anti-Persian forces, and adds to it as a sequel a sort of simplified version of the Greek invasion of Crete. After Minos was killed, almost all the forces of Crete besieged the Sicilian city. On their way home, after failing, they were wrecked by a storm on the coast of Italy, where the survivors stayed to form a colony, and Crete, now undefended, was settled by the Greeks, shortly (Herodotus says) before the Trojan War.

Minos as judge of the dead continues to haunt the mythology, and indeed makes an unforgettable reappearance in that capacity in Dante, by which route also many of the other figures of Greek myth have passed into European literature.

As in so many other cases, but here to a much more remarkable degree, the whole complex of the Cretan myths has benefited during this century by the reinstating and revitalizing process of archaeological discovery. Both the digs of Evans and the translations of Ventris and Chadwick have shown us in quite indubitable form the extent of the greatness and power of Crete in very early times, a realm in the physical world paralleling the aspects of awe and might surrounding the figure of Minos conveyed to us by the myths. This new dimension restores to the matter an element which was missing from it even for Homer and the classical Greeks. It reunites the distillation and abstraction of Crete's past with the facts of the physical place.

In spite of their very great antiquity, the palace-towns of Minoan Crete are not so unfamiliar as one would expect. Their

I

plan is not more complex and tightly meshed than that of many
modern Greek island villages, for instance that intricate jumble
of buildings crowning the clifftop on Santorini, where houses are
interwoven and stacked up on each other in such a way that were
their foundations to be excavated some thousands of years hence
they would, no doubt, resemble a complicated single building.
Similarly one finds with many old Arab towns, for instance the
casbahs in the middle of southern Moroccan cities, that the space
available is so densely filled that it is impossible to distinguish
one from another the buildings making up the rabbit-warren
through which one winds one's way, down those enclosing
passageways, as if down the corridors of a complicated building.

There is plenty of evidence that the Minoan (like the
Mycenaean) complexes were centred on a royal residence, and
for that reason they are customarily referred to as palaces. More
correctly one should see the palace as being only a part, though a
central one, of the town—rather as the public buildings on the
central square would be in the standard town plans of several
other centuries elsewhere. The settlement-unit hangs together
fairly closely, but that does not really make it best viewed as a
single building, as the term 'palace' would suggest. There is a
palace there in the sense that the main part of it consists of official
rooms and royal apartments; around this area the rest of the
town spreads out, closely connected and conjoined, expanded by
a beehive process of cellular addition and infilling.

Knossos is not just the best-known of the sites of Crete, but
the one which best represents the various characteristics of the
Minoan towns. In structure it is much simpler than it looks, its
labyrinthine form being the result of the denseness of the building
pattern and, no doubt, the long period of its use. Its core consists
of two main sets of rooms, either side of a large central court.
When in its complete form it must have presented an impressive
skyline, seen both from the approaches and from the central court
itself. Some of the buildings were up to five storeys high, with
hanging gardens, painted columns of a downward tapering shape
(which has been reproduced for us in the reconstruction) and a
great deal of colour in the form of frescoes and decorations.

The court, and the layout around it, belong to the first palatial period, the time when, about 1900 B.C., the original Neolithic settlement on this hill was levelled—its remains in fact forming the foundation, to a depth of as much as twenty feet, of this broad flat area. One gets one's bearings best by going straight to that central court, and working outwards in various directions from there. The modern entrance to the palace (as, for want of a better word, I shall continue to call the whole conglomeration) is by means of what was originally the western entrance, one of the four ways in, joining with that from the south to approach the central court via a series of colonnades, with flanking anterooms, the walls of which were beautifully frescoed. The southern entrance was that at which the main road approach to Knossos terminated, approaching across a viaduct of which the uprights can still be seen, flanked by a drinking and washing complex known as 'the Caravanserai'; this road approach ends here at steps, since (as becomes immediately apparent) Knossos was set on the slope of a spur jutting over a valley. There were watch-towers over some of the entrances, but no walls to be penetrated, and so nothing of the form of the Lion Gate at Mycenae or the equally impressive passage and doorway at Tiryns. It is a well-known testimony to the effectiveness of Minoan sea power that none of the cities were fortified.

Around the central complex of the royal residence are several other associated structures, such as the theatre immediately outside the north extremity, and the more distant group of buildings known as 'the little palace', the other side of the modern road; and many outlying houses, all of which, taken together, must have seemed an impressively urban complex in a rural world.

The main official rooms of the palace are in the block to the west of the central court, the opposite side to the steep drop of the hill. It is there that we find the clearly ceremonial rooms connected with kingship, the throne room with its anteroom, and the adjoining shrine. If Minos was a priest-king, it was here that he undertook his protective rituals.

Precautions are taken now against over-use, and one cannot

any longer enter the throne room itself. Perhaps it was always inappropriate that one could, that any unsanctified and un-crowned mortal could then sit, as we used to, on that tall and narrow, straight-backed throne, looking around at the delicately decorated room, the close constriction of this inner cell, with a Minos-eye view. What was so striking about that view, in fact, was its lack of grandeur, its domesticity and ungodly scale. One did not feel particularly exalted, on that throne; and indeed in the courts and state rooms of Knossos as a whole there is no feeling of super-normal proportion, of the sort of magnificence which the term 'palatial' leads one to expect. In the throne room in parti-cular there is a personal, private-feeling scale of proportion, which suggests at once that only a few people at a time attended the occupant of this gypsum throne, here in what was evidently an exclusive ritual shrine, and not an audience chamber or a council seat.

One of the reasons for this intimacy of proportion through most of the palace begins to become apparent when one considers the proportions of the throne itself. It feels, when sat on, to have been made for a short, small-limbed, neatly built person. It suggests a delicacy of frame, almost a diminutiveness. And if this form was characteristic of the Minoan people as a whole, a great deal is explained. Viewing them as small and delicate, like the Japanese, one begins to understand their architectural and artistic style in a way that one otherwise lacks. The layout of Knossos is not in fact very labyrinthine, but simply rather neat and small. On examination it turns out to be quite orderly, with rooms tucked away in the corners of public spaces, and open areas just sufficient to give light and air. Its meticulous tidiness makes a modern Cretan village look positively maze-like.

On the opposite side of the courtyard, the eastern section of the palace (the latest to be built) contains some rather grander features, the great descending staircase and the royal rooms at its bottom. Here there is an echo of the key-pattern maze-form in the arrangement of the passages and staircases of the suite of royal rooms, which form the flank of the palace along the contour of the slope. The corridor for some reason refuses to lead one directly from one room to another, so that one's sense of direction is foiled and it becomes easy to lose the way. After a little of this apparent doubling-back you get the uncomfortable impression that you have come out into the room which you have just left.

These royal rooms contain a hall, known as the Hall of the Double Axes from the occurrence of that symbol on its walls, another throne room, this time more public and open, another such room attributed to the queen, and a bathroom. The much-restored bath in the latter again gives us a view of rather small and delicate people.

Since the excavations of a Minoan town on the island of Thera (also called Santorini), which have revealed many remarkable wall paintings in their complete form, we now know even more certainly what these people looked like—or at least what they thought they looked like, since perhaps one should count in a possible element of style and idealization. The Thera frescoes are remarkably detailed, and show us a number of people all with the same characteristics. They have long, flattish faces, with slightly slanting eyes set below prominent foreheads. They are (in confirmation of the inference from Knossos) noticeably slight in build, with something definitely delicate about them. There is something delicate too about their art, which shows a love of colour and of neat decorativeness. Swallows and dolphins dance in the frescoes, dancing among lily-like flowers and fronds. This sort of Japaneseness pervades all their artefacts, as if these things were the trappings of a world inhabited by small and sensitive people.

That the depicting of the figures and faces both on Thera and in the Cretan frescoes is reminiscent of Egyptian work is not really surprising. We know that Minos did business with Pharaoh; and in fact Sir Arthur Evans traced connections with Egypt from a very early stage of Cretan development. At least some of the relation with Egypt seems likely to be stylistic, rather than to prove that the Minoans and Egyptians were of the same stock. The long curved eyebrow, the almond-shaped eye, for instance: these are features which, when drawn, are aesthetically pleasing, and might be emphasized in the frescoes for that reason.

Not only do we know now what they looked like, but, since the decipherment of the Linear B tablets, we know too what they did, at any rate in the later period. It is tantalizing that the earlier tablets (written in another script not surprisingly known as Linear A) have not yet been interpreted. What is known is that that earlier language was not Greek, a fact every bit as interesting as the much-applauded discovery that the language of the later tablets *was* Greek. The difference tells us firmly that Crete was invaded by Greek-speaking people, who adopted, and adapted, the form of writing. This event accords well with the destruction of the main palatial sites in Crete, and the re-occupation and alteration of Knossos, in about 1450 B.C.

From the Cretan Linear B tablets we have a picture of the inhabitants of Knossos, during at any rate this later period, occupying a territory consisting of a number of subordinate areas governed from this central headquarters. The economy was largely agricultural, and we have evidence of the growing of cereals, olives, figs, the production of wine and the extensive herding of sheep; but it was also at least incipiently industrial, since the organization of textile workers (no doubt a result of the large flocks) seems to have occupied some of the officials of that Minoan bureaucracy which the tablets firmly suggest.

This highly developed culture, located in this well-designed structure with its light shafts, windows, drains, and running water brought by aqueducts and pipelines across the hills, is, we must remember, the outcome of a long sequence of urban development on this spot, beginning perhaps in the early third millennium, expanding from about 1900 B.C. to become, in effect, one of the earliest great cities. Evans, in rebuilding some of it, has given us some assistance in imagining what it would have been like to live there. However much his concrete and rather prosaic-looking structure may seem to us distasteful, even comic, the fact remains that (as one discovers to one's loss elsewhere) only the trained archaeologist can read the character of a room from the base of its walls.

What has of course remained much as it was, to be appreciated now as then, is the outlook and surroundings of this place, which, more than the stones of it themselves, make it so remarkable in atmosphere. You look out on to those rather ominous slopes, to see in concise form the contrasting gentleness and severity of Crete. The valley hangs like a gulf between the palace and the bare high hill, with a distancing, isolating effect. Looking down you see cypresses and vines; looking up you are faced with the hard strata of the escarpment. Its harshness is not disguised by the attempts at cultivation of the lower slopes, but instead seems to defeat and negate attempts at taming it. Olive trees fade into mountainside among the erosion. They precariously stabilize a fragile sandy soil, which the wind when it comes whips up to fill the air with pale ochre dust. It is, above all, a strange, uneasy place.

The last phase of the palace, succeeding the great destruction of about 1450, only lasted for, relatively, an instant of time. Many of the the objects and preserved tablets which Evans disinterred were of course from this end-period, buried under the fallen palace when a great fire savaged it in about 1400 B.C. The beams and columns were mostly made of wood, perhaps as a result of unfortunate earlier experiences with more fragile material in a land often shaken by earthquakes. It is amazing that the whole then lay concealed for more than three thousand years, until Sir Arthur Evans came to Crete in the 1890s. Political trouble at first obstructed him, but he persevered, and on the achievement of Cretan independence at the end of the century he was at last enabled to dig. Starting in 1900 he dug away for thirty years, building a house for himself, the famous Villa Ariadne, near the site, his headquarters from 1906. In 1911 he was rewarded with a knighthood, and remains both an outstanding figure in archaeo-logical history and perhaps the last example of the rich and dedi-cated amateur, both able and willing to finance his own under-takings. The trouble with his much-criticized (and much defended) reconstructions, is that inevitably one has to take his word for their correctness. Sometimes he seems to have been working on the basis of inspiration rather than evidence, with the result that many people have the uncomfortable feeling that they are visiting Evans's Knossos rather than Minos'.

At least in the museum we can see the artefacts of those very distant times much as they were. Rightly the Heraclion museum is regarded as one of the world's best and most important, and almost by itself it would make a visit to the island worthwhile.

The finds span the long stretch of Crete's prehistory, from the times before the building of the palaces to the immediate prelude of the classical age. It is a very consistent collection, most of it showing the distinctive Cretan flair for subtle workmanship. The delicate patterning, the fringes and flowers painted on the vases, and particularly the habit of making little models of things—a model of a house, a model of an acrobat, a model of a religious service, of men and animals—in itself illustrates the element of charm which pervades Cretan art. The famous faience figurines of the goddess herself, in one case brandishing her sacred snakes, add to the delicate workmanship an element of fierceness. The dark power lying behind their thinking seems to obtrude, too, in the black bull's head, with its aloof dignity, its shining crystal eyes and tall gold horns. This, from the sixteenth century B.C., is one of the most impressive of the exhibits, combining naturalism with the implication of some larger meaning. In one room we are overwhelmed by the sombre symbol of the double axe. The fragments of the frescoes from Knossos have been reconstructed on the upper floor, where one can see more of those delicate Minoan faces and, perhaps most striking, the scene of the bull-jumping episode with its vast stylized monster and its lightweight acrobats.

No doubt one does get to know something about the people from their artefacts, though probably not so much the sort of thing they would have found important themselves as something rather more latent or unconscious. I feel too that a view of the nature of the people who gave rise to the sinister myths of Minos can be gained from experiencing the feeling of the places where they lived—not just Knossos (which to some extent obstructs such a direct contact by its fame and its air of being too much visited) but more those open and rural sites, and particularly the simpler ones which can be enjoyed without the encumbrance of a guidebook.

Foremost among these of course is Phaestos, where the situation alone is a source of pleasure, its confident out-jutting stance over the wide valley of Messara. In such places it is perhaps neither necessary nor desirable to try to reconstruct, and in fact the effort of imagination involved in believing that those little stone pens were ever really rooms and houses spoils the enjoyment of appreciating what it would be like to live in such a spot. At several sites in Crete one has this choice of attitude, and Evans was no doubt right to build up the one palace, so that we can see what they were like, and leave the others flat, so that we can walk around them unobstructed in the sweet Cretan air.

Phaestos is set in powerful scenery, terraced above the grand scope of its view. Idyllic in a different way is its neighbour, Agia Triada, perhaps at one time its port, lying just over the hill and nearer to the soft luxury of the plain. Phaestos has grandeur, Agia Triada a contrasting air of urbanity and intimate scale. It seems very much like what it probably was, the private residence of a royal personage, rather than the seat of the monarchy. Here a luxurious country house has outgrown its status, and become a stately home. It bears the unusual Minoan intricacy of plan, superficially warren-shaped and characterized by density of use. How small the rooms are, we feel, and how closely packed. The intensity of its construction is relieved here and there, as it always is in the palaces, by open spaces; but here these too are as if private, rather than grand.

It is in such places, where the original intention has not become disguised by a long succession of rebuildings, that one can best get a feeling of the Minoan mind. Crete is literally dotted with Minoan sites, many of them (such as the villa on the road up to Anogia) being no more than large country houses or perhaps farmsteads, some of these merging into a small village form usually dominated by one major building, as if one house had come in the course of time to be superior to its neighbours, absorbing them into its precincts. Among the best-preserved settlements is the coastal town of Gournia, a set of closely stacked boxes on a hillside, which represents perhaps better than any that particular beehive quality, the combination of order and complexity, which all Minoan settlements display.

Gournia presents a honeycomb of closely packed rooms, most of them the size of cubbyholes, impressively intact, the narrow alleys between buildings, the paved ways, staircases and stepped streets still feeling very much like a place that has been lived in. The over-all impression here, however, is not so much that of majesty or might, as at Knossos and Phaestos, or of civilized domesticity, as at Agia Triada, as of a people with an obsession about broom cupboards. Sometimes the Minoans seem too obsessive to be worthy of respect. Here there is something unattractively fussy about these meticulously enclosed small spaces. Why did they feel the need to fit so many walls into so small an area? Why did they need to have so many walls at all?

The palace-town of Mallia, also on the north coast, appears much grander than Gournia, though lacking anything imposing in its setting. Here again many maze-like passages end rather puzzlingly in tiny rooms, which seem in fact to have been mostly cellars. The main life (to judge by the staircases now leading grandly to nowhere) went on on the floor above, now entirely defunct. This assumption helps to clarify the thinking behind the remains. But in the end we cannot entirely grasp it. Why such complexity? Why so much confusion and congestion among the serene order of the public spaces and more eminent rooms? But of course to judge from such remnants, rather than a know-ledge of what the original was like, is unfair. In the end, I suppose, all that will remain of your house, too, will be the parts of it which cannot fall down—the foundations and perhaps the basement floor. And if revealed with exquisite patience by little men in straw hats these unseen bases of your life would not be recognizable to you as anything familiar. In a sense which is neither picturesque nor metaphoric, time is a great leveller, since entropy infallibly increases and it takes less effort to fall down than to go on standing up. Ground level asserts itself in the end.

Some of the sites seem to have been chosen for their beauty rather than their convenience. Out at the far eastern end of the island, at the extremity of ever smaller and rougher roads, the most remote and (perhaps for that reason) the most recently investigated, is Kato Zakro, a place so difficult to get to that it must, when in use, have relied on supply by sea. It lies at the side of a small flat valley on a bay, backed all around by hard mountain country, the road down to it skirting the edge of the terrifying Zakros gorge. The site forms a striking contrast to the country around, being a sudden fertile patch of green among the miles of rocky wilderness.

Many of the palaces and settlements were by the seaside. Some, like Kato Zakro, were almost on the sea. They came to a sudden and universal end in about 1450 B.C., and it is now thought credible to relate this destruction to the vast eruption of Thera, which must have had far-reaching and devastating effects. One of these effects would be a monstrous tidal wave, which could both have damaged the coastal settlements and, much more significantly, destroyed the Minoan fleet. The theory fits with the change which then took place at Knossos, which alone among the Minoan sites was restored and reoccupied. It was after this destruction that the new form of writing, known to us as Linear B, replaced the earlier script; since this, though found in Crete only at Knossos, is also the form used at the mainland Mycenaean palaces of Pylos, Thebes and Mycenae, we cannot really argue with the theory that the Achaeans took the opportunity to invade Crete after the disaster, occupied Knossos and prevented the rebuilding of the other palaces.

One slight weakness of this theory, though, is the time lag, since the explosion appears to have taken place some fifty years before the downfall of the palaces; but we may assume both that it left the Cretans in a weakened and demoralized state, and that they were unable to rebuild their defensive navy. Crete owed its sea power originally to its extensive native cypress forests, and Sir Arthur Evans gave the opinion that it was the deforestation caused by the over-exploitation of these, as much as any natural or outside human cause, which led to the eventual weakening of its maritime supremacy. If the Cretans' fleet had not been rebuilt, the effects of this on their powers in Greece must have accelerated during those fifty years, at the same time producing an equivalent increase in the power, influence, and wealth of the Achaeans, and by the end of such a period the change in the balance must have been sufficiently obvious as to be irresistible to the Mycenaean kings, who had had ample time to prepare and organize an attacking force.

It is wrong, in my opinion, to involve these restrained and credible theories with the high-flown business of Atlantis. That argument, as first put forward by the Greek archaeologist Professor Marinatos in 1948 and since made much of by others, says, briefly, that the legend of Atlantis recorded by Plato from the Egyptian historical tradition, must refer to the destruction of the ancient Cretan civilization. Nowhere else, it is argued, could there have been such a highly developed and powerful nation as that referred to by the myth, and one moreover which met a sudden end. The argument then goes on to fit the drowning of Atlantis with the eruption of Thera which destroyed the Minoan world, and gains some strength from the recent discovery of a Minoan town on the island of Thera itself.

There are, however, many things wrong with this, even as a piece of reasoning. It involves a highly selective treatment of the details given by Plato, accepting those which fit the theory and rejecting those which do not. In particular Plato insisted, as has always been assumed, that Atlantis was outside the Mediterranean. It was an island the size of a continent, and it sank into the sea. None of this fits at all well with Crete, and the difficulties of making it do so are so great as to be not worth the effort.

Atlantis is, of course, the summary and epitome of many such lost kingdoms. No doubt Plato's tradition set it out in the Atlantic mainly because there was room for it there. One should look upon the Atlantis of his legend as being a general term for a phenomenon of which there are countless particular instances. Several such golden and irrevocable kingdoms lie off the coast of Britain—Llys Helig, Cantref Gwaelod, Lyonesse—and there is probably no coastal country which does not possess them. The myth of course expresses, on several levels, facts of a real situation: that the land does disappear under the sea or the flooding of basins (as both low-lying areas and land bridges did disappear in the eastern Mediterranean in geological times); that great powers and cultures (of which Bronze Age Crete and its dependencies must have been a specially definite example) do come to an end; and perhaps also that the past is a drowned land itself, where everything was lovelier and richer than it is in these parts now.

The Greeks had their own flood myth, much like the one involving Noah, related almost certainly to other Asian examples. In this version Zeus unleashes a total flood designed to destroy the human race, which has made him furious with its crimes. One man, Deucalion, son of Prometheus, being warned in time, built himself a boat and survived, together with his wife. The boat floated across the flooded world, in which only the tops of high mountains protruded, and eventually came to rest on one of these, in some versions specified as Mount Parnassus. The water subsided, Zeus was appeased by worship and sacrifice, and the race was renewed.

The picture given by the Deucalion myth is strikingly paralleled by evidence that the surviving Mediterranean islands are, as it were, the mountaintops of lost connecting ridges; so that (for instance) a large number of animals from both Europe and Africa, including some species now extinct, found themselves marooned in very crowded conditions on the island of Malta, where one may now see their bones washed by a torrent into a cave. The point is perhaps that being flooded is a primordial and permanent feature of life, and if it happened to Minos too then that is simply another example of a long and recurrent Atlantis tradition. This kingdom, however, fortunately for us, did not disappear for ever into a lost realm of past time. Its remains sit firmly in a very real and durable landscape, much as they did in the time referred to by the myths.

One still cannot help feeling, after seeing the palace sites and the skilful artefacts, that there is a paradox about the whole Minoan business which is not fully explained. The deeply rooted fear which pervades the myth, and the implications of various sorts of unpleasantness, do not quite mesh with the orderly and highly civilized lives which the Cretans of ancient times had clearly developed. But that is the paradox of Crete, and the surrounding countryside helps to make it slightly less incomprehensible. Crete is a savage and beautiful country, at the same time hard and gentle.

The fierceness of its terrain gives a sharp edge to the lives of its people, while its lovely valleys and often friendly climate give them too a sort of luxurious softness of manner. By being both fierce and beautiful the country produces the tension of many contradictions. Paradoxes are not at all out of place here, and one can perhaps best describe the Cretans (as one could perhaps describe the Minoans) as having a ferocious gentleness about them, a sort of resilience coupled with warmth. They have voices which come from the stomach, behave with a dignified courtesy, yet when they do the authentically Cretan dances—light-stepped circular measures—they are seen to be capable of the meticulous delicacy of their predecessors. Most of all one feels that their life is subject to some constant inner tension, perhaps the tension of that dualistic make-up which the figure of the Minotaur expresses in extreme form. If Crete exaggerates in its people the elements of the animal and the human, then it would certainly be appropriate if the myth expressed, in a particularly strong and incisive form, the same fundamental and disturbing idea.

SELECT BIBLIOGRAPHY

SELECT BIBLIOGRAPHY

Almost all the main classical texts are to be found in the Penguin Classics series, and so need not be mentioned in detail. Penguin have unfortunately allowed Peter Levi's delightful and valuable translation of Pausanias' *Guide to Greece* to go out of print, but this situation (1977) may yet be rectified. There are of course many other translations available of almost all the texts, and among these I would mention particularly (as having given me special pleasure) Richmond Lattimore's version of the Odes of Pindar (University of Chicago Press) and the Folio Society editions of Herodotus and Plutarch.

Writing on a subject which has been as deeply investigated as this inevitably involves referring to a very large number of books. Here I give details of only those to which reference is made, directly or implicitly, in the text, and of those only the main ones:

Albert Camus, *The Myth of Sisyphus* (Hamish Hamilton, 1955)
C. P. Cavafy, *The Complete Poems*, trans. Rae Dalven (Hogarth Press, 1961)
John Chadwick, *The Mycenaean World* (Cambridge University Press, 1976)
J. G. Frazer, *The Golden Bough* (Macmillan, 1933)
Sigmund Freud, *Totem and Taboo* (Routledge, 1960)
Robert Graves, *The Greek Myths* (Penguin, 1955)
——, *The White Goddess* (Faber, 1961)
C. G. Jung, *Psychological Types* (Routledge, 1962)
——, *Symbols of Transformation* (Routledge, 1956)
G. S. Kirk, *Myth, Its Meaning and Function in Ancient and Other Cultures* (Cambridge University Press, 1973)
——, *The Nature of the Greek Myths* (Pelican, 1974)
J. V. Lucas, *The End of Atlantis* (Paladin, 1975)

Spiros Marinatos, *Some Words about the Legend of Atlantis* (Athens, 1971)

George E. Mylonas, *Eleusis, and the Eleusinian Mysteries* (Princeton University Press, 1974)

W. B. Stanford and J. V. Lucas, *The Quest for Ulysses* (Phaidon, 1974)

INDEXES

INDEX OF CHARACTERS IN GREEK MYTH

(bold face figures indicate main reference)

INDEX OF PLACES IN GREEK MYTH

GENERAL INDEX